ALSO BY MARK R. LEVIN

Men in Black

Rescuing Sprite

Liberty and Tyranny

Ameritopia

The Liberty Amendments

Plunder and Deceit

Rediscovering Americanism

Unfreedom of the Press

AMERICAN MARXISM

MARK R. LEVIN

THRESHOLD EDITIONS

NEW YORK LONDON TORONTO SYDNEY NEW DELHI

Threshold Editions
An Imprint of Simon & Schuster, Inc.
1230 Avenue of the Americas
New York, NY 10020

First Threshold Editions hardcover edition July 2021

THRESHOLD EDITIONS and colophon are trademarks of Simon & Schuster, Inc.

For information about special discounts for bulk purchases, please contact Simon & Schuster Special Sales at 1-866-506-1949 or business@simonandschuster.com.

The Simon & Schuster Speakers Bureau can bring authors to your live event. For more information, or to book an event, contact the Simon & Schuster Speakers Bureau at 1-866-248-3049 or visit our website at www.simonspeakers.com.

Interior design by Jaime Putorti

Manufactured in the United States of America

10 9 8 7 6 5

Library of Congress Cataloging-in-Publication Data

ISBN 978-1-5011-3597-2
ISBN 978-1-5011-3601-6 (ebook)

CONTENTS

CHAPTER ONE

IT'S HERE

The counterrevolution to the American Revolution is in full force. And it can no longer be dismissed or ignored, for it is devouring our society and culture, swirling around our everyday lives, and ubiquitous in our politics, schools, media, and entertainment. Once a mostly unrelatable, fringe, and subterranean movement, it is here—it is everywhere. You, your children, and your grandchildren are now immersed in it, and it threatens to destroy the greatest nation ever established, along with your freedom, family, and security. Of course, the primary difference between the counterrevolution and the American Revolution is that the former seeks to destroy American society and impose autocratic rule, and the latter sought to protect American society and institute representative government.

The counterrevolution or movement of which I speak is Marxism. I have written about Marxism at length in two earlier books—*Ameritopia* and *Rediscovering Americanism and the Tyranny of Progressivism*—and discuss it regularly on my radio and television shows. There are also untold numbers of books written about Marxism. It is not my purpose to contribute yet another long treatise to the many that exist, nor is it possible given the focus and limitations of this book. But the application and adaption of *core* Marxist teachings to American society and culture—what I call *American* Marxism—must be addressed and confronted, lest we are smothered by its modern manifestations. And make no mistake, the situation today is dire.

In America, many Marxists cloak themselves in phrases like "progressives," "Democratic Socialists," "social activists," "community activists," etc., as most Americans remain openly hostile to the name Marxism. They operate under myriad newly minted organizational or identifying nomenclatures, such as "Black Lives Matter" (BLM), "Antifa," "The Squad," etc. And they claim to promote "economic justice," "environmental justice," "racial equity," "gender equity," etc. They have invented new theories, like Critical Race Theory, and phrases and terminologies, linked to or fit into a Marxist construct. Moreover, they claim "the dominant culture" and capitalist system are unjust and inequitable, racist and sexist, colonialist and imperialist, materialistic and destructive of the environment. Of course, the purpose is to tear down and tear apart the nation for a thousand reasons and in a thousand ways, thereby dispiriting and demoralizing the public; undermining the citizenry's confidence in the nation's institutions, traditions, and customs; creating one calamity after another; weakening the nation from within; and ultimately, destroying what we know as American republicanism and capitalism.

However, there should be no mistake that various leaders of this counterrevolution are increasingly outspoken and brazen about who they are, including bands of openly Marxist professors and activists, and they are supported by a core group of zombie-like "woke" followers. Whatever their labels and self-descriptions, the essential characteristics of their beliefs, statements, and policies exhibit core Marxist dogma. Moreover, they occupy our colleges and universities, newsrooms and social media, boardrooms, and entertainment, and their ideas are prominent within the Democratic Party, the Oval Office, and the halls of Congress. Their influence is seen and felt among the mostly witting as well as the unsuspecting, and in news reporting, movies, television shows and commercials, publishing, and sports, as well as teacher training and classroom curriculum throughout America's public school system. They use the tactics of propaganda and indoctrination, and demand conformity and compliance, silencing contrary voices through repressive tactics, such as "the cancel culture," which destroys reputations and careers, censoring and banning mostly patriotic and contrary viewpoints on social media, even including former president Donald Trump, and attacking academic freedom and intellectual interchange in higher education. Indeed, they take aim at all aspects of the culture—historical monuments (including memorials to Abraham Lincoln, George Washington, abolitionist Frederick Douglass, and the 54th Massachusetts black Union regiment), Mark Twain, William Shakespeare, Mr. Potato Head, Dr. Seuss, Disney cartoons, ad infinitum. Pronouns are banned and replaced with nondescript words so as not to offend fifty-eight flavors of gender identification. Past social media posts are scrutinized for early indications of insufficient fealty to the present-day Marxist hegemony. Journalism and editorial pages are sanitized of nonbelievers.

And yet, historical and present-day experience shows that Marxism and its supposed "worker's paradise" are responsible for the death of tens of millions of human beings, and the impoverishment and enslavement of over a billion more. Indeed, Marx was wrong about almost everything. The Industrial Revolution created a vast middle class unmatched at any time in world history, as opposed to an army of angry proletariat revolutionaries hell-bent on overthrowing the capitalist system. And despite the Marxist class warfare rhetoric of Democratic Party politicians and their surrogates, with technological and other advances capitalism has created unimaginable and unparalleled wealth for more people in all walks of life than any other economic system.

Marx's insistence that labor alone creates value is also incorrect. If that were the case, the Third World would not be the Third World. It would be flourishing. Longer workdays do not ensure wealth creation or growth. Of course, labor is a very important part of economic value and production, but without capital investment, entrepreneurship and sensible risk taking, wise management, etc., businesses would fail—as many do. As any businessman will tell you, there are many decisions that go into running a successful enterprise. Furthermore, all labor is not alike—that is, there are different specialties, backgrounds, and approaches both within the workforce and applicable to certain businesses that make references to "*the* proletariat" nonsensical.

In addition, labor alone does not determine the value of a product or service. Obviously, it contributes to it. However, consumers play the major role. They create the demand. And depending on the demand, business and labor provide the supply. In other words, capitalism caters to desires and needs of "the masses." Also, profit does not create worker exploitation, as Marx insisted. On the contrary. It makes possible increased worker pay, benefits, security, and job opportunities.

Nor was America's early economic success built on imperialism or colonialism. The very resources America is falsely accused of plundering from other countries have not, in and of themselves, made those countries wealthy, even though they are the repository of the resources. American know-how and ingenuity, born of freedom and capitalism, are the source of societal and economic development and advancement.

What, then, is the appeal of Marxism? American Marxism has adapted the language and allure of *utopianism*, which I wrote about at length in my book *Ameritopia*. It is "tyranny disguised as a desirable, workable, and even paradisiacal governing ideology. There are . . . unlimited utopian constructs, for the mind is capable of infinite fantasies. But there are common themes. The fantasies take the form of grand social plans or experiments, the impracticability and impossibility of which, in small ways and large, lead to the individual's subjugation."[1] Indeed, the economic and cultural agenda driven by President Joe Biden and the Democratic Party provide ample examples of this ideology and behavior at work. They include massive deficit spending, confiscatory taxation, and the regulation of all things large and small—drenched in Marxist class-warfare propaganda—and a slew of executive orders claiming to end numerous historical and cultural injustices.

So, too, does their demand for absolute one-party control over the body politic through various extra-constitutional schemes and other means, as Marxism does not tolerate the competition of ideas or political parties. These efforts include changing the voting system to ensure Democratic Party control for decades, which has as its purpose the eradication of the Republican Party and political competition; attempting to eliminate the Senate filibuster rule so all manner of laws can be imposed on the country without effective deliberation or challenge; threatening to breach separation of powers and judicial independence by plotting to pack the Supreme Court with like-minded ideologues; planning to add Democratic seats to the Senate to ensure its control over that body; using tens of billions in taxpayer funds to subsidize and strengthen core parts of the Democratic Party base (such as unions and political activists); and facilitating massive illegal immigration, the purpose of which is to, among other things, alter the nation's demographics and eventually add significantly to the pro–Democratic Party voting base. These actions and designs, among others, are evidence of an autocratic, power-hungry, ideological movement that rejects political and traditional comity and seeks to permanently crush its opposition—and emerge as the sole political and governmental power.

The latter explains the true motivation of the obsessive and unremitting war against the candidacy and presidency of Donald Trump, and his tens of millions of supporters. The Democratic Party, aligned with its surrogates in the media, academia, and the bureaucratic Leviathan, colluded to discredit and cripple Trump's presidency, and destroy him personally, by unleashing an onslaught of slanders, conspiracy theories, criminal and congressional investigations, impeachments, and coup attempts, the likes of which this nation has never experienced. The unremitting, harmonized, and ferocious blitz was aimed not only at the former president, but his followers and voters. Their purpose was to break the back and spirit of the political opposition, and clear the field of obstacles to power and governance. Indeed, the Democratic Party continues to pursue now-private-citizen Trump, having gained access to his tax returns through the offices of elected Democratic officials, including the Manhattan district attorney, an aggressive partisan.

The campaign to delegitimize and marginalize the Democratic Party's political opposition is further evidenced by Biden's reckless racial rhetoric in accusing Republicans in Georgia of instituting Jim Crow laws to prevent black citizens from voting, a contemptible lie intended to upset minorities and turn them against the Republican Party. Although weaponizing race is not new to the Democratic Party, given its historic pedigree—from supporting slavery to segregation—and Biden's vocal and active opposition to integration early in his Senate career, it is shocking to witness its grotesque rebirth as a political tool.

And during the violent riots last summer and this spring, which involved looting, arson, and even murder in multiple cities over the course of several months, and where Antifa and BLM had prominent organizational roles, the Democratic Party's leadership mostly regurgitated the rhetoric and claims of the anarchist/Marxist groups and rioters, including the broad condemnation of law enforcement as "systemically racist," and were not only loath to denounce the violence, but, incredibly, declared the rioters as "mostly peaceful" and their demand to defund the police (later, changed to slash their budgets) as legitimate. In fact, a BLM cofounder declared in the summer of 2020 that one of their "goal[s] is to get Trump out now."[2] Democratic-controlled cities named streets after the group. And numerous Biden campaign staffers donated to a fund that paid the bail for the release of those who were arrested and jailed.[3] Obviously, the Democratic Party and Biden campaign perceived an overlap or synergy of political interests and objectives with the rioters.

The Democratic Party seeks to empower *itself* by breaching constitutional firewalls; skirting if not eradicating rules, traditions, and customs; adopting Marx's language of class warfare; and aligning with certain avowedly Marxist groups and ideological causes, among other things. Moreover, it is using the instrumentalities of the government for its political empowerment and purposes. The truth is that the interests of the Democratic Party come before those of the country. And allegiance to the party is more important than fidelity to the country. It holds these characteristics in common with other autocratic and communist parties throughout the world.

Marxism is especially alluring to, and actively supported by, individuals who find Marxism's oppressor-oppressed class warfare construct appealing for several reasons. First, the fact is people want to belong to groups, including ethnic, racial, religious, and economic groups. People find identity, commonality, purpose, and even self-worth with such attachments. Indeed, I believe this to be the most potent of Marx's paradigms, because he exploits this instinctively human and psychologically emotional appeal to create passionate and even fanatical adherents and revolutionaries. This is another characteristic of American Marxism and the Democratic Party.

This brings me to my second point. Within this class warfare construct, Marxism's adherents and would-be followers are encouraged to view themselves and the groups with which they identify as the oppressed—that is, the victims. And their oppressors are found in the existing society, culture, and economic system, from which the oppressed must liberate themselves and their fellow travelers, meaning those victims who identify with or are also members of the same group. This is a primary reason why Marxism stresses classism over individualism. The individual is dehumanized and is nothing unless he identifies with a group—the oppressed and victimized group. And the individuals who make up opposing or nonconforming groups are collectively dehumanized, condemned, and loathed as the enemy. Again, this is a trait of American Marxism and the Democratic Party.

Of course, this formulation is especially seductive to the malcontented, disenchanted, disaffected, and dissatisfied. For them, individual liberty and capitalism expose their own shortcomings and failings, and their difficulty and perhaps inability to function in an open society. Marxism provides a theoretical and institutional framework through which they can project their own limitations and weaknesses onto "the system" and their "oppressors" rather than take responsibility for their own real or perceived plight. Again, as I wrote in *Ameritopia*, these individuals are "lured by the false hopes and promises of the utopian transformation and the criticisms of the existing society, to which their connection is tentative or nonexistent. Improving the malcontents' lot becomes linked to the utopian cause."[4] Many in this population are susceptible to manipulation, especially by demagogues and propagandists, and the lure of revolutionary transformation.

Importantly, whether one identifies with or is among the class of oppressed or victimized is a matter of self-determination and self-actualization. In other words, there are no hard and fast rules. Furthermore, they and their group can also define and identify what and whom, for them, are their oppressors. In the end, Marx and his modern-day surrogates direct their wrath at the existing society and culture, which must be toppled if life is to have meaning and start over in the newly minted egalitarian paradise.

Thus, those in the existing society who are successful, content, and happy are tormented and targeted, for they are either among the oppressors or oppressor groups, and therefore support and sustain the status quo. Moreover, those who sanction the existing society, or refuse to support or acquiesce to the agenda and demands of the oppressed, are also subjected to damaging and destructive pressures and conduct. Either you are part of the righteous revolution for liberation and transformation or you are not. Hence, the allegedly oppressed become the real oppressors, and wield substantial power throughout society and the culture despite their limited appeal and smaller numbers. And they become more belligerent, demanding, and even violent as their appetite for control and revolution grows and must be constantly satiated.

This also explains, but only in part, the cowardice of corporatists, professional athletes, broadcasters, artists, actors, writers, and journalists who, in the face of such tumult, buckle under the pressure, seek to avoid the mob's notice through various forms of appeasement and capitulation, and in some cases participate in their own transfiguration and even disembowelment. For others, their boardrooms, management, and workforce are sympathetic and "down for the revolution," populated from the ranks of ideologically indoctrinated college and university students, particularly among the Ivy School elite, teachers' unions, or the increasingly radicalized Democratic Party, of which they are members, sympathizers, and/or supporters. And, of course, many corporatists have simply abandoned capitalism for statism and government/economic centralization, and support groups like BLM and various radical causes, as a way to curry favor if not partner with political and bureaucratic autocrats to destroy their competition and improve their financial positions.

Ted McAllister, professor of public policy at Pepperdine University, makes a persuasive case that today's ruling class or elites disdain our country. In a 2021 essay titled "Thus Always to Bad Elites," he writes:

> Today, we have a very different elite than America did as recently as the 1980s in terms of their nature, goals, ambitions, style, and ways of exercising power. The deepest fact of our time is that America has a bad elite, a mendacious one whose skills, values, goals, tastes, and types of knowledge are hostile to our nation's inherited cultures and plural people. The new elite that has emerged in the last generation or two has no interest in preserving anything but perhaps their own power. They lack historical knowledge and vision, which they supplant by, or exchange for, the powers of transformation and change. Intoxicated by the power possible with emerging technologies, inspired by visions that only a deracinated globalist perspective could make attractive, this elite thinks of creative destruction as applied to culture.

> As winners in what they imagine to be a meritocratic struggle, they can see nothing of an inherited world worth preserving for their very success. The peculiar characteristics of their evolving power have given to our new elite the soul of adolescent art applied to a global canvas. They lack any experiential or historical ballast to weigh them down, to slow them in remaking everything according to their desires. For them, streamlining power is key to creation and the annoying obstacles to their new creations are not really checks to prevent tyranny but, rather, limitations—unnecessary friction in the headlong rush to transform.
>
> For this new elite, for instance, the good of free speech has become invisible because, for them, free speech is simply friction, resistance to their goals. The elimination of hate speech is the goal, the unimpeachable good, that the openness of free speech prevents. In half a generation, the work of centuries is undone and the levers of tyranny put in place.[5]

Actually, this is the best that can be said of the contemporary elite.

Unfortunately, too many among us take false comfort in the belief that there could never be a Marxist-based or oriented revolution in America, and what they are witnessing is just another in a cycle of liberal movements, which contribute to the evolution of American society and culture and, therefore, are worthy of approval and passive support.

Collectively, these are America's "useful idiots" on whom Marxists rely—that is, individuals and organizations that are unserious and unaroused by the ominous clouds of tyranny, and even worse, are participants in their own demise and that of the country.

For many, Marxism has a way of sneaking up on them. They are not yet personally threatened and, at least for now, are unmolested or personally unaffected by it; or there are those who are too busy in their everyday lives to realize what is transpiring, or may dismiss these threats as amorphous, distant, or passing events; and there are still more who cannot believe their country would succumb to Marxist influences and despotism.

The purpose of this book is to *awaken* the millions of patriotic Americans, who love their country, freedom, and family, to the *reality* of Marxism's rapidly spreading influence throughout our nation. What is occurring in our country is not a temporary fad or passing event. American Marxism exists, it is here and now, and indeed it is pervasive, and its multitude of hybrid but often interlocking movements are actively working to destroy our society and culture, and overthrow the country as we know it. Many of the individuals and groups who collectively make up this movement are unknown to most Americans, or operate in ways in which most Americans are unaware. Thus, this book is written to introduce you to a representative sample of them, some perhaps more familiar than others, and to provide you with specific examples of *their* writings, ideas, and activities, so you can know of them and hear from them. Of course, I provide commentary and analysis throughout. I also provide some thoughts about tactical actions that might be taken to help stem the nation's slide and reverse course. Although this is the longest book I have written, there is much more to be said about this subject. Therefore, I anticipate writing a second volume.

American Marxism has made great progress toward instituting its goals over the last several years. If it is to be defeated, as it must—albeit a daunting and complex mission—its existence must first be acknowledged and labeled for what it is, the urgency of the moment must be realized, and the emergence of a unified, patriotic front of previously docile, divergent, and/or disputatious societal, cultural, and political factions and forces, which have in common their belief that America is worth defending, must immediately galvanize around and rally to the cause. We must rise to the challenge, as did our Founding Fathers, when they confronted the most powerful force on earth, the British Empire, and defeated it. Admittedly, in numerous ways today's threat is more byzantine, as it now inhabits most of our institutions and menaces from within, making engagement difficult and complicated. Nonetheless, I fervently believe America as we know it will be forever lost if we do not prevail.

I closed my book *Liberty and Tyranny*, which was published a short twelve years ago, with President Ronald Reagan's fateful and prescient observation, which compels our attention especially now for it is more imperative than ever: "Freedom is never more than one generation away from extinction. We didn't pass it to our children in the bloodstream. It must be fought for, protected, and handed on for them to do the same, or one day we will spend our sunset years telling our children and children's children what it was once like in the United States where men were free."[6]

PATRIOTS OF AMERICA, UNITE!

CHAPTER TWO

BREEDING MOBS

Almost a decade ago, and before Antifa was widely known and Black Lives Matter (BLM) was established, I wrote of mass movements in my book *Ameritopia* in the framework of utopianism. Utopianism, whether in the form of Marxism, fascism, or some other form of autocratic statism, is alluring to many because at their core they make glorious claims of a paradisiacal future and the perfectibility of man, if only the existing society and culture are radically transformed or abandoned altogether, and the individual surrenders more of his liberty, free will, and security to the cause. Such is the nature of mass movements.

I explained further that mass movements attempt to devour the individual in two ways: consume his identity and uniqueness, thereby making him indistinguishable from "the masses," but also assigning him a group identity based on race, age, income, etc., to draw class distinctions. "This way [the demagogues and propagandists] can speak to the well-being of 'the people' as a whole while dividing them against themselves, thereby stampeding them in one direction or another as necessary to collapse the existing society or rule over the new one."[1]

And who among us is attracted to such mass movements? Again, as I noted: "[A] receptive audience [is found] among the society's disenchanted, disaffected, dissatisfied, and maladjusted who are unwilling or unable to assume responsibility for their own real or perceived conditions but instead blame their surroundings, 'the system,' and others. They are lured by the false hopes and promises of utopian transformation and the criticisms of the existing society, to which their connection is tentative or nonexistent. Improving the malcontent's lot becomes linked to the utopian cause. Moreover, disparaging and diminishing the successful and accomplished becomes an essential tactic. No one should be better than anyone else, regardless of the merits or value of his contribution. By exploiting human frailties, frustrations, jealousies, and inequities, a sense of meaning and self-worth is created in the malcontent's otherwise unhappy and directionless life."[2]

Furthermore, in mass movements "[t]he individual is inconsequential as a person and useful only as an insignificant part of an agglomeration of insignificant parts. He is a worker, part of a mass; nothing more, nothing less. His existence is soulless. Absolute obedience is the highest virtue. After all, only an army of drones is capable of building a rainbow to paradise."[3]

Almost a century ago, the French philosopher and essayist Julien Benda observed that mass movements form frequently around individuals who share the same political hatred. He wrote: "Thanks to the progress of communication and, still more, to the group spirit, it is clear that the holders of the same political hatred now form a compact impassioned mass, every individual of which feels himself in touch with the infinite numbers of others, whereas a century ago such people were comparatively out of touch with each other and hated in a 'scattered' way. . . . It may be asserted that these coherences will tend to develop still further, for the will to group is one of the most profound characteristics of the modern world, which even in the most unexpected domains (for instance, the domain of thought) is more and more becoming the world of leagues, of 'unions' and of 'groups.' Is it necessary to say that the passion of the individual is strengthened by feeling itself in proximity to these thousands of similar passions? . . . [T]he individual bestows a mystic personality on the association of which he feels himself a member, and gives it a religious adoration, which is simply the deification of his own passion and no small stimulus to its intensity."[4]

Benda also concluded that such movements are often cultlike. "The coherence just described might be called a surface coherence, but there is added to it a coherence of essence. For the very reason that the holders of the same political passion form a more compact, impassioned group, they also form a more *homogeneous*, impassioned group, in which the individual ways of feeling disappear and the zeal of each member more and more takes on the color of the others."[5]

Today, clearly the Antifa movement is populated with indistinguishable "soldiers" dressed uniformly in black clothing and face coverings. Their identities and names are unknown. They are indoctrinated in a Marxist-anarchist ideology, trained in violence, and said to be "an idea." Obviously, it is more than an idea. It is a dangerous and brutal movement populated by angry zealots.[6]

BLM is also a Marxist-anarchist movement. However, it has self-identified as a black power or black liberation movement when, in fact, its agenda extends well beyond race into the usual Marxist demands for the destruction of the existing society.[7]

Of course, these movements, like all mass movements, cannot tolerate or survive competing or rival ideas or voices. They demand groupthink and conformity. We have even seen this orthodoxy spread throughout our culture, with the widespread firing, shaming, banning, intimidating, and otherwise abusing those who dare to voice contrary or different views, or question or challenge, for example, BLM's mission. So ubiquitous is this assault on individualism and nonconformism in today's society that it has acquired its own modern nomenclature—the "cancel culture." However, this is not new, just more prevalent, open, and intense.

Again, I wrote nearly a decade ago that these mass movements are "intolerant of diversity, uniqueness, debate, etc., for [their] purpose requires a singular focus. There can be no competing voices or causes slowing or obstructing society's long and righteous march. [They rely] on deceit, propaganda, dependence, intimidation, and force. In its more aggressive state, as the malignancy of the enterprise becomes more painful and its impossibility more obvious, it incites violence inasmuch as avenues for free expression and civil dissent are cut off. Violence becomes the individual's primary recourse and the state's primary response. Ultimately, the only way out is the state's termination."[8]

Thus, mass movements rely significantly on indoctrination and brainwashing. They are ignited and motivated "by an enthusiastic intelligentsia or 'experts' professionally engaged in developing and spreading utopian fantasies. . . . [They] are immune from the impracticability and consequences of their blueprints for they rarely present themselves for public office. Instead, they seek to influence those who do. They legislate without accountability."[9]

Where are these "experts" found? As we shall see, primarily among tenured faculty in our colleges and universities, whose intellectual and emotional fealty are mostly aligned, at least in significant part, with the ideological prescriptions of Jean-Jacques Rousseau, Georg Wilhelm Friedrich Hegel, and, of course, Karl Marx.

Rousseau, Hegel, and Marx, in their own ways, argue for the individual's subjugation into a general will, or greater good, or bigger cause built on radical egalitarianism—that is, "the collective." Of course, as logic, reason, and experience demonstrate, this is a building block for totalitarian causes and regimes. As the state becomes increasingly authoritarian and despotic, controlling speech, mobility, and even thought where possible, it is said to perpetuate and celebrate a kind of popular or people-oriented will and liberation.

To better understand the philosophical underpinnings of the Antifa, BLM, and similar anti-American movements, let us take a brief look at Rousseau, Hegel, and Marx in this context. Rousseau explained: "I conceive of two kinds of inequality in the human species: one that I call natural and physical, because it is established by nature and consists in the difference of age, health, bodily strength, and qualities of mind or soul. The other may be called moral or political inequality, because it depends on a kind of convention and is established, or at least authorized, by the consent of men. This latter type of inequality consists in the different privileges enjoyed by some at the expense of others, such as being richer, more honored, more powerful than they, or even causing themselves to be obeyed by them."[10]

Rousseau argued further that "[i]f we follow the progress of inequality [in the history of governing systems], we will find that the first stage was the establishment of the law and of the right of property, the second stage was the institution of magistracy, and the third and final stage was the transformation of legitimate power into arbitrary power. Thus the condition of rich and poor was authorized by the first epoch, that of the strong and weak by the second, and that of the master and slave by the third: the ultimate degree of inequality and the limit to which all the others finally lead, until new revolutions completely dissolve the government or bring it nearer to a legitimate institution."[11]

How will we know when the "legitimate institution" has been achieved beyond the theoretical construct? Rousseau does not tell us.

For Hegel, the individual finds his actualization—liberty, happiness, fulfillment—through the state. But not just any state. States evolve over time, ultimately leading to a fully developed state, or the "final end." In such a state, the individual becomes part of a universalized, collective whole. That which preceded the final end is of no consequence. Again, the individual is subservient to the state for both his own realization and the greater good of the collective.

At this point, "[t]he state as a completed reality is the ethical whole and the actualization of freedom. It is the absolute purpose of reason that freedom should be actualized, the state is the spirit, which abides in the world and there realizes itself consciously. . . . Only when it is present in consciousness, knowing itself as an existing object, is it the state. In thinking of freedom, we must not take our departure from individuality or the individual's self-consciousness, but from the essence of self-consciousness. Let man be aware of it or not, this essence realizes itself as an independent power, in which particular persons are only phases. The state is the march of God in the world; its ground or cause is the power of reason realizing itself as well."[12]

How do we know when we have reached the "final end" beyond the theoretical construct? Hegel does not tell us.

Marx, with his emphasis on historic materialism, wrote: "The modern bourgeois society that has sprouted from the ruins of feudal society has not done away with class antagonisms. Society as a whole is more and more splitting up into two great hostile camps, into two great classes directly facing each other: Bourgeoisie [the capitalists, the owners of property and the means of production] and Proletariat [laborer, the industrial working class] . . ."[13]

Marx argues that "[n]ot only are [the proletarians] slaves of the bourgeois class, and the bourgeois State, they are daily and hourly enslaved by the machine, by the over-seer, and above all, the individual bourgeois manufacturer himself."[14] Consequently, the proletariat's fate is at a dead end. Unless, of course, he adopts the revolution prescribed by Marx. It is the only way out.

If the proletariat is to eliminate economic classes and transform society into an egalitarian paradise, he must wipe clean the present from the past—first, by overthrowing the existing regime and smashing capitalism, replacing them with a centralized proletariat state, and once society and the culture are cleansed of the past, the state will wither away and what follows is an amorphous utopian state powered by the people through the collective. As Marx declares: "Of course, in the beginning this cannot be effected except by means of despotic inroads on the rights of property and on the conditions of the bourgeois production; by means of measures, therefore, which appear economically insufficient and untenable, but which, in the course of the movement, outstrip themselves, necessitate further inroads upon the old social order and are unavoidable as a means of entirely revolutionizing the mode of production."[15]

Again, Marx insists that the individual's realization and salvation are discovered through his identity with the proletarian revolution and, then, the perfected existence under the people's collective will, which somehow and some way develops from a police state that precedes the withering away of the state altogether.

How do we know when we have reached the "workers' paradise" beyond a theoretical construct? Marx does not tell us.

The impracticability and, in fact, impossibility of these ideologies appear to be strangely alluring to those who crusade for them. Moreover, the paradise each promises, once the revolution succeeds in dissolving the status quo and existing state, fails to move beyond the point of a centralized police state, in which the individual is indeed expendable and "the masses" are compelled to serve the purposes of the party or individuals in charge of that state. Examples of such states include China, North Korea, Venezuela, Cuba, etc.

Seventy years ago, Eric Hoffer wrote an iconic book, *The True Believer*, on the nature of mass movements. Hoffer explained that mass movements are built of deeply flawed individuals with deeply flawed ideas. He noted that "[a] mass movement attracts and holds a following not because it can satisfy the desire for self-advancement, but because it can satisfy the passion for self-renunciation. People who see their lives as irremediably spoiled cannot find a worthwhile purpose in self-advancement. . . . They look on self-interest as something tainted and evil; something unclean and unlucky. Anything undertaken under the auspices of the self seems to them foredoomed. Nothing that has its roots and reasons in the self can be good and noble."[16]

Moreover, most mass movements are angry and gloomy movements, hostile toward well-adjusted, happy, and successful individuals. Again, this is evident in the Antifa and BLM movements, among others. Hoffer observed that "[n]ot only does a mass movement depict the present as mean and miserable—it deliberately makes it so. It fashions a pattern of individual existence that is dour, hard, repressive and dull. It decries pleasures and comforts and extols the rigorous life. It views ordinary enjoyment as trivial or even discreditable, and represents the pursuit of personal happiness as immoral. . . . The prime objective of the ascetic ideal preached by most movements is to breed contempt for the present. . . ."[17]

Indeed, there is a kind of psychotic pleasure and excitement in wrecking the present-day society, including if not especially one as free, humane, tolerant, and virtuous as ours. "What surprises one, when listening to the frustrated as they decry the present and all its works," wrote Hoffer, "is the enormous joy they derive from doing so. Such delight cannot come from the mere venting of a grievance. . . . By expatiating upon the incurable baseness and vileness of the times, the frustrated soften their feeling of failure and isolation. . . . Thus by deprecating the present they acquire a vague sense of equality."[18]

The "cause" itself becomes the reason for one's existence. As Hoffer pointed out, "[t]he means . . . a mass movement uses to make the present unpalatable strike a responsive chord in the frustrated. The self-mastery needed in overcoming their appetites gives them an illusion of strength. They feel that in mastering themselves they have mastered the world. . . . [19] One gains the impression that the frustrated derive as much satisfaction—if not more—from the means a mass movement uses as from the end it advocates. . . ."[20]

This also explains why "the end" of such revolutions is never in sight. Even when the revolutionaries have seized power, the revolution perseveres, for the cause has no end as it is ultimately unachievable as man and society are not perfectible. But the true believer's appetite for revolution is insatiable.

Nonetheless, as Hoffer points out, and as Rousseau, Hegel, and Marx advocated, "[t]he [radical] ha[s] a passionate faith in the infinite perfectibility of human nature. He believes that by changing man's environment and by perfecting a technique of soul forming, a society can be wrought that is wholly new and unprecedented. . . ."[21]

And, of course, brainwashing and idolatry to the cause are the lifeblood of mass movements. For example, when presented with statistical evidence that law enforcement is not systemically racist, "It is the true believer's ability to 'shut his eyes and stop his ears' to facts that do not deserve to be either seen or heard which is the source of his unequaled fortitude and constancy. He cannot be frightened by danger nor disheartened by obstacles nor baffled by contradictions because he denies their existence. . . . And it is the certitude of his infallible doctrine that renders the true believer impervious to the uncertainties, surprises and the unpleasant realities of the world around him. . . ."[22] "It is obvious . . . that in order to be effective a doctrine must not be understood, but has rather to be believed in. . . . The devout are always urged to seek the absolute truth with their hearts and not their minds."[23]

Thus, Hoffer is describing a fanatic and fanaticism. "[The fanatic's] passionate attachment is the essence of his blind devotion and religiosity, and he sees in it the source of all virtue and strength. Though his single-minded dedication is a holding on for dear life, he easily sees himself as the supporter and defender of the holy cause to which he clings. . . ."[24]

When the fanatic is confronted with facts, statistics, history, experience, ethics, faith, or what have you, it is of no consequence. He has found his calling and he will not be dissuaded from it. Again, "the cause" is greater than all things.

Hoffer explains it this way: "The fanatic cannot be weaned away from his cause by an appeal to his reason or moral sense. He fears compromise and cannot be persuaded to qualify the certitude and righteousness of his holy cause. . . . His passionate attachment is more vital than the quality of the cause to which he is attached."[25] He continues, "To live without an ardent dedication is to be adrift and abandoned. He sees in tolerance a sign of weakness, frivolity and ignorance. He hungers for the deep assurance which comes with total surrender—with the wholehearted clinging to a creed and a cause. What matters is not the contents of the cause but the total dedication and the communion with the congregation."[26]

The fanatic comes from all walks of life and all backgrounds. For example, multi-billionaire George Soros pours enormous sums of money into radical causes and groups[27]; professional athletes such as Colin Kaepernick and LeBron James are vociferous vilifiers and disparagers of American society; many college and university professors are purveyors of revisionist American history and radical anti-American ideologies; college and university students from middle-class and wealthy families are increasingly militant opponents of the civil society; and, of course, various communities are ever more radicalized by racial, economic, educational, and other distinctions and disparities.

Like Benda, Hoffer sees the fanatic and the mass movement as centered on an intense if not obsessive hatred. "Passionate hatred can give meaning and purpose to an empty life," explained Hoffer. "Thus people haunted by the purposelessness of their lives try to find a new content not only by dedicating themselves to a holy cause but also by nursing a fanatical grievance. A mass movement offers them unlimited opportunities for both."[28] Indeed, the dangerousness of this hatred, when tied to a cause, can have calamitous societal and human consequences. It leads to scapegoating, balkanization, violence, and, in its more aggressive form, ethnic cleansing. More broadly and simultaneously, this hatred seeks to malign, debase, debauch, and, ultimately, topple the status quo and the civil society—for example, the American founding (the "1619 Project," which is addressed in Chapter 4), the Constitution, capitalism, law enforcement, etc.

Hoffer described the model by which the groundwork is set for the rise of mass movements: "1) by discrediting prevailing creeds and institutions and detaching from them the allegiance of the people; 2) by indirectly creating a hunger for faith in the hearts of those who cannot live without it, so that when the new faith is preached it finds an eager response among the disillusioned masses; 3) by furnishing the doctrine and the slogans of the new faith; 4) by undermining the convictions of the 'better people'—those who can get along without faith—so that when the new fanaticism makes its appearance they are without the capacity to resist it."[29]

In the end, if such mass movements succeed, the result is totalitarianism. Hannah Arendt, in her book *The Origins of Totalitarianism*, argued these mass movements are the foundation for violence and despotism: "The attraction of evil and crime for the mob mentality is nothing new. It has always been true that the mob will greet deeds of violence with the admiring remark: 'it may be mean but it is very clever.' The disturbing factor in the success of totalitarianism is rather the true selflessness of its adherents. . . ."[30]

In point of fact, mass movements are the necessary precursors to building revolutions and overthrowing governments—in the immediate instance, our own republic—by various and competing tactical approaches. But as described earlier, there is a commonality and essential methodology to this counterrevolution and societal transformation—the promotion of the "the collective" into which all revolutionaries or "social activists" are to be absorbed.

Unbeknownst to most, this subject, loosely called "social movement theory" among academics, is widely analyzed, debated, taught, and promoted by the professoriate throughout that nation's colleges and universities. Moreover, revolution and mass movements are frequently romanticized and glamorized as righteous and irreproachable responses to an oppressive, inequitable, unjust, racist, and immoral society. Of course, this matters greatly because of the effect that education on the college campus and communication through formal textbooks and scholarly essays—which, too often, take the form of indoctrination and brainwashing—have on the ideas that saturate and engulf not just students but the culture and society, and manifest themselves in America's streets, corporate boardrooms, politics, and newsrooms. Hence, it is necessary to briefly examine examples of this pedagogy.

Frontiers in Social Movement Theory (1992) is a compilation of such essays authored by numerous social activist scholars, most of whom are professors. As will become apparent, these scholars have essentially built their arguments and propositions for social activism and even revolution on the foundational ideological writings of Rousseau, Hegel, and Marx, and mostly follow the characteristics and formula of mass movements described by Benda, Hoffer, and me.

The book's preface sums up its overarching premise: "[W]e hope this volume illuminates some fundamental issues regarding an important topic, for, as Lewis Coser [a prominent socialist, sociologist, and social conflict advocate] reminded us . . . , 'social movements are instrumentalities to abolish, or at least weaken, structures of political and social domination.' He also made the point that many people who participate in social movements do so at great sacrifice because 'they draw their sustenance not from the enhancement of present satisfaction but from long-term time perspective sustained by the firm belief in the coming of a society embodying justice and democratic equality instead of the here and now of exploitation and denial of human dignity.' "[31]

One of the essayists, Professor William A. Gamson of Boston College, emphasizes, much like Rousseau, the significance of *the collective identity*. He writes, in part, that "[p]articipation in social movements frequently involves an enlargement of personal identity for participants and offers fulfillment and realization of self. Participation in the civil rights movement, women's movement, and New Left, for example, was frequently a transformative experience, central to the self-definition of many participants in their later lives."[32] "[T]he construction of a collective identity is the most central task of 'new' social movements."[33]

Group identity is necessary and critical to the success of the movement. "When people bind their fate to the fate of a group," argues Gamson, "they feel personally threatened when the group is threatened. Solidarity and collective identity operate to blur the distinction between individual and group interest, undermining the premises on which such utilitarian models operate."[34]

Gamson insists that for a movement to effectively mobilize, it must be viewed and, in fact, must become the identity through which the individual views himself. "Collective identity is a concept at the cultural level, but to operate in mobilization, individuals must make it part of their personal identity. Solidarity centers on the ways in which individuals commit themselves and the resources they control to some kind of collective actor—an organization or advocacy network. Adopting a collective action frame involves incorporating a product of the cultural system—a particular shared understanding of the world—into the political consciousness of individuals. Individual and sociocultural levels are linked through mobilizing acts in face-to-face encounters."[35]

Assistant Professor Debra Friedman and Professor Doug McAdam, then of the University of Arizona, bluntly declare: "The collective identity of social movement organization is a shorthand designation announcing a status—a set of attitudes, commitments, and rules for behavior—that those who assume the identity can be expected to subscribe to."[36] They continue, "It is also an individual announcement of affiliation, of connection with others. To partake of a collective identity is to reconstitute the individual self around a new and valued identity."[37]

In essence, therefore, the individual is being reinvented and remade, he is being conditioned and programmed, into a devoted social activist or revolutionary tied inextricably to the cause through the movement. "As regards a social movement," write Friedman and McAdam, "collective identity refers to that identity or status that attaches to the individual by virtue of his or her participation in movement activities. One of the most powerful motivators of individual action is the desire to confirm through behavior a cherished identity. In the case of a movement, the opportunity to do so can be seen as selective incentive more available to those who are integrated into activist networks than those who are not. Integration into these networks makes it more likely that the individual will value the identity of 'activist' and choose to act in accordance with it."[38]

In addition to collective identity, the movement's *collective beliefs* must be drilled into the individual. Professor Bert Klandermans of the Free University in the Netherlands, argues: "Collective beliefs and the way they are formed and transformed are the core of the social construction of protest; interpersonal networks submerged in multiorganizational fields are the conduits of this process of meaning construction. Collective beliefs are constructed and reconstructed over and over; in public discourse, during the mobilization of consensus, and in the process of consciousness raising during episodes of collective action. Because collective beliefs are formed and transformed in interpersonal interactions, attempts to change the mind of a single individual would not be very effective in changing the collective beliefs unless that individual is influential in his or her interpersonal circle. Incoming information is processed and anchored in existing collective beliefs through interpersonal interaction. Only when actors are able to direct this interaction so that their message becomes anchored in existing beliefs can they transform collective beliefs. Thus every actor will be able to mobilize consensus more easily in some groups or categories than others."[39]

And then there is *class consciousness*, including class and group identity, as yet another means to absorb the individual into the collective—that is, the mass movement and revolution. Professor Aldon D. Morris of Northwestern University contends: "Empirical studies using diverse methodologies and conceptual frameworks have demonstrated that class consciousness has developed in a variety of societies and historical periods and that it has affected major revolutions and social movements. Indeed, class consciousness has been one of the key determinants of social and historical change."[40]

Morris's observations reflect, in a significant way, the teachings of Marx in that he sees society and culture broken down into classes that are in a constant state of competition and conflict. "Class consciousness," he writes, "is important precisely because it influences the very nature of class conflict and helps determine the kinds of social structures—unions, political parties, workers' associations—that will be erected and that affect the outcome of class conflict."[41]

Consequently, groups are dominated and oppressed by looking at society's and the culture's structural and historical prejudices and inequities, and the effect on their political influence. Morris declares that "[g]roups['] interests become paramount because systems of domination have no meaning outside the accumulation and defense of such interests. The task of precisely identifying the groups who benefit from such a system is complex because several groups usually benefit, although unequally. An important task, therefore, is to establish the relative positions of privilege enjoyed by groups hierarchically positioned within systems of domination and to show how such relative positions affect their political consciousness. In this approach, scholarly attention is directed squarely toward the long-standing cleavages within a society and the structural preconditions (threats of violence, polity membership, economic resources such as the control of jobs, and so on) inherent to systems of domination that enable certain groups to rule. By the same token, attention is focused on the structural preconditions (networks of communications, formal and informal social organization, availability of leadership, financial resources, and so on) central to effective and sustained protest by oppressed groups."[42]

Given the injustices, prejudices, and inequality imposed by society's dominant groups against oppressed groups, the oppressed groups must awaken to their inferior status, become politically aware, and then rise up in protest and even revolution against the existing society. Morris argues, "My approach directs attention to culture—political consciousness. Such consciousness is also analyzed within the context of major social cleavages and systems of domination. . . . [B]oth dominant and oppressed groups have long-standing traditions of political consciousness. Hegemonic consciousness is always present but often unrecognized because of its ability to successfully masquerade as the general outlook while simultaneously protecting the interests of dominant groups. But effective social protest informed by a mature oppositional consciousness enables challenging groups to strip away the garments of universality from hegemonic consciousness, revealing its essential characteristics. This is precisely what the modern civil rights movement accomplished in the South, forcing the nation to decide publicly on the world stage whether it would continue to be guided by blatant white supremacy ideology."[43]

The oppressed must be encouraged to rise up and join in protest and even revolution. "Oppositional consciousness," explains Morris, "often lie[s] dormant within the institutions, life-styles, and culture of oppressed groups. Members of such groups are usually not without basic collective identities, injustice frames, and the like that are conducive to individual and collective social protest."[44]

Morris contends that the seeds of oppositional protest and revolution already exist in oppressed communities, which makes possible the birth of new and more effective forms of collective activism. "[C]ultural phenomena are not reducible simply to organization and structural dynamics. Indeed, varied forms of oppositional consciousness are important precisely because they are able to survive under the most adverse structural conditions. In many ways, oppressed communities nurture oppositional ideas during intense periods of repression, thereby creating the social and cultural space for the emergence of more favorable structural conditions conducive to collective action. . . ."[45]

Moreover, much can be learned from the experiences of successful "combat-ready" oppositional protests—that is, veterans of protest movements—that help spread and sustain activism. Morris writes, "Combat-ready oppositional consciousness can have an independent effect on structural determinants of collective action. Once a successful instance of protest has occurred . . . , it affects collection action in two ways: It provides those activists who participated directly with an understanding of how it happened and why it worked, and it attracts other non-participants who wish to internalize these lessons so as to transplant the model to other locales, thereby increasing the volume of collective action. Thus, both sets of actors become cultural workers for the movement by further hammering out the set of viewpoints that previously lay dormant within the historic oppositional consciousness, making them relevant for the contemporary scene. In the manner, these viewpoints become the defining ideas about how to initiate and sustain social protests."[46]

Ultimately, these arguments for collective identity, collective beliefs, and class consciousness, in support of mass movements, wittingly or otherwise have a Marxist formulation, and form the basis not only for peaceful protests but violence, riots, and revolution—of the sort we have seen in our cities and towns with the likes of Antifa, BLM, and other violent radical groups. In fact, they attempt to provide the veneer of an expertise or scholarly approach to societal disruption, the undermining of civil institutions, and flat-out rebellion.

Professors Frances Fox Piven and the late Richard A. Cloward wrote less about social movement theory and more extensively and openly in support of militant uprisings. And they were more forthright and detailed than many others in their prescriptions for using activism to develop disruption, create crises, collapse institutions, and excite riots as legitimate and necessary to transform society. Therefore, given their extensive writings and influence on radical and even violent revolutionary strategies, they require more substantial exposition here.

In 1966, the professors wrote what is considered by radical activists a seminal essay in the far-left *Nation*, entitled "The Weight of the Poor: A Strategy to End Poverty," focused on race and poverty. They bluntly stated their intention: "It is our purpose to advance a strategy which affords the basis for a convergence of civil rights organizations, militant anti-poverty groups and the poor. If this strategy were implemented, a political crisis would result that could lead to legislation for a guaranteed annual income and thus an end to poverty."[47]

The pair laid the predicate by arguing that welfare is a right, the welfare payments recipients receive are less than what they are entitled to, and efforts to reduce the welfare rolls are an assault on the well-being of the poor and minorities. They contend that more people should enter the system, indeed flood it, and those in the system should demand more benefits to which they are entitled. This would create a major societal crisis. Piven and Cloward wrote that "a vast discrepancy exists between the benefits to which people are entitled under public welfare programs and the sums which they actually receive. This gulf is not recognized in a society that is wholly and self-righteously oriented toward getting people off the welfare rolls. . . . This discrepancy is not an accident stemming from bureaucratic inefficiency; rather, it is an integral feature of the welfare system which, if challenged, would precipitate a profound financial and political crisis. The force for that challenge, and the strategy we propose, is a massive drive to recruit the poor onto the welfare rolls."[48]

Piven and Cloward also argued that in certain past periods, the Democratic Party was the political institution through which radical change was realized as a result of economic crises and that the party must again be targeted and effectively hijacked for such purposes. Moreover, the reforms were also instituted to build and strengthen a new Democratic coalition. "The legislative reforms of the depression years, for example, were impelled not so much by organized interests exercised through regular electoral processes as by widespread economic crisis. That crisis precipitated the disruption of the regionally based coalitions underlying the old national parties. During the realignments of 1932, a new Democratic coalition was formed, based heavily on urban working-class groups. Once in power, the national Democratic leadership proposed and implemented the economic reforms of the New Deal. Although these measures were a response to the imperative of economic crisis, the types of measures enacted were designed to secure and stabilize the new Democratic coalition."[49]

For Piven and Cloward, revolution is tied, at least in part, to radicalized black communities influencing and tied to the Democratic Party. "In the face of such a crisis, urban political leaders may well be paralyzed by a party apparatus which ties them to older constituent groups, even while the ranks of these groups are diminishing. The national Democratic leadership, however, is alert to the importance of the urban Negro vote, especially in national contests where the loyalty of other urban groups is weakening. Indeed, many of the legislative reforms of the Great Society can be understood as efforts, however feeble, to reinforce the allegiance of growing ghetto constituencies to the national Democratic Administration."[50]

Indeed, today the allegiance of the black community to the Democratic Party is overwhelming. And a similar strategy is playing out with respect to the Hispanic and Asian communities.

In 1968, Piven and Cloward also wrote of "Movements and Dissensus Politics," explicitly arguing that, among other things, "incendiarism" and "riots" are legitimate and necessary acts of mass movements. They declared that "poor people win mainly when they mobilize in disruptive protests, for the obvious reason that they lack the resources to exert influence in conventional ways, such as forming organizations, petitioning, lobbying, influencing the media, buying politicians. By disruptive protest, we mean acts such as incendiarism, riots, sit-ins and other forms of civil disobedience, great surges in demands for relief benefits, rent strikes, wildcat strikes, or obstructing production on assembly lines."[51]

The goal is to force the weakening of the system or, as they call it, the "regime," making it vulnerable to the movement's demands. "Mass disruption, both its emergence and its successes, is closely related to electoral politics. . . . When a regime is insecure . . . it is more likely to bargain actively for support, and may then issue appeals which signal its vulnerability to demands from the bottom."[52]

"Social movements thrive on conflict," wrote Piven and Cloward. "By contrast, electoral politics demands strategies of consensus and coalition. [M]ovements have the impact they do on electoral politics mainly because the issues they raise and the strife they generate widen cleavages among voter groups. We call this 'dissensus politics' to differentiate it from the usual process of building electoral influence by recruiting adherents and assembling coalitions, or what might be called 'consensus' politics. . . . Movements are not likely to have much impact unless economic and social conditions are already eroding established electoral allegiances and coalitions. But then it is also the case that significant change-oriented movements are not likely to emerge except during periods of economic and social instability."[53]

If this seems familiar, it is. This strategy has also largely played out in America's streets and politics, as Antifa, BLM, and other Marxist-anarchist groups exploited both the initial economic collapse due to the coronavirus and the death of George Floyd. These groups and others have been key in fomenting violent rioting mostly but not exclusively in the inner cities, militant confrontations with law enforcement, the destruction of public monuments and targeting of a federal courthouse and the White House, occupying parts of cities, and assaulting and threatening citizens at restaurants and other public places.

Piven and Cloward also see opportunity in the transformation of the Democratic Party. "The discontinuities between social experience and electoral politics that result from a static party system may well set the stage for realignment. And signs of electoral discontent may even prompt some rhetorical shifts in campaign appeals by major party operatives."[54] Indeed, this transformation occurred during the last election cycle, where the leadership of the Democratic Party was reluctant to criticize the violent, revolutionary movements and, indeed, frequently disparaged efforts to control them. Furthermore, within the Democratic Party there is a growing allegiance to these movements and their causes, as Piven and Cloward had hoped, which is reflected, in part, by the party's rhetorical and policy radicalization, including the Biden-Sanders 110-page "unity" agenda released during the campaign[55] and the slew of executive orders and legislative initiatives. Moreover, there is clearly a growing radicalization of the party's elected membership, including the likes of the so-called Squad members—Representatives Alexandria Ocasio-Cortez,

Ilhan Omar, Ayanna Pressley, and Rashida Tlaib. But for Piven and Cloward, still more is required, and the pace must quicken.

The professors argue that the progress of mass movements will always be too slow as the American system is too difficult to mold into a truly revolutionary force. However, there will be opportunities to use the system against the system, and to create turmoil from within and without, bringing pressure for revolutionary change. "Still, overall, political leaders remain timid and conservative, trying to suppress the potential for realignment by bridging potential cleavages with general symbols and vague promises. Under these confusing conditions, discontented voters may be as atomized and ineffective as all voters are said to be in the absence of parties."[56]

Social activists must be prepared to abandon the political parties as another way of putting pressure on them. "Just as people have to be mobilized to support parties and the issues and candidates they put forward," they declare, "so do they have to be mobilized to desert them. Social movements are often the mobilizers of disaffection. In particular, . . . social movements are politically effective precisely when they mobilize electoral disaffection."[57]

Nonetheless, the duet proclaim that the party system is problematic in that even the losing party retains some power, blunting or slowing revolutionary progress. "A fragmented governmental system in the United States means that the opposition party usually continues to control some part of the government apparatus, and so it is itself constrained by the need to hold together a majority by promoting consensus."[58] Consequently, there is a need for constant upheaval to bring pressure for change.

Piven and Cloward write that since political parties seek consensus, there will always be cleavages and discordant issues between and among groups that should be exploited by social activists. "To appreciate the role of social movements in helping to precipitate electoral convulsion and realignment, we have to pay attention to the distinctive dynamics of social movements that enable them to do what party politicians do not do. . . . [59] Social movements, even movements that are not particularly disruptive, can do what party leaders and contenders for office in a two-party system will not do: They can raise deeply divisive issues. In fact, social movements thrive on the drama and urgency and solidarity that result from raising divisive issues. If conflict is deadly to the strategy of a party trying to build a majority coalition, it is the very stuff that makes social movements grow."[60] Hence, as we see today, the spawning of numerous movements based on, for example, race, gender, income inequality, environmental justice, etc.

Again, when economic conditions have weakened, causing social conditions to do the same, the political system is said to be ripe for transformation. "[S]ocial movements tend to emerge at moments when the electoral system itself signals the emergence of new potential conflicts. Signs of increased volatility appear in electoral politics, usually traceable to changes in the economy or social life that generate new discontents or encourage new aspirations. The evidence of voter volatility in turn may prompt party leaders to do what they characteristically do, to attempt to hold together their coalition. Only now they will employ more expansive rhetoric, acknowledging grievances among their constituents that are ordinarily ignored or naming and thus perhaps fueling the aspirations that are only beginning to emerge. Even the threat of defections that jeopardize a majority can prompt electoral leaders to make the pronouncements that contribute to the climate of change and possibility that nourish movements."[61]

Indeed, the coronavirus pandemic and the shutting down of our economy, schools, and social activities, and the collective economic and psychological effects on our society, created an environment ripe for exploitation. And that exploitation has occurred both in the halls of power, with far-reaching legislative and executive actions, and in the streets, where organized violence is becoming all too common.

Having created conflict and strife, the movements must control the narrative. Piven and Cloward explained: "[P]oliticians are not the only communicators. The conflicts that movements generate often lend them considerable communicative force. This is no small thing. Ordinarily, political communication is dominated by political leaders and the mass media, who together define the parameters of the political universe, including understandings of which sorts of problems should properly be considered political problems and which sorts of remedies are available. . . . [I]t is hard to dispute the monopoly by the powerful on public and political communication, at least in the absence of movements.[62] Movements can break that monopoly, at least for a brief moment. Movements mount marches and rallies, strikes and sit-ins, theatrical and sometimes violent confrontations. The inflammatory rhetoric and dramatic representations of collective indignation associated with these tactics project new definitions of social reality, or definitions of social reality of new groups, into public discourse. They change understandings not only of what is real but of what is possible and of what is just. As a result, grievances that are otherwise naturalized or submerged become political issues."[63]

For example, BLM has succeeded hugely in controlling the narrative. Time and again, violent confrontations with police are said by the media to be "mostly peaceful protests."[64] Looting is all but ignored and certainly tolerated. Driving the narrative and creating new divisions are key ingredients in expanding and further empowering revolutionary movements. "Movements raise new issues," write Piven and Cloward, "and when new issues take center stage in politics, the balance of political forces changes, in two ways. First, by raising new issues or articulating latent issues, movements activate groups that might otherwise remain inactive. Second, new issues are likely to create new cleavages, with far-reaching consequences for the balance between contending forces. Cleavages are what electoral politicians seek to avoid, but they are the key to understanding the impact of movements on electoral politics and, in particular, to understanding why movements sometimes win victories."[65]

Moreover, hitherto moderate or reluctant politicians can be pressured into accommodating and embracing radical movements if their own political survival is at stake. The professors explained that "[m]ovements wrest concessions from reluctant political leaders when concessions are seen as a way to avert threatened disaffections, or to staunch [*sic*] the flow of defections already occurring, or sometimes when concessions are viewed as a way to rebuild an already fragmented coalition by enlarging or solidifying support from one side of the cleavage line."[66]

Recently, Piven returned to the *Nation* magazine to specifically take aim at "stopping Trump," whom she and the vast majority of academia loathe, of course. In her 2017 article, titled "Throw Sand in the Gears of Everything," Piven wrote, in part: "[W]hat makes movements a force—when they are a force—is the deployment of a distinctive power that arises from the ability of angry and indignant people to at times defy the rules that usually ensure their cooperation and quiescence. Movements can mobilize people to refuse, to disobey, in effect to strike. In other words, people in motion, in movements, can throw sand in the gears of the institutions that depend on their cooperation. It therefore follows that movements need numbers, but they also need a strategy that maps the impact of their defiance and the ensuing disruptions on the authority of decision-makers."[67] ". . . [B]y blocking or sabotaging the policy initiatives of the regime, resistance movements can create or deepen elite and electoral cleavages."[68]

Once again, form and activate a violent mob, create societal fissures, attack racial and economic distinctions, undermine civic life and social associations, etc. In other words, use the freedom secured by the Constitution to attack that which the Constitution is intended to protect. Particularly ready for unrest, Piven posits, are the large cities with their leftist mayors. Indeed, events have rolled out as Piven encouraged, with Antifa and BLM followers, among others, rioting and the left-wing, Democratic mayors who run these cities tolerating most of it. Piven declared: "The repercussions of such mass refusals can be far-reaching, simply because social life depends on systems of intricate cooperation. So does our system of governance. Perhaps the U.S. government, with its famous separation of powers on the national level and its decentralized federal structure, is especially vulnerable to collective defiance. . . . [T]he big cities, where a majority of the population lives, have not been captured [by the 'right wing']. Center-left mayors preside over cities like New York, Los Angeles, Boston, Seattle, and San Francisco, for example. And that fact can nourish urban resistance movements."[69]

More recently, as if leading a resistance movement herself against President Trump and his supporters, this senior-citizen revolutionary insisted that mass action must be taken immediately against them: "Resistance movements are hard: They must mobilize defiant collective action against what seem formidable odds, and they risk triggering tough reprisals. Moreover, they often operate in the dark, not knowing the weak points of the regime they confront or the strains among its allies. This describes our own situation: We don't really know much about the potential fissures among this parade of groups and individuals that Trump is inviting into the national government. . . . But we do know something about the political dangers of a Trump administration that is allowed to move forward without mass resistance."[70]

As if addressing Piven and the literally hundreds of like-minded revolutionaries populating our college and university facilities, the late philosopher and professor Allan Bloom wrote in his 1987 book, *The Closing of the American Mind*, that "[e]very educational system has a moral goal that it tries to attain and that informs its curriculum. It wants to produce a certain kind of human being. This intention is more or less explicit, more or less a result of reflection; but even the neutral subjects, like reading and writing and arithmetic, take their place in a vision of the educated person. . . . Democratic education . . . wants and needs to produce men and women [who are] supportive of a democratic regime."[71] Bloom warned that "we have a culture in which to root education, but we have begun to undermine it. The idealism of the American founding has been explained away as mythical, selfishly motivated, and racist. And so our culture has been devalued."[72] "Nobody believes that the old books do, or even could, contain the truth. . . . Tradition has become superfluous."[73]

Indeed, America's college and university faculties have turned their classrooms into breeding grounds for resistance, rebellion, and revolution against American society, as well as receptors for Marxist or Marxist-like indoctrination and propaganda. Academic freedom exists first and foremost for the militant professors, and the competition of ideas is mostly a quaint concept of what higher education used to be and should be. But Marxism is not about free speech and debate, it is about domination, repression, indoctrination, conformity, and compliance. The existing society and culture and those who prosper within it (intellectually, spiritually, and economically), as well as those who defend it, must be denounced and defamed. Disillusion with the status quo is key. Marxism presents a "new faith," if you will, which promises a new and better society, for which a passion if not obsession is inculcated in future generations—despite its trail of mass death, enslavement, and impoverishment.

CHAPTER THREE

HATE AMERICA, INC.

The progressive intellectuals of the late 1800s and early 1900s laid the foundation for the present-day acceptance and indoctrination of the Marxist ideology throughout academia, society, and the culture. They made clear their hostility toward capitalism and the constitutional-republican system that established barriers against tyrannies of various kinds, including that which is born from the mob or centralized autocracy—and, of course, what would become known as progressivism. They understood that the citizenry generally was not amenable to their alien objectives. Thus, they undertook a long campaign to educate, or better stated, reeducate and indoctrinate future armies of radicals and revolutionaries, such as students and student advocates, through government schools and institutions of higher learning.

Early progressive intellectuals were sympathetic toward the Marxist ideology, as they are today, and even embraced its core themes. And they more or less adopted the Rousseauian approach to educational indoctrination—that is, while contending the student should be free to learn what interests and motivates him as an individual, in fact the instructor should cleverly manipulate what interests and motivates the student. For the ultimate purpose of public education is to subsume the individual's will into the general will. Hence, the progressive frequently intones on behalf of the individual's needs and desires but only in the sense or context of "the greater good" and "the community's best interests."

More recently, but over three decades ago, in a little-remembered article on Marxism's influence in American colleges and universities, *New York Times* education writer Felicity Barringer penned "The Mainstreaming of Marxism in U.S. Colleges" (October 29, 1989). She revealed, in part, that "[a]s Karl Marx's ideological heirs in Communist nations struggle to transform his political legacy, his intellectual heirs on American campuses have virtually completed their own transformation from brash, beleaguered outsiders to assimilated academic insiders. It could be considered a success story for the students of class struggle, who were once regarded as subversives. But some scholars say that as Marxists have adapted, their ties to the 19th-century German philosopher have fragmented into a loosely knit collection of theories with little in common. And in the past decade, while the prosperity of Western economies has made Marxism irrelevant to many, new rival radical theories have arisen to challenge the Marxists themselves."[1]

Thus, there has been an "Americanized" adaption of Marxism, which uses Marx's core precepts and contextualizes them to the American system, in order to effectively overthrow the system—governmental, economic, social, and cultural. Indeed, the report goes on to say: " 'Marxism and feminism, Marxism and deconstruction, Marxism and race—this is where the exciting debates are,' said Jonathan M. Wiener, a professor of history at the University of California at Irvine."[2] Indeed, in 1989, at the time of this article's publication, the seeds of a radical-fringe ideology, Critical Theory, which I discuss at length in a subsequent chapter, and the unraveling of the existing society by weaponizing the culture against itself, began their early bloom throughout the American landscape, but with little public notice.

In fact, Barringer unknowingly exposes what will become a central tenet of Critical Race Theory and other adaptations of Marxism to Americanism—that is, the assault on American history, institutions, and traditions or "the dominant white culture," including by her own employer and publisher, the *New York Times*, in such schemes as the 1619 Project. She wrote: "[D]econstructionists deny that one can understand any experience of the past because the evidence for any conclusion comes from people's observations, most of which appear in a text. Deconstructionists maintain that texts are only stories told by people who leave out what they deem unimportant, and that such omissions keep written history from being reliable evidence about reality."[3] Thus, the war on the traditional teaching of history begins its metastization throughout academia.

In American colleges and universities, there is no limit to how professors can and do use Marxism as a doctrinal tool. Barringer explained: "[D]iversity is now the signature of once-monolithic Marxism. Professor [Gayatri] Spivak, [who teaches] . . . English at the University of Pittsburgh, calls herself a Marxist feminist, Professor [John] Roemer, economics professor at the University of California at Davis, designs Marxist market-driven economies, and Erik Olin Wright, a sociology professor at the University of Wisconsin, calls himself an analytic Marxist, seeking to break Marx's grand theories down into their components."[4]

While Barringer's exposé is quite accurate, and the consequences of multifaceted applications of Marxism are manifest today throughout modern America, the "brash" Marxists still exist and their numbers are growing both on campus and throughout the society, culture, and government.

Moreover, the early progressives understood that they must institutionalize their educational activism by, among other things, controlling the administration of education and the classroom through a tenured and unionized legion of teachers, where like-minded instructors armed with ideologically driven ("social activism") curricula populate all levels of educational institutions, often choose their successors, and are protected from scrutiny or competition. For these reasons and more, they adamantly oppose standardized testing, merit-based teacher evaluations, school choice, and the like. After all, their purpose is to uproot traditional, pre-progressive oriented educational approaches and clear the way for progressive/Marxist-oriented, ideologically based doctrinal approaches instead.

It also bears reminding that the early progressives, like their modern progeny, are the intellectual offspring of Rousseau, Hegel, and Marx. They share the overarching view that the individual must be subjugated to the greater community. Herbert Croly (1869–1930), a leading progressive mastermind and founder of the *New Republic*, explained in his 1909 book, *The Promise of American Life*, that "[t]he better future to which Americans propose to build is nothing if not an idea which must in certain essential respects emancipate them from their past. American history contains much matter for pride and congratulation, and much matter for regret and humiliation. . . . [Americans] must be prepared to sacrifice that traditional vision, even the traditional American way of realizing it."[5] Hence, Croly denounces America's past and insists that it not only be rejected, but that the American people learn to reject it. In other words, as Marx preached, the citizenry must condemn and cast off their own history if there is to be individual and societal progress. Of course, this attitude has now taken firm hold throughout academia and has spilled over into much of our culture.

Croly continued: "It is the economic individualism of our existing national system which inflicts the most serious damage on American individuality; and American individual achievement in politics and science and the arts will remain partially impoverished as long as our fellow countrymen neglect or refuse systematically to regulate the distribution of wealth in the national interest. . . . Americans have always associated individual freedom with the unlimited popular enjoyment of all available economic opportunities. Yet it would be far more true to say that the popular enjoyment of practically unrestricted economic opportunities is precisely the condition which makes for individual bondage. . . ."[6]

Of course, this is a core theme of Rousseau, Hegel, and Marx—that is, the individual must sacrifice his independence, free will, and personal pursuits to the greater good, and in that way not only will he become more fulfilled and self-realized, but the entire community will benefit as well. In America, capitalism and constitutionalism are ramparts that stand against Marxism and progressivism and, therefore, must be discredited and ultimately demolished. For the progressive, like the Marxist, economic and political power must be in the same hands, the hands of a relative few in charge of the state.

However, much groundwork must be done to create broad acquiescence or acceptance to this alien transformation, where the philosopher kings and intellectual masterminds disassemble and, thereafter, remake society. The solution: indoctrinate "the masses," who have been raised to respect and revere the ideals of tradition, custom, faith, and patriotism, to abandon their supposedly obsolete beliefs for a promise of an organized, collective utopia. Change the people to accommodate and eventually support an autocratic government that can allegedly manage their lives better than they can. This necessitates the transformation and seizing of the culture and governing instrumentalities.

Croly wrote that "[i]t can hardly be claimed that the greater proportion of the millions who are insufficiently educated are not as capable of being better educated as the thousands to whom science [the centralized administrative state run by 'expert' masterminds] comes to have a real meaning. Society has merely deprived them of the opportunity. There may be certain good reasons for this negligence on the part of society; but as long as it exists, it must be recognized as in itself a good reason for unpopularity of experts. The best way to popularize [progressivism], and to enable the democracy to consider highly educated officials as representatives, is to popularize the higher education. An expert administration cannot be sufficiently representative until it comes to represent a better educated constituency."[7]

This explains, in part, the push in the Democratic Party for free college education for all, or the canceling of student loans to encourage more attendance at colleges and universities. The purpose is less about teaching classical liberal education or science, technology, engineering, and mathematics to a larger number of students, than doing exactly as Croly urged—indoctrinating as many young people as possible to support their radical dogma.

Moreover, although there has been a huge increase in the number of young people who have graduated from a four-year college (less than 6 percent in 1940)[8], still, only about one-third of the adult population today actually graduates from a four-year college.[9] Therefore, it is necessary to begin the indoctrination process at an earlier age. Thus, the widening of ideologically driven course work and textbooks in government-run primary and secondary schools. This also explains the war on true academic freedom and campus free speech, through intimidation and even violence against those who teach, write, or speak well of Americanism, or merely challenge, or do not conform to, the Marxist-centric orthodoxy.

Even more prolific and prominent than Croly, John Dewey's (1859–1952) role in drastically altering the traditional purposes of education into a social activism movement is manifest throughout education today. Dewey acknowledged and approved of Marxism's influence on, and relationship to, the progressive movement: "[T]he issue which [Marx] raised—the relation of the economic structure to political—is one that actively persists. Indeed, it forms the only basis of present political questions. . . . We are in for some kind of socialism, call it by whatever name we please, and no matter what it will be called when it is realized. Economic determinism [Marx's theory of economic class struggle between, among others, the capitalist and the proletariat] is now a fact, not a theory. But there is a difference and a choice between a blind, chaotic and unplanned determinism, issuing from business conducted for pecuniary profit, and the determination of a socially planned and ordered development. It is the difference and the choice between a socialism that is public and one that is capitalistic."[10]

But there is no "economic determinism" when individuals are free to pursue their own goals and dreams. "Economic struggle" is a false label given to hard work, competition, free will, personal responsibility, and life's lessons—the exercise of free will, personal motivations, the satisfaction of individual needs and desires, the creation and pursuit of opportunities, personal responsibility and accountability, etc. That is, the yearnings and complexity of each human being. And in this context, individual liberty and capitalism go hand in hand. Therefore, capitalism must be maligned and ultimately disemboweled if the individual is to accept and conform to the demands of the few in the name of the many. Hence, Dewey's call for a public, top-down, government-managed "socialism," as opposed to a messy socialism that slow-creeps into the capitalist economy.

Of course, capitalism is a spontaneous form of commerce arising from individuals voluntarily entering into economic relationships. It is not a planned economic system imposed on people by a governmental regime. For Dewey et al., that is the problem. Authority, social engineering, grandiose plans, etc., can only "work" if imposed on the population, which requires usurping the very foundation of America's purpose. Constitutionalism and capitalism limit the role or possibility of a centralized authoritarianism and, conversely, empower the individual within the framework of the civil society. As such, they are utterly incompatible with Marxism and Marxism's offspring—progressivism, which seek the widest latitude over the development and future state of a society. The party controls the government and the government controls the society. There is little room for philosophical or political diversity.

In recent days, this has been demonstrated by threats from the highest levels of the Democratic Party to destroy the independence of the judiciary by packing the courts with progressive ideologues; permanently instituting a Democratic Party majority in the Senate by expanding the chamber's numbers with additional members from Democratic Party strongholds; eliminating the Senate's filibuster rule in order to impose, without effective debate or challenge, far-reaching progressive legislation; and, nationalizing the electoral system in ways that ensure permanent Democratic Party control over the elected parts of our government. Together, these policies would disenfranchise, disunite, and marginalize tens of millions of citizens from more conservative and Republican areas of the country from any role in the nation's governance. Republicanism and representative government would be effectively dead.

It is further evidenced with the flood of market-killing, anticapitalist plans from the infinite government-centric, socialist-type programs promoted by the Democratic Party, which fall under the newly minted nomenclature of the "Green New Deal" and the war on "man-made climate change," which I discuss in a later chapter. So far-reaching are these plans that the principle of private property rights would be gutted—again, in the name of the greater good and the larger community.

Moreover, since the institution of the federal income tax over a century ago, at the birth of American progressivism, redistribution of wealth through the heavy taxation of labor, income, and wealth, supported by Marxist-like class-warfare political propaganda, is a central objective of the Democratic Party. Unfortunately, it resonates today with a significant portion of the population. Indeed, under the guise of the coronavirus pandemic, the Democratic Party has widely expanded the scope and reach of the welfare state, not only doling out trillions of dollars to shore up its political and ideological base, but also ensnaring an ever-larger pool of individuals to government subsidies and transfer payments.

The educational transformation has led, in many ways, to the societal transformation intended by the early progressive intellectuals. Dewey had condemned the educational system of his day and insisted on its conversion into a progressive-thought mill. While he attempted to portray his intentions as training students how to think, much like Socrates, in truth his ambition was the opposite: the indoctrination of children, much like Rousseau had hoped and Marx had demanded. It also has a kinship with *The Republic*, Plato's version of a utopian society, which was nothing more than a form of organized tyranny. As Dewey wrote: "The pupil learns symbols without the key to their meaning. He acquired a technical body of information without ability to trace its connections with the objects and operations with which he is familiar—often he acquires simply a peculiar vocabulary. There is a strong temptation to assume that presenting subject matter in its perfected form provides a royal road to learning. What's more natural than to suppose that the immature can be saved time and energy and be protected from needless error by commencing where competent inquires have left off? The outcome is written large in the history of education. Pupils begin their study of science with texts in which the subject is organized into topics according to the order of the specialist. Technical concepts, with their definitions, are introduced at the outset. Laws are introduced at a very early stage, with at best a few indications of the way in which they were arrived at. The pupils learn a 'science' instead of learning the scientific way of treating familiar material of ordinary experience. The method of the advanced student dominates college teaching; the approach of the college is transferred into the high school, and so down the line, with such omissions as may make the subject easier. . . ."[11]

Therefore, Dewey, argued, as Marx had, that the nation's youth must be freed from existing mores, values, belief systems, traditions, customs, and the like, through public education, and made ready for another sort of programming. And why not? The classroom provides a captive audience of millions of children, a perfect setting for Marxist-oriented indoctrination. Dewey, like his intellectual peers, described this as applying "science" and "reason." As Dewey wrote: "Under the influence of conditions created by the non-existence of experimental science, experience was opposed in all the ruling philosophies of the past to reason and the truly rational. Empirical knowledge meant the knowledge accumulated by a multitude of past instances without intelligence insight into the principles of any of them. . . . Science is experience becoming rational. The effect of science is thus to change men's idea of the nature and inherent possibilities of experience. . . . It aims to free an experience from all which is purely personal and strictly immediate; it aims to detach whatever it has in common with the subject matter of other experiences, and which, being common, may be saved for further use. . . . From the standpoint of science, this material is accidental, while the features which are widely shared are essential. . . . In emancipating an idea from the particular context in which it originated and giving it a wider reference the results of the experience of any individual are put at the disposal of all men. Thus ultimately and philosophically science is the organ of general social progress."[12]

In other words, Dewey sought to relinquish what is and what has been, for an ideology disguised as science and reason. Of course, the arrogance of the progressives, like that of the Marxists, is boundless, which one would expect from those who would rule over us. That said, to be clear, people of tradition, faith, and custom do not reject science or reason, but they do not worship them, either. They have learned and experienced the value of eternal truths and past wisdom, including from the ancients, which reflects the basis of America's founding, as concisely set forth in the Declaration of Independence.

Like Rousseau, Dewey framed his educational approach as both opening the student's mind and insisting on his obedience; or, more accurately stated, opening the mind to surrender to indoctrination and conformity. As Dewey declared, "The fundamental conclusion is that the school must be made itself into a vital social institution to a much greater extent than obtains at present. . . . Interest in the community's welfare, an interest which is intellectual and practical, as well as emotional—an interest that is to say, in perceiving whatever makes for social order and progress, and for carrying these principles into execution—is the ultimate ethical habit to which all the special school habits must be related."[13]

Unsurprisingly, Dewey was an early fan of the Soviet Union and its "educational system"—or more precisely, its massive propaganda efforts where obedience and conformity were contorted as a new unity. He visited the communist regime and in December 1928 wrote in the *New Republic* that "in the 'transitional' state of Russia (of course, communist regimes are always in 'transitional states') chief significance attaches to the mental and moral (*pace* the Marxians) change that is taking place; that while in the end this transformation is supposed to be a means to economic and political change, for the present it is the other way around. The consideration is equivalent to saying that the import of all institutions is educational in the broad sense—that of their effects upon disposition and attitude. Their function is to create habits so that persons will act cooperatively and collectively as readily as now in capitalistic countries they act 'individualistically.' "[14]

So, here is one of the founding fathers of America's progressive movement, who had lectured about "science and reason," praising the forced brainwashing of the Russian population by the brutal regime of communist dictator Joseph Stalin. And keep in mind, Dewey remains central to progressive thought in academia, the media, and elsewhere.

Dewey continued: "The same consideration defines the importance and the purpose of the narrower education agencies, the schools. They represent a direct and concentrated effort to obtain the effect which other institutions develop in a diffused and roundabout manner. The schools are, in current phase, the 'ideological arm of the Revolution.' In consequence, the activities of the schools dovetail in the most extraordinary way, both in administration and organization and in aim and spirit, into all other social agencies and interests."[15]

Ah, "the revolution." Again, the objective is to control the schools and the curriculum, control the teachers and the classroom, and you will, in time, control the minds and hearts of the population. Is not that the state of affairs in education that we confront in the United States today? And as we shall see later, the radicalization of the culture through education and media propaganda with radical, Marxist-based ideologies, such as Critical Theory.

"During the transitional regime," wrote Dewey, "the school cannot count upon the larger education to create in any single and wholehearted way the required collective and cooperative mentality. The traditional customs and institutions of the peasant, his small tracts, his three-system farming, the influence of home and Church, all work automatically to create in him an individualistic ideology. In spite of the greater inclination of the city worker towards collectivism, even his social environment works adversely in many respects. Hence the great task of the school is to counteract and transform those domestic and neighborhood tendencies that are still so strong, even in a nominally collectivist regime."[16]

This is an extraordinarily blunt proclamation by Dewey of what public schools should be and, in fact, have now become. "The required collective and cooperative mentality?" Marx would have been so proud of his progressive descendants. Indeed, it is startling that Dewey would specifically point to the peasant farmers as an obstacle to the collective utopia. In 1932, about four years after the publication of Dewey's article, Stalin targeted the Ukrainian population, especially the peasant farmers, for extinction through a campaign of massive and ruthless starvation, because they would not surrender their "small tracts" of land to the communist regime and would not buckle to Stalin's collectivist agenda. Millions lost their lives. Indeed, in an effort to protect the stated ideas and supposed principles behind the Russian Revolution, including liberating the people, promoting equality, and instituting justice, the *New York Times*, one of the most influential newspapers in the United States, was a propaganda sheet for Stalin's early regime and helped cover up the genocide and atrocities against the Ukrainians.[17]

Again, it could not be clearer that the ideological underpinnings of the modern progressive movement were spawned from the Marxist womb. The bond is indisputable. Of course, all of Marxism's incarnations, as practiced and where imposed, need not be identical in every respect and, in fact, differ. But the same core beliefs and vocalized arguments are unmistakable among America's progressives. And the resulting decades-long process of progressive indoctrination and manipulation, throughout the culture and government, has taken its toll. Rather than learning allegiance to the nation's founding and ideals, and celebrating a free and civil society, successive generations of students are taught disdain for their own country, its history and its founding, and are encouraged to renounce it.

Many parents who send their children to government-mandated schools, or later voluntarily support their children's attendance at schools of higher learning, hoping they will improve their future job opportunities in society post-education, are often appalled to see the transformation of their children from what they were raised to believe as part of a family, to what they have been indoctrinated to believe as part of a third-party indoctrination effort and ideological movement.

As the progressive control over education, the culture, and society began taking hold, in 1948, University of Chicago professor Richard M. Weaver, in his book, *Ideas Have Consequences*, warned that education and the civil society were crumbling. He wrote: "Surely we are justified in saying of our time: If you seek the monument to our folly, look about you."[18] He condemned what he rightly saw as the rejection of olden truths and faith, resulting in unimaginable inhumanity. "In our own day," Weaver explained, "we have seen cities obliterated and ancient faiths stricken. We may well ask, in the words of Matthew, whether we are not faced with 'great tribulation, such as was not since the beginning of the world.' We have for many years moved with brash confidence that man had achieved a position of independence which rendered the ancient restraints needless. Now, in the first half of the twentieth century, at the height of modern progress, we behold unprecedented outbreaks of hatred and violence; we have seen whole nations desolated by war and turned into penal camps by their conquerors; we find half of mankind looking upon the other half as criminal. Everywhere occur symptoms of mass psychosis. Most portentous of all, there appear diverging bases of values, so that our single planetary globe is mocked by worlds of different understanding. These signs of disintegration arouse fear, and fear leads to desperate unilateral efforts toward survival, which only forward the process."[19]

Weaver explained that "religion begins to assume an ambiguous dignity, and the question of whether it can endure at all in a world of rationalism and science has to be faced." Born is "the anomaly of a 'humanized' religion."[20] Indeed, mankind was now to be defined by his surroundings and, in particular, materialism—the foundational principle behind Marxism, also known as material historicism. "Materialism loomed . . . on the horizon, for it was implicit in what had already been framed. Thus it soon became imperative to explain man by his environment. . . . If man came into this century trailing clouds of transcendental glory, he was now accounted for in a way that would satisfy the positivists."[21] That is, by those intellectuals who reject eternal truths and experience through the ages for the social engineering by supposed experts and their administrative state—which claim to use data, science, and empiricism to analyze, manage, and control society.

Weaver also referenced Charles Darwin and his theory of evolution, writing that "[b]iological necessity, issuing in the survival of the fittest, was offered as the *causa causans* [the primary cause of action], after the important question of human origin had been decided in favor of scientific materialism. After it has been granted that man is molded entirely by environmental pressures, one is obligated to extend the same theory of causality to his institutions. The social philosophers of the nineteenth century found in Darwin powerful support for their thesis that human beings act always out of economic incentives, and it was they who completed the abolishment of freedom of will. The great pageant of history thus became reducible to the economic endeavors of individuals and classes; and elaborate prognoses were constructed on the theory of economic conflicts and resolution. Man created in the divine image, the protagonists of a great drama in which his soul was at stake, was replaced by man the wealth-seeking and-consuming animal."[22]

In other words, the complexity and nature of human existence is reduced to nothing more than a simplistic and defective economic theory in which the individual is little more than a one-dimensional creature, focused solely on material consumption.

"Finally came psychological behaviorism," wrote Weaver, "which denied not only freedom of the will but even such elementary means of direction as instinct." What is happening now "is a reduction to absurdity of the line of reasoning which began when man bade a cheerful goodbye to the concept of transcendence [that is, spirit, faith, God]. There is no term proper to describe the condition in which he is now left unless to be 'abysmality.' He is in the deep and dark abysm, and he has nothing with which to raise himself. . . . As problems crowd upon him, he deepens confusion by meeting them with *ad hoc* policies."[23]

Of course, this leads again to the subject of education. Religion was let go and replaced with education, which, as Weaver observed, "supposedly would exercise the same efficacy. The separation of education from religion, one of the proudest achievements of modernism, is but an extension of the separation of knowledge from metaphysics. And the education thus separated can provide their kind of indoctrination. We include . . . the education of the classroom, for all such institutionalized instruction proceeds on the assumptions of the state. But the education which best accomplishes their purpose is the systematic indoctrination from day to day of the whole citizenry through channels of information and entertainment."[24] Little did Weaver know how right he was, and how bad it would get nearly eighty years later.

This brings us to the period of the late 1950s to the early 1970s, which gave rise to the New Left movement on America's college campuses, much heralded by today's Marxists. Students for a Democratic Society (SDS), among the most prominent of the New Left groups, was founded in 1959 and issued its political manifesto, *The Port Huron Statement*, in 1962. *The Port Huron Statement* is a platitudinous, rambling, pop-psychoanalytical essay condemning capitalism and endorsing a Marxist-type revolution. The New Left "generally avoided traditional forms of political organization in favor of strategies of mass protest, direct actions, and civil disobedience."[25] The movement was greatly influenced by a German-born Marxist, Herbert Marcuse, who, expectedly, was a fierce anticapitalist. Also, unsurprisingly, Marcuse taught at several American universities during his career, including Columbia, Harvard, and Brandeis. A prolific writer, his 1964 book, *One-*

Dimensional Man, was widely read, especially among the New Left, and its success helped to transform Marcuse from a relatively unknown university professor to a prophet and father figure of the burgeoning student antiwar movement."[26] As we will later see, his influence extends well beyond the New Left to modern-day Critical Theory movements, which actively seek to undermine and ultimately supplant American society and culture. Therefore, serious attention must be paid to his writings.

Like most Marxist professors, Marcuse was not merely satisfied with indoctrination, but he urged activism—concrete revolution. Marcuse's explanation for the lack of a Marxist uprising in the United States would change from time to time. At one point he believed it would be led by "the masses." Later, he insisted that the affluence of capitalist society made such a revolution impossible. Hence, he claimed the revolution would emerge from the intellectuals working with the disenfranchised. However, with the advent of the student movement, he was more inclined toward the idea of a popular revolutionary movement.[27] In any event, Marcuse asserted, like Marx, that anything short of a full-fledged revolution would fail to dislodge the scourge of capitalism and the dominant culture.

Marcuse argued, in part, that the capitalist system or "industrial machine" was both psychologically and economically omnipresent, even to the point of devouring and co-opting the working class and labor movements. "By virtue of the way it has organized its technological base," declared Marcuse, "contemporary industrial society tends to be totalitarian. For 'totalitarian' is not only a terroristic political coordination in society, but also a non-terroristic economic-technical coordination which operates through the manipulation of needs by bested interests. It thus precludes the emergence of an effective opposition against the whole. Not only a specific form of government or party rule makes for totalitarianism, but also a specific system of production and distribution which may well be compatible with a 'pluralism' of parties, newspapers, 'countervailing powers,' etc."[28]

Indeed, so powerful is capitalism's grasp, Marcuse claimed, that it is used by the government to manage and control society. "Today political power asserts itself through its power over the machine process and over the technical organization of the apparatus," wrote Marcuse. "The government of advanced and advancing industrial societies can maintain and secure itself only when it succeeds in mobilizing, organizing, and exploiting the technical, scientific, and mechanical productivity available to industrial civilization. And this productivity mobilizes society as a whole, above and beyond any particular individual or group of interests. The brute fact that the machine's physical . . . power surpasses that of the industrial, and of any particular groups of individuals, makes the machine the most effective political instrument in any society whose basic organization is that of the machine process."[29]

But Marcuse argued that there is a way out of "the machine's" clutches. "New modes of realization are needed, corresponding to the new capabilities of society. Such new modes can be indicated only in negative terms because they would amount to the negation of the prevailing modes. Thus economic freedom would mean freedom *from* the economy—from being controlled by economic forces and relationships; freedom from the daily struggle for existence, from earning a living. Political freedom would mean liberation of the individuals *from* politics over which they have no effective control. . . . The most effective and enduring form of warfare against liberation is the implanting of material and intellectual needs that perpetuate obsolete forms of struggle for existence."[30]

The internal contradictions of Marxism and its advocates,

like Marcuse, are stark. Individual and economic freedom mean forsaking free-market capitalism for collectivism? The individual is fulfilled and free from want and struggle? The government will eventually wither away? Is this how Marxism has worked throughout the world or anywhere? Of course not. For example, is there a Marxist regime anyplace on earth that is not a police state? China, North Korea, Cuba, Venezuela? The imposition of the Marxist ideology, from an abstraction to reality, has left tens of millions of suffering and dead human beings in its wake.

Nonetheless, Marcuse argued, having failed to actually overthrow the existing society, there are now serious cracks in its foundation. "[T]here are indications that the 'message' of the New Left has spread and been heard beyond its own spheres. There are, of course, reasons for that. The stability of capitalism has been upset, and indeed on an international scale; the system exposes more and more of its inherent destructiveness and irrationality. It is from this point that protest grows and spreads, even if it is largely unorganized, diffuse, unconnected and still without any evident socialist aims at first. Among workers, the protest expresses itself in the form of wildcat strikes, absenteeism and in undercover sabotage, or appears in flare-ups against the union leadership; it appears as well in the struggles of oppressed social minorities and finally, in the women's liberation movement. It is obvious that there is a general disintegration of worker morale, a mistrust of the basic values of capitalist society and its hypocritical morality; the overall breakdown of confidence in the priorities and hierarchies set by capitalism is apparent."[31]

In the last several decades, building on Dewey's work, and adopting Marxist ideas developed and espoused by the likes of Marcuse and others, and adapting them for American society and culture, the teaching and promotion of Marxism and Marxist notions in the classroom have been open and pervasive on

America's college campuses. As I noted earlier, it even merited an exposé in the *New York Times* some thirty years ago.[32]

Lest anyone be misled, the issue is not whether Marxist teachings in our classrooms have devolved into "a loosely knit collection of theories with little in common," as the *Times* reported back then, thereby making the messages and impact less concerning, but that the tenets of Marxism are being used in numerous ways to attack American society and culture on myriad fronts, making these movements much more difficult to confront and challenge.

It is well worth underscoring what Professor Jonathan M. Wiener told the *Times*: " 'Marxism and feminism, Marxism and deconstruction, Marxism and race—this is where the exciting debates are.'[33] And diversity is now the signature of once-monolithic Marxism."[34]

Indeed, as Marxism has borne various iterations of itself, with its advocates seeking to overturn one or another aspect of cultural and societal life, with their constant exploitation of societal imperfections and individual dissatisfaction, and the Marxist archetype of class struggle theory of the oppressor and the oppressed (bourgeoisie versus proletariat), Marxism's tentacles have reached deeply into American society. And its ubiquity has led to a kind of acquiescence or passive embrace, from corporate boardrooms and professional sports, to most newsrooms and beyond—or is even openly celebrated, albeit under different nomenclatures. At its core, however, Marxism is named for the man and the ideology he propounded at great length in numerous writings. Its principles and arguments provide the foundation for the unmaking of our constitutional republic and market-based economy, regardless of and despite its various permutations in academia and elsewhere.

As underscored in this chapter, however, it is academia and its rule over the education of generations of students that serves as the most potent force for Marxist indoctrination and advocacy, and the most powerful impetus for its acceptance and spread. And it is these students, the real target of Marxist thought, who form the basis for resistance, rebellion, and even revolution.

In his 2011 book, *Heaven on Earth*, Professor Richard Landes of Boston University explains, among other things, the emotional, intellectual, religious, and spiritual drive of millennialists. While he intends for the word "millennialist" to mean more than what I address here, it is very helpful in describing the mind-set and motivations of younger people, especially college and university students, drawn to Marxism and revolutionary movements. As I highlight some of his writing, keep in mind that his use of the word "millennialist" is intended to incorporate "millennials" of a sort; but for my analytical purposes here, if you prefer, substitute the word millennialist with millennials. Either way, Landes's scholarship is important and relevant in understanding the mentality that breeds societal upheaval on college and university campuses.

Landes explains that "[m]illennialists have a passion for justice. They think they know good and evil well. When they look at humanity, many see not a wide and nuanced spectrum of people, but a few saints and a vast sea of sinners, some redeemable, some (most) not. They are quite clear on who will suffer punishment, and who will gain reward at the final Revelation. And when they believe the moment has come, they do not believe in compromise. They anticipate the absolute eradication of evil—corruption, violence, oppression—and the wondrous bliss of the just kingdom for the good. . . . For millennialists, the gray world of the *corpus permixtum* [mixed body of believers and unbelievers] is an illusion in which the 'bad guys' are only first for the time being; it will—it *must*—pass away. Then the last, the meek, the humble, the powerless, will be first."[35]

This makes Marxism a uniquely alluring ideology in that Marx wraps his ideology in the language of the underdog and oppressed, and calls for the eradication of the status quo for it is said to be corrupt through and through.

"All millennialists hope that commitment to their beliefs will spread far and wide," writes Landes, "enough to bring about a transformation of the social and political universe. That is the very essence of millennialism, as opposed to other forms of eschatology: *the just will live free in this world.* It is a collective salvation, a social mysticism. It might come by and by, but such a promise is not pie in the sky. It imagines a transformation of humanity, an evolutionary leap to a different way of human interaction that can have enormous emotional appeal. To use language of political science, millennialism is a (perhaps the first) revolutionary ideology."[36]

Thus, for its preachers and followers, there is a theological-like aspect to Marxism. A promised fundamental transformation of society and the purification of man's nature through a rebirth of society, replaced with a "collective salvation" found in communal egalitarianism.

Landes continues: "Revolutionary ideologies only begin to appeal to large numbers (i.e., the *meme* only spreads widely) when people feel themselves close to the moment of transformation. Indeed, while many of us are millennialists in some way (i.e., we hope that eventually humankind will enter a new stage of peace and justice), very few of us are apocalyptic millennialists (i.e., believe that this world-historical event is about to happen). Only in those relatively rare moments when large numbers are convinced and mobilized by the conviction that at last *the time has come*, does millennialism become a movement that has entered the apocalyptic vortex."[37]

Of course, we saw this play out during the summer of 2020, with widespread violent riots initiated and organized by Black Lives Matter (BLM), Antifa, and other Marxist-oriented groups, among others. We also saw acceptance of and support for BLM spread throughout the culture, including in the Democratic Party, corporations, professional sports, and newsrooms, to name a few.

"For the people who have entered apocalyptic time," explains Landes, "everything quickens, enlivens, coheres. They become semiotically aroused—everything has meaning, patterns. The smallest incident can have immense importance and open the way to an entirely new vision of the world, one in which forces unseen by other mortals operate. If the warrior lives with death at his shoulder, then apocalyptic warriors live with cosmic salvation before them, just beyond their grasp."[38]

Moreover, the revolutionary is intolerant of differing beliefs or ideas, of intellectual challenges or opposition. He demands conformity, which he declares as unity and communality. Landes argues that "[m]illennialists are prolific in what they do. They live in an enchanted and exciting world, and they want nothing more than to bring the rest of us into it. Or, if we refuse, they will bring it to us. And if we still resist, alas too often, they will strike us down as the apocalyptic enemy or force us to strike them down."[39]

Consequently, it is unsurprising that the world's most renowned and notorious Marxist revolutionaries were greatly influenced by their college experiences and studies. For example, the biography of Russia's Vladimir Ilyich Ulyanov, aka Lenin, includes that he "was born . . . into a well-educated family. He excelled at school and went on to study law. At university, he was exposed to radical thinking, and his views were also influenced by the execution of his elder brother, a member of a revolutionary group. Expelled from university for his radical policies, Lenin completed his law degree as an external student in 1891. He moved to St Petersburg and became a professional revolutionary."[40]

Although China's Mao Zedong was born into a peasant family, his biography explains that "he train[ed] as a teacher, [and] he travelled to Beijing where he worked in the University Library. It was during this time that he began to read Marxist literature. In 1921, he became a founding member of the Chinese Communist Party (CCP) and set up a branch in Hunan."[41]

Cambodia's Pol Pot came from a relatively prosperous family. His biography states that he "was educated in a series of French-speaking schools. In 1949, he won a scholarship to study in Paris where he became involved in communist politics."[42]

What occurs in our colleges and universities is largely ignored or abided by most Americans, including parents who often subsidize their children's attendance at these schools, and taxpayers who subsidize these institutions to the tune of tens of billions of dollars every year. This is a grave failure of accountability and responsibility, even a multigenerational debacle.

It is necessary, therefore, to undertake a brief, albeit incomplete, review of Marxist and Marxist-related influences occurring today in higher education. It is enough, for now, to focus on the teachings and writings of the late professor Jean Anyon. Anyon was a professor of social and education policy in the Urban Education Doctoral Program at the Graduate Center of the City University of New York. While unknown to most outside academia, and one of many professors who use their classrooms to promote Marxist or Marxist-related indoctrination, her influence in higher education is well established and lingers to this day.

Writing of her longtime friend, Lois Weis, Ph.D., University at Buffalo, explained: "Relatively few graduate students over the past thirty-five years in the US, Canada, Australia, New Zealand and the UK in the areas of Urban Education, Sociology of Education, Curriculum Studies, and Anthropology of Education have not encountered [Anyon's] work. Since the late 1970's, Jean Anyon sits at the very center of a scholarly movement to unpack the nature of what later is called the 'official curriculum': what is it; how it comes to attain this status; and who it serves. Spurred by calls in England in the early 1970's for a 'new sociology of education,' scholars began to address questions related to what constitutes 'official' knowledge and the ways in which such knowledge is differentially distributed through schools. The theoretical starting point for most of these analyses is articulated by Michael F. D. Young (1971), who argues that there is a 'dialectical relationship between access to power and the opportunity to legitimate dominant categories, and the processes by which the availability of such categories to some groups enable them to assert power and control over others.' Extending this general framework, numerous writers argue that the organization of knowledge, the forms of its transmission, and the assessment of its acquisition are factors in the reproduction of class relationships in advanced capitalist societies."[43]

In plain English, Anyon promoted her dumbed-down brand of Marxist ideology in the classroom in lieu of a traditional approach to attaining knowledge. For example, she wrote: "Capitalism's private ownership of production is . . . distinct from a socialist/communist system as imagined by Marx, in which everyone contributes to the production of economic goods according to their ability, and is provided profits and goods according to what each person needs."[44]

She trumpeted the usual bourgeoisie (property-owning capitalists) versus the proletariat (wage-earning laborers) class warfare struggle, as if a complex world and complicated relationships are so easily broken down into such a caste system. In her 2011 book, *Marx and Education*, she claimed, "An important insight of Marx was that capitalism is an economic system that cannot function without fundamental inequality—meaning that inequity is built into the way the system works. Business owners must make a profit to survive, and those who do not own businesses must find jobs and work in these enterprises, if they are to provide for themselves and their families. Workers (and other employees) are commodities, bought and sold in the market place like any other, at the lowest price. In order to make a profit, the capitalist must pay the worker less than the product s/he made can be sold for. (If the product is a service like health care or computer work, the owner of the business must take in more money than is paid to the employees, if the business is to survive.) The extra money from selling the product or providing the service is the profit that is kept by the capitalist. It is important to note that while the profit margin of small businesses is often relatively small, large corporations—and the shareholders, executives, and managers of these businesses—typically enjoy huge profits, that dwarf the wages and salaries of employees. . . . This profoundly unequal relationship between workers/employees and owners is at the base of the system and, for Marx, is fundamental to its definition."[45]

Obviously, this theory rejects, among other things, all evidence of economic and social mobility that exists in capitalist societies, and especially the United States. The "rags to riches" and "riches to rags" stories are infinite. Indeed, the extent to which individuals by the millions seek refuge in America, risking their lives and the lives of their families, particularly those fleeing so-called communist paradises throughout the world, for a better life are also limitless. Where are the concomitant examples of the opposite—that is, individuals "escaping" the "inequalities of America capitalism" for a better life in communist regimes? The entire ideology is built on a fairy tale, yet delivers a nightmare of horrors.

Anyon, like all Marxists, also exploits the fact of human inequality, which exists for myriad reasons, many having nothing to do with economic oppression or dislocation, historic discrimination, or injustice, but the nature and consequences of individual conduct, motivation, work ethic, luck (good or bad), etc. Moreover, actual equality in the economic context is both impracticable and impossible. What precisely is meant by economic equality? To what extent can it be imposed upon a population of unique and diverse individuals? And by what means and methods shall it be imposed? How do we measure when economic equality has been achieved? And how do we ensure it endures from one generation to the next? Is not economic equality in the eye of the beholder? And what effect will economic equality, whatever it means and however enforced, have on the economic growth, opportunity, and well-being of the general society? In over 190 countries, including communist regimes, where does economic equality actually exist? The questions are endless, yet profoundly important in addressing Marxist theory and its implications for real societies.

Furthermore, the "owner versus worker" paradigm is not a rational paradigm at all. Frequently, the line or distinction between an "owner" and "worker" is ambiguous if nonexistent. Is a person who owns a small retail shop or online business who is self-employed an owner, worker, or both? Most people would answer both. Is a worker who invests in stocks issued by a publicly held business who employs him, or who purchases stock through their own investments and pension plan, also an owner in these businesses? The answer is yes. And why is it assumed, as a matter of empirical fact, that an employer is exploiting his employees in a capitalist economic system? For example, who is better off—employees working for American businesses large and small, or those working in slave-labor conditions in North Korea, Cuba, and Venezuela? Or, let's look at Communist China. Chinese citizens are not free to change jobs; they are assigned social credits based on their strict compliance with governmental dictates; they must worship China's brutal dictator, Xi Jinping, as a supreme leader; religion is all but banned; the judicial system exists to enforce Communist Party orthodoxy; there exists an extensive network of concentration camps; etc. For most cogent people, this is far from the idyllic nirvana promised by Marxist propagandists, especially university professors.

The late Raymond Aron, who was a philosopher and journalist, had a keen insight into the thinking of Marxist intellectuals and elites. In 1955, he wrote in *The Opium of the Intellectuals*, "In the myth of the Revolution, this inconclusive struggle is represented as an ineluctable necessity. The resistance of vested interests, of elements hostile to the radiant, lyrical future, can only be broken by force. On the face of it, Revolution and Reason are diametrically opposed: the latter suggests discussion, the former, violence. Either one argues and ends up by convincing one's opponent, or one renounces argument and resorts to arms. Yet violence has been and continues to be the last resort of a certain rationalist impatience. Those who claim to know the form which institutions should be made to assume are enraged by the blindness of their fellow-men and lose faith in words, forgetting that the same obstacles arising from the nature of individuals and societies will always be there and the revolutionaries, when they have made themselves the masters of the State, will be faced with the same alternative of compromise or despotism."[46]

Nonetheless, despite the world's experience with the reality of Marxism, professors like Anyon march on. For example, she wrote, which is basic Marxist orthodoxy, that "[s]ince higher salaries and employee benefits would reduce the profit margin of owners, capitalists are (by definition and in most actual cases) diametrically opposed to the interests of workers—who generally desire unions, higher minimum wages, and stronger benefits. Thus the worker/owner economic relationship can be seen as a contradictory relationship. The contradictions between the main classes (working and capitalist classes) lead to tension and continual battles (strikes, slow-downs, political demonstrations) and it is by winning these class struggles that workers can be freed from the 'chains' Marx saw holding them down in factories, offices, and other capitalist enterprises. It is this class struggle which Marx saw as ultimately leading to the overthrow of capitalism and the possible development of socialism and communism—a democratic sharing of resources and profits. Marx argued that in a socialist system, 'In place of the old bourgeois society, with its classes and class antagonisms, we shall have an association in which the free development of each is the condition for the free development of all' (Marx and Engels, 1848)."[47]

Actually, the vast majority of private sector employees are not members of unions[48] not because of some conspiracy to prevent the spread of unions but because unions are outdated in many industries, job-killing in other industries, and serve no purpose in additional industries. Furthermore, many if not most employers understand that mistreating your workforce is self-destructive, as it becomes difficult to fill jobs, retain employees in whom much time, training, and resources have been invested, and maintain a loyal and productive work environment. For the American Marxist, however, they are useful in centralizing labor control in the hands of a relative few who mostly share their collectivist agenda. Too often, the union becomes more of a voice for the state than the members it claims to represent, as witnessed in many totalitarian regimes. In the end, however, the decline of private-sector unions is a natural consequence of the preferences and needs of both management and individual employees in an open society.[49]

Anyon asserted that "[i]n capitalism, according to Marx, economic class relations strongly influence the social situation outside the work place, affecting the domestic and civic worlds in which people live. . . . He argued that, 'The mode of production of material life conditions the social, political and intellectual life process in general. It is not the consciousness of men that determines their being, but, on the contrary, their social being that determines their consciousness." (1859) . . . Marx argued, in this vein, that the economic relation and social context in which the working class exists limits the worker's ability to transcend her or his social situation. . . . Men and women, Marx argued, do have some freedom and agency, but are not as free to determine their own life chances as living in a (capitalist) democracy would suggest. 'Men [and women] make their own history,' he said, 'but they do not make it as they please, they do not make it under self-selected circumstances, but under circumstances existing already, given and transmitted from the past.' "[50]

Most obvious in this fallacy is the assertion that our nation exists in some kind of caste or class system, that our entire existence is determined by our economic condition at a given moment in our life, and that there is no ability or hope in transcending this supposed condition. Yet, in a relatively free society, with a relatively free economic system, the opposite is true. Indeed, the examples of individual mobility up and down the social and economic chain are infinite. There simply are no static economic or social caste or class systems. That is not to say that social snobbery and the like is nonexistent, which occurs in every society. However, nowhere does an impenetrable caste or class system exist more profoundly than in communist regimes around the world, where a party and governmental aristocracy lead lives that the populations they lord over can never hope to enjoy.

Aron uncloaks this, as well. He wrote: "The mission assigned to the proletariat bespeaks a lesser degree of hope than the virtue which used to be ascribed to the people. To believe in the people was to believe in humanity as a whole. To believe in the proletariat is to believe in election by suffering. People and proletariat both symbolize the truth of simple creatures, but the people remain, in law, universal—one can conceive at a pinch that the privileged themselves could be included in the communion—while the proletariat is one class among many others, it achieves its triumph by liquidating the other classes and cannot become identified with the social whole except after much strife and bloodshed. Whoever speaks in the name of the proletariat will recall, throughout the centuries, slaves at grips with their masters; he cannot believe any longer in the progressive development of a natural order, but counts on the crowning revolt of the slaves to eliminate slavery."[51]

Despite these observable facts, Anyon repeats Marxist propaganda by writing that "[s]ocial class is another concept of Marx which neo-Marxists in education have made extensive use of. Social class is defined as a person's or group's relation to the means of production—that is, whether your relation to factories, corporations, and other businesses is one of ownership and control, or one of worker as dependent on being hired. Marx described two main classes as characterizing the capitalist system. Members of the working class . . . are in an unequal and contradictory relation to the owners who hire them. Capitalists are in ownership positions, and obtain income not from labor, but from appropriating the surplus money produced by the workers. Marx saw social class as a fundamental social category, based on the way production of goods and services is organized and distributed in the economy."[52]

Anyon continued: "Marx argued . . . that 'the class which has the means of material production at its disposal [i.e., industrial and financial capital], has control at the same time over the means of mental production [that is, of schools, book printing, news outlets, etc.]' . . . These ideologies are expressed and legitimated in the institutions in which we live and learn (in schools, for example, as curriculum and individual competition). It was because of the power of ideologies promulgated by those with economic power to mold a society's children and youth that Marx said that we need to 'rescue education from the influence of the ruling class.' "[53]

This declaration is simply wrong. Teachers and students in our primary and secondary schools are of all backgrounds and economic conditions. They are not mouthpieces or figureheads for the wealthy, whoever they may be. Indeed, "the ruling class" in our public schools consists mostly of teachers who are overwhelmingly "progressive" and teachers' unions that are the bulwark for American Marxism.[54] Moreover, school curriculum is often taught with the political bias of these teachers[55]—including Critical Race Theory, which I discuss in a subsequent chapter. What Anyon objects to is that Marx's revolution, and the overthrow of the existing society, is not pressed harder and faster in public schools. Therefore, the failure to live up to her radical standards is, absurdly, evidence of bourgeois control over the classrooms.

"My generation came of age in the rebellious 1960s, and that may be one reason that as academics many of us were attracted to a theory that challenged what we had been taught about U.S. society. Rather than focusing on meritocracy, democracy, and patriotism, as our school books had taught us, we focused on what seemed to us structural inequalities—and what we saw as systematic means by which whole groups and cultures (e.g., workers, African Americans, women) were excluded from the American Dream."[56]

"Structural inequalities" and "systemic means." Sound familiar? Of course, these terms characterize our society as interminably dissolute, unjust, and immoral. There can be no justice or improvement. The entire enterprise was irredeemable from the start, and nothing since has or can significantly improve the society. It must be relentlessly attacked and condemned, assaulted in small ways and large, and ultimately uprooted for a fantasy society that has delivered, through its entire history and various impositions, nothing but human agony.

Anyon and her ilk see the entire American society as an interlocking system of universal and inescapable oppression serving dark and archaic forces desperately holding on to their power. Moreover, these objectives are said to be formally instituted and enshrined by the Constitution and the capitalist system. Everywhere she looks, there is discrimination, injustice, and subjugation. But, again, the key to advancing "the cause" is indoctrination.

Anyon explains, "A central tenet of critical pedagogy is that students are not always incorporated into the dominant ideology, they sometimes resist. Indeed, they may resist more than we know."[57] Anyon wrote that neo-Marxist scholarship from the late 1970s to 1989 established that "U.S. schools were not neutral in regard to social oppression or exclusion, but were critically implicated in the reproduction of economic inequalities and social ideologies. The next period, 1990–2005, attended to the criticism that race and gender were missing from our analysis and took neo-Marxism in new directions." Anyon argued that her own work evolved from "analysis of social class manifestations in schooling to investigation of ways in which the economic and political decisions of powerful corporations and legislative bodies fundamentally shape school systems and the opportunities they present (or deny) various groups of students."[58]

"[I]n addition to extending Marxist theory," wrote Anyon, "new conditions require an extension of our practice. Critical pedagogy is an enduring, important form of neo-Marxist practice for education at all levels. In order to make this practice more effective in encouraging political participation by young people in struggles for social justice, we need to move our work beyond classroom walls and into the worlds in which low-income, black and Latino, and immigrant students live. We can . . . involve our students in contestation in public places—public struggles over rights, injustice, and opportunity."[59]

Consequently, it is not enough to teach Marxism, but the students must be enlisted into the revolution. Anyon contended there are several reasons for people to become involved in political contention. It "has to do with how they interpret their political and economic surroundings—and changes in those. To be willing to engage in social protest, people must view current developments as presenting opportunities for waging struggle. . . . Situations that were previously understood as oppressive but immutable can be reimagined and viewed as useful."[60] "Critical educators today have an important role to play in helping students apprehend possibility in what, at first glance, might appear overdetermined or unchangeable racial, class, or gender subordination."[61]

Anyon and others have introduced the word "re-imagine" into the Marxist lexicon, the purpose of which is to soften the iron first of Marxism with a nonthreatening appeal. This description has also become popular among Democratic Party politicians and the media, as well. You have heard it more recently in the application to defunding police departments. For example, "it is time to re-imagine law enforcement." Thus, writes Anyon, "Critical educators are involved in [the] vital process of reimagining schools and classrooms as social justice building spaces. This work is incredibly difficult but . . . not any more impossible than the re-imagining of economic relations, the church, and culture that black Americans undertook to achieve the victories in the civil rights movement."[62]

Re-imagine an entirely new society, built on Marxist precepts, leaving no societal stone unturned. Of course, there is no reason to re-imagine such a place, given mankind's infernal experience with Marxist totalitarianism and genocide. Nonetheless, little is mentioned of this knowledge despite its familiarity and real-world consequences, and on those rare occasions when it is mentioned, it is framed in a way to deflect from its consistently inhumane outcomes. Frequently, the diversion involves statements like, "Well, Stalin was a flawed person and not a real communist," or "Mao improved the lot of the peasants," or "Castro's Cuba has universal health care," etc. In other words, semantic digression is used to excuse the horrors of despotism.

Again, Anyon was no mere academic, like so many in her profession. She urged, as did Marx, charging the civil society's ramparts. "Re-imagining economic change and institutions as potentially oppositional does not, by itself, bring social change. And developing critical consciousness in people through information, readings, and discussion does not, by itself, induce them to participate in transgressive politics—although it provides a critical basis for understanding. To activate people to create or join public contention, it is important to actually involve them in protest activity of some kind."[63] Indeed, wrote Anyon, "shifts in political identity do not so much motivate contentious political action, as develop a logical consequence of it. One develops a political identity and commitment—a change in consciousness—from joining demonstrations, marching, singing, joining the activities of social justice organizations in one's neighborhood, etc. Participation creates individual participants; and it also leads to groups developing their own collective identity as social change agents."[64]

If you wondered why college-age people were participating

in the violent uprisings during the summer of 2020 and since, certainly a primary reason was the indoctrination they had been receiving to "join the revolution" and "resistance," led by such groups as BLM and Antifa. And given that most college and university campuses had been closed to physical attendance due to the coronavirus, they had both the time and opportunity to join in the "mostly peaceful protests."

Indeed, as Anyon wrote: "In order to develop a sense of themselves as change agents, as active political players, youth also need opportunities to engage in such activity. . . . Engagement itself, then, is a necessary part of taking up further engagements. Like riding a bike, one has to do it to learn to do it. . . . There is an addition[al], very important reason that people become active, and that is that they are part of organizations or networks that are already active."[65]

Brainwashing against the American founding and civil society, and indoctrination about activism and protest—even violent if necessary—are constantly preached throughout academia. The goal is to create a generation of revolutionaries. Anyon argues that "although critical educators do well to share with students information about systemic causes of subordination, that is not enough to get students involved in the struggle for social justice. . . . [There is] the need to assist students in interpreting economic and political developments as opportunities for participation, helping them to appropriate existing institutional and organization forms for providing physical and emotional support for . . . actual public contention and the development of themselves as active agents in their own and their communities' futures. . . . By giving students direct experience with social justice work, we can educate them to appreciate and value those forms of democratic process that are aimed specifically at creating a more equitable society—public contention toward progressive social change. By setting up situations in the school experience that allow practice of, and assisting students to acquire skill with, public political contention, we legitimize this work and develop students' predisposition to engage in it."[66]

Thus, the agenda for the Marxist faculty member is clear: to create an army of anti-American youth who will do the bidding of the Marxist faculty as they emerge from academia and enter the workplace. Anyon proclaimed: "Re-imaging economic change, institutions, and cultural forms as potentially oppositional does not by itself bring social change. And developing 'critical consciousness' in people through information, readings, and discussion does not by itself induce them to participate in transgressive politics—although it provides a crucial base of understanding. To activate people to create or join a social movement, it is important to actually involve them in protest activity of some kind. . . . One develops a political identity and commitment—a change in consciousness—from talking, walking, marching, singing, attempting to vote, 'sitting in,' or otherwise demonstrating with others."[67]

In his 2020 book, *The Breakdown of Higher Education*, John M. Ellis, distinguished professor emeritus at University of California, Santa Cruz, cites a 2006 survey conducted by Neil Gross and Solon Simmons, of a very large sample of faculty from 927 different institutions, in which Ellis studied the survey's data and concluded that "the faculty in their sample were 9 percent conservative (though only mildly so on average), while 80 percent were solidly left, with well over half of those being extreme left. . . . They found that one in five professors in the social sciences self-identified as 'Marxist.' (In the field of sociology, the ratio was more than one in four.)" . . . "Astonishing as this statistic is," writes Ellis, "it almost certainly understates the matter. The word 'Marxist' does not play at all well with the general public, and many whose mental framework has been largely formed by Marx's ideas prefer to describe themselves as 'socialist' and 'progressives,' or simply 'activists.' We can assume, therefore, that the real number of people motivated by Marxist ideas among social science professors is higher—anything up to double the Gross and Simmons number, but certainly a good deal more than one in five."[68]

Ellis declares that "[i]t is safe to say that self-identified Marxists are no more than a tiny fraction of the general public of the United States, which means that there is a huge discrepancy between this very small group in the population and the very large one found among social science professors."[69] This helps explain why the Democratic Party generally, and Sen. Bernie Sanders in particular, push for free college and the cancellation of student loans. The more young people who are processed through America's colleges and universities, the greater the chance for their revolution.

CHAPTER FOUR

RACISM, GENDERISM, AND MARXISM

The foundational question: what is Critical Theory, from which these other Critical Theory/Marxist movements sprang? Uri Harris at *Quillette* explains: "Critical theory draws heavily on Karl Marx's notion of *ideology*. Because the bourgeoisie controlled the means of production, Marx suggested, they controlled the culture. Consequently, the laws, beliefs, and morality of society reflected the interests of the bourgeoisie. And importantly, people were unaware that this was the case. In other words, capitalism created a situation where the interests of a particular group of people—those who controlled society—were made to *appear* to be universal truths and values, when in fact they were not."[1]

Harris continues: "The founders of critical theory developed this notion. By identifying the distorting effects power had on society's beliefs and values, they believed they could achieve a more accurate picture of the world. And when people saw things as they really were, they would liberate themselves. 'Theory,' they suggested, always serves the interests of certain people; *traditional* theory, because it is uncritical towards power, automatically serves the powerful, while *critical* theory, because it unmasks these interests, serves the powerless. All theory is political, they said, and by choosing critical theory over traditional theory one chooses to challenge the status quo, in accordance with Marx's famous statement: 'Philosophers have hitherto only interpreted the world in various ways; the point is to change it.'"[2]

Herbert Marcuse is credited with hatching the Critical Theory ideology from which the racial, gender, and other Critical Theory–based movements were launched in America. As mentioned earlier, he was a German-born Hegelian-Marxist ideologue of the Franklin School of political theorists. He is best known for attempting to explain why the so-called proletariat (workers) in the United States and elsewhere have not risen up to overthrow the capitalist system of the ruling bourgeoisie. Therefore, we must plunge further into Marcuse's "scholarship."

In his 1965 paper, "Repressive Tolerance," the title of which is a truly perverse if not bizarre twist on logic and reality, Marcuse wrote, in part: "This essay examines the idea of tolerance in our advanced industrial society. The conclusion reached is that the realization of the objective of tolerance would call for intolerance toward prevailing policies, attitudes, opinions, and the extension of tolerance to policies, attitudes, and opinions which are outlawed or suppressed. In other words, today tolerance appears again as what it was in its origins, at the beginning of the modern period—a partisan goal, a subversive liberating notion and practice. Conversely, what is proclaimed and practiced as tolerance today, is in many of its most effective manifestations serving the cause of oppression."[3]

Thus, for Marcuse, tolerance is actually a ploy instituted by the powerful and conniving forces of the bourgeoisie against the unsuspecting proletariat, in which the masses are duped and programmed to support their oppressors. In short, tolerance is used to suppress the people.

"Tolerance is an end in itself," declared Marcuse. "The elimination of violence, and the reduction of suppression to the extent required for protecting man and animals from cruelty and aggression are preconditions for the creation of a humane society. Such a society does not yet exist; progress toward it is perhaps more than before arrested by violence and suppression on a global scale. As deterrents against nuclear war, as police action against subversion, as technical aid in the fight against imperialism and communism, as methods of pacification in neo-colonial massacres, violence and suppression are promulgated, practiced, and defended by democratic and authoritarian governments alike, and the people subjected to these governments are educated to sustain such practices as necessary for the preservation of the status quo."[4]

Therefore, the public in non-Marxist or nonrevolutionary societies are too senseless to realize that they are oppressed and their existence is at the service of the rich and powerful who control the society.

Marcuse claims that "[t]olerance is extended to policies, conditions, and modes of behavior which should not be tolerated because they are impeding, if not destroying, the chances of creating an existence without fear and misery. This sort of tolerance strengthens the tyranny of the majority against which authentic liberals protested. The political locus of tolerance has changed: while it is more or less quietly and constitutionally withdrawn from the opposition, it is made compulsory behavior with respect to established policies. Tolerance is turned from an active into a passive state, from practice to non-practice: laissez-faire the constituted authorities. It is the people who tolerate the government, which in turn tolerates opposition within the framework determined by the constituted authorities. Tolerance toward that which is radically evil now appears as good because it serves the cohesion of the whole on the road to affluence or more affluence. The toleration of the systematic moronization of children and adults alike by publicity and propaganda, the release of destructiveness in aggressive driving, the recruitment for and training of special forces, the impotent and benevolent tolerance toward outright deception in merchandising, waste, and planned obsolescence are not distortions and aberrations: they are the essence of a system which fosters tolerance as a means for perpetuating the struggle for existence and suppressing the alternatives. The authorities in education, morals, and psychology are vociferous against the increase in juvenile delinquency; they are less vociferous against the proud presentation, in word and deed and pictures, of ever more powerful missiles, rockets, bombs—the mature delinquency of a whole civilization."[5]

In other words, America as a land of opportunity and freedom is a fiction, and the citizen-majority that accepts this fiction is made up of mindless zombies, unable to think for themselves—unwitting servants of their own persecutors, who themselves are undermining the cause of economic and political liberation. Tolerance is the means by which this supposed con is accomplished.

Indeed, Marcuse insisted that "[t]he tolerance which enlarged the range and content of freedom was always partisan—intolerant toward the protagonists of the repressive *status quo*. The issue was only the degree and extent of intolerance. In the firmly established liberal society of England and the United States, freedom of speech and assembly was granted even to the radical enemies of society, provided they did not make the transition from word to deed, from speech to action."[6]

Hence, if American society does not tolerate its own demise or overthrow at the hands of Marxist ideologues and movements, it cannot be said to be truly tolerant. Therefore, Marcuse insists that a society is not truly tolerant if it does not sow the seeds of its own demise by Marxist revolutionaries.

Marcuse makes excuses for the failure of his ideology to take root among the American people. He adds: "With the actual decline of dissenting forces in the society, the opposition is insulated in small and frequently antagonistic groups who, even where tolerated within the narrow limits set by the hierarchical structure of society, are powerless while they keep within these limits. But the tolerance shown to them is deceptive and promotes coordination. And on the firm foundations of a coordinated society all but closed against qualitative change, tolerance itself serves to contain such change rather than to promote it. These same conditions render the critique of such tolerance abstract and academic, and the proposition that the balance between tolerance toward the Right and toward the Left would have to be radically redressed in order to restore the liberating function of tolerance becomes only an unrealistic speculation. Indeed, such a redressing seems to be tantamount to the establishment of a 'right of resistance' to the point of subversion. There is not, there cannot be any such right for any group or individual against a constitutional government sustained by a majority of the population."[7]

Moreover, since a republic would not consent to its own subversion and dissolution, thereby rejecting true tolerance, Marxists must resort to other means to overthrow it, including violence. Marcuse declared: "I believe that there is a 'natural right' of resistance for oppressed and overpowered minorities to use extralegal means if the legal ones have proved to be inadequate. Law and order are always and everywhere the law and order which protect the established hierarchy; it is nonsensical to invoke the absolute authority of this law and this order against those who suffer from it and struggle against it—not for personal advantages and revenge, but for their share of humanity. There is no other judge over them than the constituted authorities, the police, and their own conscience. If they use violence, they do not start a new chain of violence but try to break an established one. Since they will be punished, they know the risk, and when they are willing to take it, no third person, and least of all the educator and intellectual, has the right to preach them abstention."[8]

The inescapable conclusion is that in the end, Marcuse was urging the violent overthrow of American society in which the "established hierarchy" was using tolerance to perpetuate oppression against the minority. This nonsensical argument has served as the foundational catalyst for various critical theories that have grown into Marxist-related ideological movements—which, in turn, have been embraced and promoted by the Biden administration, the Democratic Party, the media, and institutions throughout our society and culture. One of the most destructive among these movements is Critical Race Theory (CRT).

In short, CRT is an insidious and racist Marxist ideology spreading throughout our culture and society. The Heritage Foundation's Jonathan Butcher and Mike Gonzalez write in their study, "The New Intolerance, and Its Grip on America," that it promotes, among other things:

- "The Marxist analysis of society made up of categories of oppressors and oppressed;
- The idea that the oppressed impede revolution when they adhere to the cultural beliefs of their oppressors—and must be put through re-education sessions;
- The concomitant need to dismantle all societal norms through relentless criticism; and

- The replacement of all systems of power and even the descriptions of those systems with a worldview that describes only oppressors and the oppressed.

Far from being merely esoteric academic exercises, these philosophies have real-life consequences."[9]

George R. La Noue, research professor of public policy and political science at the University of Maryland, describes CRT through the writings of "the two best-selling proponents of CRT, Robin DiAngelo and Ibram X. Kendi. . . . CRT begins with the presumption that race is the primary way to identify and analyze people and consequently posits a racial hierarchy that supposedly exists with whites on top and blacks at the bottom. Individual behavior is insignificant because everyone in America functions within a society of systemic racism, structural racism, and institutional racism. CRT affirms this perspective by pointing to various existing racial disparities, which it claims are the result of racist discrimination. According to this perspective, efforts by public and private organizations to enforce civil rights laws in employment, housing, contracting, education, etc. are either insufficient or pointless. CRT offers two responses to this situation. First, all whites must admit their culpability by confessing the advantages white supremacy confers on them. Failure to do so reflects 'white fragility'—an instinctive defensiveness that whites are said to display after they have been trained about their investment in racism. Second, individual whites cannot hide behind any personal history of non-discrimination or the desirability of race-neutral laws or policies because the collective action of their race has been oppressive."[10]

In acknowledging their white privilege, La Noue explains that "[w]hites . . . must support 'anti-racist' policies that require various forms of race preferences for non-whites across a variety of fields for an indefinite period. This is required even where whites are a local minority and power structures are controlled by non-whites or Blacks, Indigenous, and People of Color—'BIPOCs' in the current terminology."[11]

In his book *Intellectuals and Society*, Dr. Thomas Sowell, author, scholar, and professor, denounces the entire multicultural/identity politics movement. He explains that "[t]he kind of collective justice demanded for racial or ethnic groups is often espoused as 'social justice,' since it seeks to undo disparities created by circumstances, as well as those created by the injustices of human beings. Moreover, cosmic justice not only extends from individuals to groups, it extends beyond contemporary groups to intertemporal abstractions, of which today's groups are conceived as being the current embodiments."[12]

"Among intellectuals who confuse blame with causation," writes Sowell, "the question-begging phrase 'blaming the victim' has become a staple in discussions of intergroup differences. No individual or group can be blamed for being born into circumstances (including cultures) that lack the advantages that other people's circumstances have. But neither can 'society' be automatically assumed to be either the cause or the cure for such disparities. Still less can a particular institution whose employment, pricing, or lending decisions *convey* intergroup differences be automatically presumed to be *causing* those differences."[13] Indeed, CRT takes blame to a new and dangerously hateful level—that is, white privilege and the white dominant culture are responsible for all manner of black and minority grievances and disaffection.

Moreover, the claim is that the existing system has been permanently rigged against blacks and minorities from its founding by white racists. Sowell explains that "[e]ven if one believes that environment is the key to intergroup differences, that environment includes a cultural legacy from the past—and the past is as much beyond our control as the geographic settings and historic happenstances that have left not only different individuals or races, but whole nations and civilizations, with very different heritages. . . ."[14]

While Marcuse and his progeny are obsessed with categorizing individuals and treating such groups as stagnant and operating within their own boxes, Sowell contends that such a belief and approach is actually destructive of the very people who are said to be oppressed. In the context of multiculturalism, Sowell argues: "If the dogmas of multiculturalism declare different cultures equally valid, and hence sacrosanct against efforts to change them, then these dogmas simply complete the sealing off of a vision from facts—and sealing off many people in lagging groups from the advances available from other cultures around them, leaving nothing but an agenda of resentment-building and crusades on the side of angels against the forces of evil—however futile or even counterproductive these may turn out to be for those who are the ostensible beneficiaries of such moral melodramas."[15]

In fact, CRT goes beyond arguing that different cultures are equally valid. It declares that society is a systemically racist white-dominant culture and enlists those who are disaffected, dissatisfied, and malcontented into a growing legion of anti-American revolutionaries, where minorities are at dagger points with the "white dominant" societal forces. In his 1964 book, *One-Dimensional Man*, Marcuse urges the expansion of Marxist ideology and revolution to include racial and ethnic groups. "Underneath the conservative popular base is the substratum of the outcasts and outsiders," he wrote, "the exploited and persecuted of other races and other colors, the unemployed and the unemployable. They exist outside the democratic process; their life is the most immediate and the most real need for ending intolerable conditions and institutions. Thus their opposition is revolutionary even if their consciousness is not. Their opposition hits the system from without and is therefore not deflected by the system; it is an elementary force which violates the rules of the game and, in doing so, reveals it is a rigged game. When they get together and go out into the streets, without arms, without protection, in order to ask for the most primitive civil rights, they know that they face dogs, stones, and bombs, jail, concentration camps, even death. Their force is behind every political demonstration for the victims of law and order. The fact which marks the beginning of the end of a period."[16]

Indeed, Marcuse and other Marxists spawned Critical Race Theory and a seemingly endless list of disgruntled, ideologically driven groups. Discrimination is based on race, ethnicity, gender, sexual preference, economics, and a potential myriad of other diverse human characteristics, qualities, preferences, and circumstances. In fact, often individuals and groups are said to be victims of more than one kind of discrimination. For example, if an individual is female, Muslim, and black, she is said to be subjected to multiple forms of discrimination. This, too, has been given a name by, among others, University of California, Los Angeles, law professor Kimberlé Crenshaw—*intersectionality*.

In an interview with CNN in 2020, Crenshaw described Critical Race Theory as "a practice. It's an approach to grappling with a history of White supremacy that rejects the belief that what's in the past is in the past, and that the laws and systems that grow from that past are detached from it."[17]

"Critical race theory attends not only to law's transformative role which is often celebrated," claimed Crenshaw, "but also to its role in establishing the very rights and privileges that legal reform was set to dismantle. Like American history itself, a proper understanding of the ground upon which we stand requires a balanced assessment, not a simplistic commitment to jingoistic accounts of our nation's past and current dynamics."[18]

In other words, CRT undermines and exploits America's unique and very successful fusion of diversity and cultural assimilation, and considers all issues in the context of past societal imperfections—regardless of enormous struggles and efforts in creating a more perfect society, including a civil war, massive economic redistribution, and groundbreaking legal changes. Even more, it incorporates and advances an increasing list of causes as new or additional reasons for eradicating society and transforming the country. Indeed, CRT repositions what is the most tolerant and beneficent society on earth as a miserably dark and impoverished nation, from its beginning to today.

Despite Marcuse's call to revolution among minority groups, some Marxist purists saw CRT as diffusing or undermining Marx's material historicism—that is, the notion of class struggle based on economic conditions. That view has all but passed. Critical race theoreticians are typically Marxists in orientation and mostly consider their theory for transitioning society as blending with the Marxist agenda. For example, for the Marxist and the critical race theoretician, the past is evidence of manipulation, exploitation, mistreatment, and corruption of different classes of people. America is, therefore, an irredeemably contemptible society that must be relentlessly condemned and ultimately toppled.

Like Marx, the CRT proponents deal in group stereotypes and prejudices, whether talking about perpetrators or victims, based on race, etc. Assumptions are made about individuals grounded on their physical, religious, ancestral, and other characteristics. But human beings are more than racial beings, just as they are more than economic beings, and the Marxist ideology preaches a monumental and deadly distortion of man's nature. Individuals are complex and complicated, unique, and spiritual. They are influenced by innumerable events, circumstances, motivations, desires, interests, etc. It is the Marxist and critical race academics and activists who create these categories for their own convenience and revolutionary purposes when demanding the dissolution of society and its rebirth as some utopian autocracy or mobocracy. Of course, this is not to say that individuals and the larger society are unaffected by racial and other such distinctions, but not to the exclusion of, and not through the sole lens of, a host of other human influences.

Among the most widely read books on CRT is, unsurprisingly, *Critical Race Theory*. The authors, Professors Richard Delgado and his wife, Jean Stefancic, both teach law at the University of Alabama. They write, in part: the CRT movement "is a collection of activists and scholars engaged in studying and transforming the relationship among race, racism, and power. The movement considers many of the same issues that conventional civil rights and ethnic studies discourses take up but places them in a broader perspective that includes economics, history, setting, group and self-interest, and emotions and the unconscious. Unlike traditional civil rights discourse, which stresses incrementalism and step-by-step progress, critical race theory questions the very foundations of the liberal order, including equality theory, legal reasoning, Enlightenment rationalism, and neutral principles of constitutional law. After the first decade, Critical Race Theory began to splinter and now includes well-developed Asian American jurisprudence, a forceful Latino-critical (LatCrit) contingent, feisty LGBT interest groups, and now a Muslim and Arab caucus. Although the groups continue to maintain good relations under the umbrella of critical race theory, each has developed its own body of literature and set of priorities."[19]

Thus, like Marx, the CRT movement openly disdains and rejects mankind's progress over the centuries if not several millennia, which serve as the underpinning of American society and other advanced societies, as well as racial progress made in our country, which is dismissed as an improvement by, for, and of the white privileged class. By rejecting "equality theory, legal reasoning, Enlightenment rationalism, and neutral principles of constitutional law," CRT reveals itself as a radical dogma and fanatical cause led by true believers.

Delgado and Stefancic break down the meaning and bases of CRT as follows: "First, racism is ordinary, not aberrational—'normal science,' the usual way society does business, the common, everyday experience of most people of color in this country."[20]

Hence, racism is rampant, ubiquitous, conscious, and unconscious. It is everywhere, and there is no escaping it. Minorities are relentlessly victimized as individuals and a class, and in all manners, by white dominance. And short of eradicating society, there is no cure. That's the mind-set, that's the doctrine.

"Second," write Delgado and Stefancic, "most would agree that our system of white-over-color ascendancy serves important purposes, both psychic and material, for the dominant groups. The first feature is that racism is difficult to cure because it is not acknowledged. Color-blind, or 'formal,' conceptions of equality, expressed in rules that insist only on treatment that is the same across the board, can thus remedy only the most blatant forms of discrimination. . . ."[21]

Therefore, goes the argument, widespread white privilege and white supremacy are a scientific fact that must be acknowledged if there is to be any true racial progress. References to and actions based on promoting "color-blindness" or "equality" are meaningless and superficial diversions away from a real cultural revolution.

"The second feature, . . . material determinism, adds a further dimension," declare Delgado and Stefancic. "Because racism advances the interests of both white elites (materially) and working-class whites (psychically), large segments of society have little incentive to eradicate it."[22] For our purposes here, Marx's "material determinism" simply means that individuals and mankind are influenced and motivated by purely material factors.

Thus, CRT borrows from Marx in promoting the concept of material determinism but further racializes it—that is, white elites and even the white working class are part of the bourgeois in Marx's class-struggle model. As such, the white majority must continue to support a racist societal-regime because they are its economic and "power" beneficiaries.

Delgado and Stefancic write that "[a] third theme . . . [is] the 'social construction' thesis, [which] holds that race and races are products of social thought and relations. Not objective, inherent, or fixed, they correspond to no biological or generic reality; rather, races are categories that society invents, manipulates, or retires when convenient. People with common origins share certain physical traits, of course, such as skin color, physique, and hair texture. But these constitute only an extremely small portion of their genetic endowment, are dwarfed by what we have in common, and have little or nothing to do with distinctly human, higher-order traits, such as personality, intelligence, and moral behavior. That society seeks to ignore these scientific truths, creates races, and endows them with pseudo-permanent characteristics is of great interest to the critical race theory."[23]

If you are somewhat perplexed by this third theme, it is understandable. The CRT theoreticians and movement try to advance two conflicting ideas at once: first, that minority groups are discriminated against based on their racial, gender, ethnicity, etc., yet these categories of minority groups are said to have been invented by the unjust society for stereotypical purposes. Actually, it is the Critical Theory advocates who talk and write about groups, and develop new groups of people, who are said to be subjected to injustice and discrimination, known and unknown, conscious and unconscious, interminable and everywhere, in a stereotypical fashion. Hence, identity politics, intersectionality, etc.

And, of course, Delgado and Stefancic celebrate intersectionality as a key element of the CRT movement—that is, discrimination frequently occurs on multiple levels. They write: "Closely related to differential racialization—the idea that each race has its own origins and ever-evolving history—is the notion of intersectionality and anti-essentialism. No person has a single, easily stated, unitary identity. . . . Everyone has potentially conflicting, overlapping identities, loyalties, and allegiances."[24] Moreover, anti-essentialism is the idea that there is not a single answer to every situation; therefore, governmental solutions to discrimination must be flexible and endless to accommodate all manner of discriminatory thinking, behavior, and practices in a racist society, now and in the future.

Clearly, academia is not merely about teaching students how to think—or, in the case of Marxism and CRT, what to think through repetition and indoctrination—but to develop an army of activist revolutionaries. Delgado and Stefancic write that "[u]nlike some academic disciplines, critical race theory contains an activist dimension. It tries not only to understand our social situation but to change it, setting out not only to ascertain how society organizes itself along racial lines and hierarchies but to transform it for the better."[25]

The late Derrick Bell, a Harvard law professor, is considered by some to be the founding father of modern Critical Race Theory. Thomas Sowell knew Bell and also had little regard for Bell or his ideological movement. He believed Bell was not competent to teach at Harvard and, earlier, Stanford Law School and denounced Bell for demanding "not only that people be hired by race, but that they be hired to fit Derek Bell's ideology."[26]

Indeed, it appears Bell's personal setbacks, and criticisms

from colleagues and students alike, affected his view of life and victimization. In his 1992 book, *Inside American Education: The Decline, the Deception, the Dogmas*, Sowell writes of Bell that "he argued that 'direct action' is more effective than law, that 'reform requires confrontation' which 'can't be intellectualized.' While admitting that 'few minority scholars have national reputations or are frequently published in the major law reviews,' Bell attributed this to whites' 'exclusion' of them. Blacks with a different outlook are dismissed by Bell as people who merely 'look black' but 'think white.'"[27]

Bell was critical of most civil rights advances that had come before, including the civil rights acts and Supreme Court decisions such as *Brown v. Board of Education*, and the ideas of color-blindness, merit, and equal opportunity. He argued that they served the interests of the white elite by masking ongoing and interminable racism—the so-called "interest-convergence dilemma."[28] For Bell and his adherents, there can be no neutral law, decisions, or actions as they are all affected by the white-dominant culture and white privilege. As with Marx, therefore, the societal slate must be wiped clean.

"It is our hope," wrote Bell, "that scholarly resistance will lay the groundwork for wide-scale resistance. We believe that standards and institutions created by and fortifying white power ought to be resisted. Decontextualization, in our view, too often masks unregulated—even unrecognized—power. We insist, for example, that abstraction, put forth as 'rational' or 'objective' truth, smuggles the privileged choice of the privileged to depersonify their claims and then pass them off as the universal authority and the universal good. To counter such assumptions, we try to bring to legal scholarship an experientially grounded, oppositionally expressed, and transformatively aspirational concern with race and other socially constructed hierarchies."[29]

And, of course, any negative critique of Bell's "righteous" cause was met with the charge of both white arrogance and white ignorance. Thus, no criticism of Bell or CRT is said to be legitimate. In fact, it is evidence of the very systemic racism of which Bell complains. Bell wrote: "Comparing critical race theory writing with the Spirituals is an unjustified conceit, but the essence of both is quite similar: to communicate understanding and reassurance to needy souls trapped in a hostile world. Moreover, the use of unorthodox structure, language, and form to make sense of the senseless is another similarity. Quite predictably, critics wedded to the existing legal canons will critique critical race theory, and the comparable work by feminists, with their standards of excellence and find this new work seriously inadequate. Many of these critics are steeped in theory and deathly afraid of experience. They seek meaning by dissecting portions of this writing—the autobiographical quality of some work, and the allegorical, story-telling characteristic of others. But all such criticisms miss the point. Critical race theory cannot be understood by claiming that it is ineffective in conveying arguments of discrimination and disadvantage to the majority. Moreover, it is presumptuous to suggest, as a few critics do, that by their attention, even negative attention, they provide this work with legitimacy so that the world will take it seriously. Even if correct, this view is both paternalistic and a pathetically poor effort to regain a position of dominance."[30]

But there were and are prominent critics of CRT who were active in the early civil rights movement, including the late Rev. Martin Luther King Jr.'s chief of staff, confidant, and friend, Dr. Wyatt Tee Walker. Walker was a legend in the civil rights movement in his own right. His friend and frequent collaborator in the school choice movement, Steve Klinsky, writes that Walker was King's " 'field general' in the organized resistance against notorious Birmingham safety commissioner 'Bull' Connor. Walker compiled and named King's 'The Letter from Birmingham Jail.' He was with King for the march on Washington that produced the 'I have a dream' speech, and in Oslo for the Nobel Peace Prize."[31] Walker emphatically rejected CRT. In 2015, Klinsky and Walker coauthored an essay in which they wrote, in part: "Today, too many 'remedies'—such as Critical Race Theory, the increasingly fashionable post-Marxist/post-modernist approach that analyzes society as institutional group power structures rather than on a spiritual or one-to-one human level—are taking us in the wrong direction: separating even elementary school children into explicit racial groups, and emphasizing differences instead of similarities."[32]

"The answer is to go deeper than race, deeper than wealth, deeper than ethnic identity, deeper than gender," they explained. "To teach ourselves to comprehend each person, not as a symbol of a group, but as a unique and special individual within a common context of shared humanity. To go to that fundamental place where we are all simply mortal creatures, seeking to create order, beauty, family and connection to the world—on its own—seems to bend too often towards randomness and entropy."[33]

Klinsky adds that "Dr. Walker was *for* a fundamental respect for all people, without regard to their ethnic group or religion or color of their skin. Dr. Walker's civil rights views tie back to religious values, to humanism, to rationalism, to the Enlightenment. The roots of CRT are planted in entirely different intellectual soil. It begins with 'blocs' (with each person assigned to an identity or economic bloc, as in Marxism). Human-to-human interactions are replaced with bloc-to-bloc interactions. . . . How can we ever find peace among the races and religions if we won't look at each other, person by person, based on actual facts and actual intentions?"[34]

Indeed, CRT is pseudo-scholarship hatched at first by a small cabal of Marxist law professors, led by Bell, based on victimization, emotional appeals, balkanization, and separatism. By now it should be clear that it is a Marxist-based ideology laced throughout with raw bigotry, antagonism, and hate.

Not surprisingly, Delgado and Stefancic promote "legal storytelling and narrative analysis" as among the most effective forms of persuasion, not serious scholarship. "Critical race theorists have built on everyday experiences with perspective, viewpoint, and the power of stories and persuasion to come to a deeper understanding of how Americans see race. They have written parables, autobiography, and 'counterstories' and have investigated the factual background of personalities, frequently ignored in the casebooks. . . . Legal storytellers, such as Derrick Bell . . . draw on a long history with roots going back to the slave narratives, talks written by black captives to describe their condition and unmask the gentility that white plantation society pretended to. . . . Although some writers criticize CRT for excessive negativity and failure to develop a positive program, legal storytelling and narrative analysis are clear-cut advances that the movement can claim. . . . One premise of legal storytellers is that members of this country's dominant racial group cannot easily grasp what it is like to be nonwhite."[35]

As the Heritage Foundation's Jonathan Butcher and Mike Gonzalez underscore, "CRT is purposely political and dispenses with the idea of rights because it blames all inequalities of outcome on what its adherents say is pervasive racism in the United States. 'White supremacy,' a term that comes up repeatedly in CRT discourse and continues to be heavily used today by leaders of the Black Lives Matter organizations, must be smashed. White supremacy does not mean an actual belief in the superiority of white people, however. It can mean anything from classical philosophers to Enlightenment thinkers to the Industrial Revolution."[36]

Butcher and Gonzalez point to CRT author Robin DiAngelo's use of term "white supremacy" to condemn all of society. DiAngelo is an affiliate associate professor of education at the University of Washington. She writes in her book, *White Fragility*: "White supremacy is a descriptive and useful term to capture the all-encompassing centrality and assumed superiority of people defined and perceived as white and the practices based on this assumption. White supremacy in this context does not refer to individual white people and their individual intentions or actions but to an overarching political, economic, and social system of domination. Again, racism is a structure, not an event. While hate groups that openly proclaim white superiority do exist and this term refers to them also, the popular consciousness solely associates white supremacy with these radical groups. This reductive definition obscures the reality of the larger system at work and prevents us from addressing this system."[37] Hence, white supremacy defines and explains the entire American experiment, not merely an extreme fringe of white supremacists.

CRT theorists and activists declare that not only is society incurably racist and white dominated, but there is no point in attempting to assert or pursue your "rights" because such rights really are not rights at all. Why? Because they do not deliver the kind of Marxist egalitarianism and people's (workers') paradise demanded by the critical race movement. Indeed, rights are used to uphold the white racial structure and deny minorities power. Delgado and Stefancic claim that "[i]n our system, rights are almost always procedural (for example, to a fair process) rather than substantive (for example, to food, housing, or education). Think how that system applauds affording everyone equality of opportunity but resists programs that assure equality of results, such as affirmative action at an elite college or university or efforts to equalize public school funding among districts in a region. Moreover, rights are almost always cut back when they conflict with the interests of the powerful. For example, hate speech, which targets mainly minorities, gays, lesbians, and other outsiders, receives legal protection, while speech that offends the interest of the empowered groups finds a ready exception in First Amendment law. . . . Moreover, rights are said to be alienating. They separate people from each other—'stay away, I've got my rights'—rather than encouraging them to form close, respectful communities."[38]

CRT activists, like Marxist revolutionaries, are intolerant of contrary arguments and challenges to their views. Therefore, free speech is particularly threatening to "the cause." Although the focus is said to be on hate speech, which is a term applied to both obvious and offensive racial smears as well as broader political and philosophical disagreements, Chris Demaske, associate professor of communication at the University of Washington Tacoma, explained that "CRT scholars have critiqued many of the assumptions that they believe constitute the ideology of the First Amendment. For example, instead of helping to achieve healthy and robust debate, the First Amendment actually serves to preserve the inequities of the status quo; there can be no such thing as an objective or content neutral interpretation in law in general or of the First Amendment in particular; some speech should be viewed in terms of the harm it causes, rather than all speech being valued on the basis of it being speech; and there is no 'equality' in 'freedom' of speech."[39]

For CRT advocates, counter-speech, more speech, and the marketplace of ideas are all poisoned by white dominance and privilege. Of course, this leads to repression, censorship, and today's "cancel culture," which I address in a later chapter.

Delgado and Stefancic state: "One of the first critical race theory proposals has to do with hate speech—the rain of insults, epithets, and name-calling that many minority people face on a daily basis. An early article documents some of the harms that this type of speech can inflict. It pointed out that courts were already affording intermittent relief for victims of hate speech under such doctrines as defamation, intentional infliction of emotional distress, and assault and battery and concluded by urging a new independent tort in which the victims of deliberate, face-to-face vituperation could sue and provide damages. Later articles and books built on this idea. One writer suggested criminalization as an answer; others urged that colleges and universities adopt student conduct rules designed to deter hate speech on campus. Still others connected hate speech to the social-construction-of-race hypothesis, pointing out that concerted racial vilification contributes to social images and ingrained preconceptions of people of color as indolent, immoral, or intellectually deficient."[40]

The answer, therefore, is the regulation of speech. Thus, governing authorities or, for example, their surrogates in Big Tech, the media, and academia, are to be in the business of determining what speech is acceptable and what speech is not. Of course, for the Marxists and the CRT ideologues, only one kind of speech is acceptable—theirs. Hence, the demand for campus speech codes, the war on academic freedom, and threats to intellectual diversity among faculty and students alike, and the demand for federal and state criminal hate speech laws. Obviously, the problem becomes the vagueness, overbreadth, and overreach of such policies and laws, and eventually governmental and governing authorities controlling speech. This is another example of the contradictions and hypocrisy of Marxism, and here the CRT movement, in that they rail against the existing society while demanding that the government intervene to accomplish their ideological ends.

Delgado and Stefancic also target the Internet. "Hate speech on the Internet is posing a difficult problem. Blogs, tweets, cartoons . . . and other messages in this medium are inexpensive and easy to circulate, often anonymously. They enable those who dislike a person or race to find others of like mind, so that reinforcement builds, often unopposed. Society polarizes, with groups distrusting each other and believing the other side wrongheaded. Of course, counter-speech is easy and inexpensive on the Internet. Still, the ready availability of an avenue for replying to a vituperative message has not completely solved the problem."[41] They have since figured out, however, the means by which to use the Internet for their ends. Again, more on that later in the book.

Moreover, the idea of merit as a just, objective, and desirable goal in society is said to be seen and applied through the eyes of white privilege. Delgado and Stefancic declare that "CRT's critique of merit takes a number of forms, all designed to show that the notion is far from the neutral standard that its supporters imagine it to be. Several writers critique standardized testing, demonstrating that tests like the SAT or LSAT are coachable and reward people from high socioeconomic levels who can afford to pay for expensive test-prep courses. Low test scores predict little more than first-year grades—and those only modestly—and do not measure other important qualities such as empathy, achievement, orientation, achievement orientation, or communication skills. These writers point out that merit is highly situational. If one moves the hoop in a basketball court up or down six inches, one radically changes the distribution of who has merit."[42]

Clearly, the CRT movement has spread not only throughout academia, but in the media, politics, and corporations, and has given rise to racialization of virtually all walks of life. I have often said that while the Soviet Union was defeated, manifestations of that totalitarian regime can be found on the American university and college campus. Butcher and Gonzalez explain why:

"Since CRT originated in post-secondary institutions, it comes as no surprise that some of the most intolerant manifestations of CRT are found on university campuses. College grounds have been the home to protests for decades, but many in the current generation of rioters are determined to have their ideas heard and not allow others to express themselves, even sometimes resorting to violence. Further, activist students and their allies issue demands to school administrators that attempt to exercise power over those in positions of authority."[43] From college and university campuses, the intolerant, speech-crushing cancel culture is now everywhere. And the endgame is the same as the Marxist goal—the destruction of the existing society.

Today, publishers are pushing out books on CRT at a brisk pace. Educational materials are being used in public school classrooms throughout America to indoctrinate and brainwash children. Schoolteachers are being "re-educated" and trained in Critical Race Theory. For example, *Is Everyone Really Equal—An Introduction to Key Concepts in Social Justice Education*, is a popular book by Ozlem Sensoy and Robin DiAngelo currently circulating throughout public education circles. In the book's foreword, James A. Banks, editor of the Multicultural Education Series, explains the agenda: "This trenchant and timely book is written to help both preservice and practicing teachers attain the knowledge, attitudes, and skills needed to work effectively with students from diverse groups, including mainstream groups. A major assumption of this book is that teachers need to develop a critical social justice perspective in order to understand the complex issues related to race, gender, class, and exceptionality in the United States and Canada and to teach in ways that will promote social justice and equality."[44]

Banks cautions that "[o]ne of the most challenging tasks that those of us who teach multicultural education courses to teacher education students experience is resistance to the knowledge and skills that we teach. This resistance has deep roots in the communities in which most teacher education students are socialized as well as in the mainstream knowledge that becomes institutionalized within the academic community and the popular culture that most students have not questioned until they enroll in a multicultural education or diversity course. . . ."[45]

The book is broken down into the following chapters:

Chapter 1: How to Engage Constructively in Courses That Take a Critical Social Justice Approach

Chapter 2: Critical Thinking and Critical Theory

Chapter 3: Culture and Socialization

Chapter 4: Prejudice and Discrimination

Chapter 5: Oppression and Power

Chapter 6: Understanding Privilege Through Ableism

Chapter 7: Understanding the Invisibility of Oppression Through Sexism

Chapter 8: Understanding the Structural Nature of Oppression Through Racism

Chapter 9: Understanding the Global Organization of Racism Through White Supremacy

Chapter 10: Understanding Intersectionality Through Classism

Chapter 11: "Yeah, But . . ." Common Rebuttals

Chapter 12: Putting It All Together[46]

Banks describes the ideological agenda intended by the book:

"We hope to take our readers on a journey that results in an increased ability to see beyond the immediate surface level to the deeply embedded injustice . . . injustice that for so many of us is normal and taken for granted. Looking head-on at injustice can be painful, especially when we understand that we all have a role in it. However, in taking our readers on this journey we do not intend to inspire guilt or assign blame. At this point in society, guilt and blame are not useful or constructive, no one reading this book had a hand in creating the systems that hold injustice in place. But each of us does have a choice about whether we are going to work to interrupt and dismantle these systems or support their existence by ignoring them. There is no neutral ground; to choose not to act against injustice is to choose to allow it. We hope that this book gives our readers the conceptual foundations from which to act against injustice."[47]

CRT is now firmly entrenched in American universities and colleges, and its reach is widespread. The website Legal Insurrection, founded by Professor William Jacobson of Cornell Law School, provides the most comprehensive database of more than two hundred colleges and universities that are using critical race training on their campuses.[48]

Moreover, CRT is spreading rapidly throughout America's public schools. Among other things, this is being accomplished with the strong advocacy and corporate machinery of the *New York Times* and the 1619 Project.

What is the 1619 Project? Writing in *Real Clear Public Affairs*, Krystina Skurk, a research assistant at Hillsdale College, explains that it is "[a] series of essays published by the *New York Times* . . . the 1619 Project reframes U.S. history by arguing that 1619, the year slaves were first brought to Jamestown, is the year of America's true founding. In partnership with the *Times*, the Pulitzer Center created a curriculum based on 1619 that they distributed to over 3,500 schools. The curriculum teaches that slavery has had a lasting impact on all U.S. institutions, according to a Pulitzer Center lesson plan. One discussion guide question asks, How do societal structures developed to support the enslavement of black people, and the anti-black racism that was cultivated in the U.S. to justify slavery, influence many aspects of modern laws, policies, systems, and culture?"[49]

Skurk continues: "In a video created for the curriculum Nikole Hannah-Jones, the creator of the 1619 Project, explains that growing up in the Midwest, she 'saw the landscape of inequality' through her school bus window. The most telling portion of the video is when Hannah-Jones discusses American history, first describing 1776 positively as the year that set in motion the most 'liberatory democratic experiment in the history of the world.' As she speaks, iconic images play of the pilgrims, the American Founders, the 1950s, and the Statue of Liberty. Then the images begin to rewind, and Hannah-Jones says, 'The only way you can believe that this country was the most liberatory democratic nation that the world has ever seen is to, of course, erase the indigenous people who were already here . . . and to ignore the enslaved Africans.'"[50]

Everywhere Hannah-Jones looks, from her *New York Times* perch, she sees racism. "Hannah-Jones claims that nearly everything in modern American life is tainted by the legacy of slavery," writes Skurk. "She points to incarceration rates, the lack of universal healthcare, the length of maternity leave, minimum wage laws, low rates of union membership, highway systems, explicitly and implicitly discriminatory laws, and poorly performing school systems in minority neighborhoods as examples of the continued effects of racism."[51]

What is the goal of this *New York Times* project? Jake Silverstein, the *Times* editor in chief, stated that it "is to reframe American history by considering what it would mean to regard 1619 as our nation's birth year [as opposed to 1776]. Doing so requires us to place the consequences of slavery and the contributions of black Americans at the very center of the story we tell ourselves about who we are as a country."[52]

In his book *1620: A Critical Response to the 1619 Project*, Peter W. Wood, president of the National Association of Scholars, and a former professor, wrote a devastating response to the 1619 Project. Among other things, he explains: "The larger aim of the 1619 Project is to change America's understanding of itself. Whether it will ultimately succeed in doing so remains to be seen, but it certainly had already succeeded in shaping how Americans now argue about key aspects of history. The 1619 Project aligns with the views of those on the progressive left who hate America and would like to transform it radically into a different kind of nation. Such a transformation would be a terrible mistake: it would endanger our hard-won liberty, our self-government, and our virtues as a people. . . ."[53] Wood observes that "the 1619 Project has taken ideas that a few years ago were exclusively fringe a good way into the realm of mainstream opinion. The idea, for example, that the American Revolution was a pro-slavery event once circulated only among conspiracy-minded activists with comic-book-style theories of history. The 1619 Project has brought it from the playground into the classroom, to the consternation of serious historians everywhere."[54]

Wood condemns the project as phony scholarship. And, of course, it is. It is Critical Race Theory dressed up as history. "The usual way for disputes about history to be resolved," says Wood, "is for historians to present their best arguments, and their sources, in journal articles; each side can then examine the evidence for themselves and hammer out the truth. The 1619 Project evades this kind of transparency. . . . Hannah-Jones, who makes some of the most audacious claims, cites no sources at all: the project as presented [originally] in the [*New York Times*] *Magazine* contains no footnotes, bibliography, or other scholarly footholds."[55]

In December 2019, in the *New York Times Magazine*, five exemplary historians "express[ed] . . . strong reservations about important aspects of the 1619 Project. The project is intended to offer a new version of American history in which slavery and white supremacy become the dominant organizing themes. The *Times* has announced ambitious plans to make the project available to schools in the form of curriculums and related instructional material."[56] They were: Victoria Bynum, distinguished emerita professor of history, Texas State University; James M. McPherson, George Henry Davis 1886 emeritus professor of American history, Princeton University; James Oakes, distinguished professor, the Graduate Center, the City University of New York; Sean Wilentz, George Henry Davis 1886 professor of American history, Princeton University; and Gordon S. Wood, Alva O. Wade University emeritus professor and emeritus professor of history, Brown University.

The historians explained that "[t]hese errors, which concern major events, cannot be described as interpretation or 'framing.' They are matters of verifiable fact, which are the foundation of both honest scholarship and honest journalism. They suggest a displacement of historical understanding by ideology. Dismissal of objections on racial grounds—that they are the objections of only 'white historians'—has affirmed that displacement."[57]

"On the American Revolution, pivotal to any account of our history," they write, "the project asserts that the founders declared the colonies' independence of Britain 'in order to ensure slavery would continue.' This is not true. If supportable, the allegation would be astounding—yet every statement offered by the project to validate it is false. Some of the other material in the project is distorted, including the claim that 'for the most part,' black Americans have fought their freedom struggles 'alone.'"[58]

The historians continued: "Still other material is misleading. The project criticizes Abraham Lincoln's views on racial equality but ignores his conviction that the Declaration of Independence proclaimed universal equality, for blacks as well as whites, a view he upheld repeatedly against powerful white supremacists who opposed him. The project also ignores Lincoln's agreement with Frederick Douglass that the Constitution was, in Douglass's words, 'a GLORIOUS LIBERTY DOCUMENT.' Instead, the project asserts that the United States was founded on racial slavery, an argument rejected by a majority of abolitionists and proclaimed by champions of slavery like John C. Calhoun."[59]

In a separate interview with the *Atlantic*, Wilentz explained: "To teach children that the American Revolution was fought in part to secure slavery would be giving a fundamental misunderstanding not only of what the American Revolution was all about but what America stood for and has stood for since the Founding." . . . "Anti-slavery ideology was a 'very new thing in the world in the 18th century,' he said, and 'there was more anti-slavery activity in the colonies than in Britain.'"[60]

It is important to remember that the *New York Times* has a disastrous record on truth and human rights. It has been a propaganda operation for some of the most heinous monsters and regimes in modern history. As I detailed in *Unfreedom of the Press*, the *Times* all but covered up Adolf Hitler's extermination of the European Jews for virtually the entire Holocaust. Earlier, Walter Duranty, its Moscow bureau chief from 1922 to 1936, was Joseph Stalin's favorite Western reporter. Duranty wrote glowingly of the genocidal dictator and the Soviet Union and helped cover up the purposeful mass starvation of millions of Ukrainians in 1932.[61] And in the late 1950s, Herbert L. Matthews, the *Times*' foreign correspondent, "was the first American reporter to interview Fidel Castro and the last to recognize the man as a ruthless and slightly mad totalitarian murderer. He created, fell in love with, and ultimately was devoured by Castro's mythology without ever really understanding what was happening."[62] Today, the *Times* gives voice to a racist, anti-American ideology built on Marxist ideas and tactics, brainwashes our children with lies, and undermines our own country.

However, even before the 1619 Project, the media embraced and promoted Critical Race Theory, setting the stage for the violent riots that have engulfed numerous cities. Zack Goldberg, a doctoral candidate in political science at Georgia State University, undertook what may be the most extensive examination of media reporting on race and racism in recent years. "In the wake of the protests, riots, and general upheaval sparked by the police killing of George Floyd in Minneapolis," wrote Goldberg, "the United States is experiencing a racial reckoning. The response from America's elite liberal institutions suggests that many have embraced the ideology of the protesters. Here, for instance, is a sampling of the titles of opinion pieces and news stories published over the past month by the country's two most influential newspapers, *The Washington Post* and *The New York Times*:

"When black people are in pain, white people just join book clubs"

"Black Activists Wonder: Is Protesting Just Trendy for White People?"

"To White People Who Want to Be 'One of the Good Ones'"

"America's Enduring Caste System: Our founding ideals promise liberty and equality for all. Our reality is an enduring racial hierarchy that has persisted for centuries."

The last entry on the list, a lengthy feature on America's "caste system" in the *New York Times Magazine*, explicitly compares the United States to Nazi Germany.[63]

Goldberg continues: "What the evidence suggests is that leading publications have not only vastly expanded the definition of racism and actively promoted a more racialized view of American society—in a period beginning under a Black president and during which many indicators showed slow and frustrating, but consistent, racial progress—but have done so, in part, by normalizing and popularizing the notion of 'white people's' collective guilt. The latest offering from the *New York Times*' popular podcast lineup . . . is called 'Nice White Parents' and perfectly illustrates the point. The *Times*' description of the podcast, focused on why reform initiatives have failed to fix the problems in American public schools, suggests it has found the source of the problem: 'Arguably the most powerful force in our schools: White parents.'"[64]

Focusing on the *Times* and the *Washington Post*, Goldberg found that "[p]rior to 2013, the terms 'white' and 'racial privilege(s)' appeared in an average of 0.000013% and 0.000015% of all words in the *Times* and *Post*, respectively. Between 2013 and 2019, these average frequencies grew by an astounding 1,200% in the *Times*, which was surpassed by nearly 1,500% increase at the *Post*. Meanwhile, the frequency at which 'privilege' shared the same lexical space as terms like 'white,' 'color,' and 'skin' reached a record high."[65]

Even if you are not a daily viewer or reader of the news, it is impossible to miss the radicalization of so-called journalism these days. Goldberg notes: "The spikes for 'white supremacy' and variant terms are remarkable given that they are by no means novel and so started from a higher baseline. Until a few years ago, their usage was likely limited to references to actual card-carrying white supremacists. But as with 'racism,' these terms have since been radically expanded by a rapid and ideologically driven concept creep. White supremacy is now a vague and all-encompassing label. Instead of describing the demonstrably discriminatory ideas and actions of particular institutions or individuals, white supremacy is now understood by many progressives to be the fundamental ethos of the American system as a whole."[66]

The media's use of "white supremacy" and related terms to describe anything or anyone who does not conform to the CRT racist ideology is pervasive. "Whatever it used to mean," writes Goldberg, "white supremacy is now everywhere and applicable to any context. Consider that until 2015, terms related to 'white supremacy' almost never registered at more than 0.001% of all words in a given year in any of the above newspapers. With the exception of *The Wall Street Journal*, whose upswing was less consistent, this ceiling has been comfortably breached in every year since. By 2019, the *Times* and *Post* were respectively using these terms approximately 17 and 18 times more frequently than they were in 2014."[67]

Moreover, the vast federal bureaucracy is inundated with the CRT agenda and training. President Donald Trump took steps last September 22, 2020, to end the spread of the ideology with Executive Order 13950. It stated, in part: "This destructive ideology is grounded in misrepresentations of our country's history and its role in the world. Although presented as new and revolutionary, they resurrect the discredited notions of the nineteenth century's apologists for slavery who, like President Lincoln's rival Stephen A. Douglas, maintained that our government 'was made on the white basis' . . . 'by white men, for the benefit of white men.' Our Founding documents rejected these racialized views of America, which were soundly defeated on the blood-stained battlefields of the Civil War. Yet they are now being repackaged and sold as cutting-edge insights. They are designed to divide us and to prevent us from uniting as one people in pursuit of one common destiny for our great country."[68]

The executive order explained that the CRT movement and its Marxist-racist agenda were consuming the government: "Unfortunately, this malign ideology is now migrating from the fringes of American society and threatens to infect core institutions of our country. Instructors and materials teaching that men and members of certain races, as well as our most venerable institutions, are inherently sexist and racist are appearing in workplace diversity trainings across the country, even in components of the Federal Government and among Federal contractors. For example, the Department of the Treasury recently held a seminar that promoted arguments that 'virtually all White people, regardless of how "woke" they are, contribute to racism,' and that instructed small group leaders to encourage employees to avoid 'narratives' that Americans should 'be more color-blind' or 'let people's skills and personalities be what differentiates them.' Training materials from Argonne National Laboratories, a Federal entity, stated that racism 'is interwoven into every fabric of America' and described statements like 'color blindness' and the 'meritocracy' as 'actions of bias.' Materials from Sandia National Laboratories, also a Federal entity, for non-minority males stated that an emphasis on 'rationality over emotionality' was a characteristic of 'white male[s],' and asked those present to 'acknowledge' their 'privilege' to each other. A Smithsonian Institution museum graphic recently claimed that concepts like '[o]bjective, rational linear thinking,' '[h]ard work' being 'the key to success,' the 'nuclear family,' and belief in a single god are not values that unite Americans of all races but are instead 'aspects and assumptions of whiteness.' The museum also stated that '[f]acing your whiteness is hard and can result in feelings of guilt, sadness, confusion, defensiveness, or fear.' "[69]

The executive order banned teaching "race or sex stereotyping or scapegoating," including:

> 1. One race or sex is inherently superior to another race or sex.
>
> 2. An individual, by virtue of his or her race or sex, is inherently racist, sexist, or oppressive, whether consciously or unconsciously.
>
> 3. An individual should be discriminated against or receive adverse treatment solely or partly because of his or her race or sex.
>
> 4. Members of one race or sex cannot and should not attempt to treat others without respect to race or sex.
>
> 5. An individual's moral character is necessarily determined by his or her race or sex.
>
> 6. An individual, by virtue of his or her race or sex, bears responsibility for actions committed in the past by other members of the same race or sex.
>
> 7. Any individual should feel discomfort, guilt, anguish, or any other form of psychological distress on account of his or her race or sex.
>
> 8. Meritocracy or traits such as a hard work ethic are racist or sexist, or were created by a particular race to oppress another race.[70]

President Joe Biden, on his first day in office, signed his own executive order to reverse and cancel President Trump's executive order, falsely claiming that Trump's order had eliminated diversity training. Among other things, in announcing this executive order, Biden replaced the phrase "racial equality" with "racial equity," a clear indication that his intentions are in line with the CRT movement's view that the goal is equal outcomes, *not* equal access and treatment. Indeed, the pursuit of "equity" makes the pursuit of equality impossible. Moreover, Biden directs the federal bureaucracy to aggressively collect all kinds of data on the characteristics of individual citizens to ensure the enforceability of equitable outcomes—often referred to as radical egalitarianism. The executive order states, in part: "Many Federal datasets are not disaggregated by race, ethnicity, gender, disability, income, veteran status, or other key demographic variables. This lack of data has cascading effects and impedes efforts to measure and advance equity. A first step to promoting equity in Government action is to gather the data necessary to inform that effort. . . . There is hereby established an Interagency Working Group on Equitable Data (Data Working Group)."[71]

The tracking of citizen behavior in government databases for the purpose of enforcing the government's social and cultural objectives, in this case the racist CRT goals, is reminiscent of Communist China's social credit system. China's program regulates its citizens' behavior based on a point system. As Fox News reported, "[u]nder this system, citizens are ranked in different areas of civil life using data collected from court documents, government or corporate records, and in some cases, citizen observers. Citizens with higher scores have had an easier time getting bank loans, free medical checkups and discounts on heating. Points have been deducted for traffic violations, selling faulty products or defaulting on loan payments. In some cases, people with bad social credit scores have been barred from buying airline or train tickets. Other infractions have included smoking in non-smoking zones, buying—or playing—too many video games and posting false news stories online."[72] Moreover, "[p]eople failing to comply have been placed on so-called 'blacklists,' which companies may reference when considering potential employees. In other cases, students may be denied entry into universities because of their parents' bad social credit scores."[73]

Furthermore, among Biden's first presidential acts was to abolish Trump's Advisory 1776 Commission, which was established to "enable a rising generation to understand the history and principles of the founding of the United States in 1776 and to strive to form a more perfect Union."[74] "The Commission's first responsibility is to produce a report summarizing the principles of the American founding and how those principles have shaped our country."[75] Prior to Biden's swearing in, the commission issued the 1776 Report, which was immediately disparaged by the media.

On January 19, 2021, NBC's Chuck Todd and MSNBC's Trymaine Lee refused to even dig into the contents of the report on air before ridiculing it. Their commitment to the Critical Race Theory ideology was obvious:

> TODD: "Well, look, we've seen it even in sports what Deion Sanders wants to do at Jackson State and sort of break some of those barriers and reestablish a lot of ways for HBCUs [Historically Black Colleges and Universities]. I know one of the things we wanted you to do was talk to students at the university to see what their reactions were about the banner that said "1776 . . ."
>
> LEE: Yeah, Chuck. We talked to a political science professor who said it's really just the response to 1619 and it's really based in a fiction, hypocrisy of America that there's no way to disentangle slavery. To present this kind of shoddily slapdash, it's a shock to no one quite frankly because they've been on this for quite some time.

TODD: It's both a shock, and sadly, I don't think we were surprised.[76]

Todd, Lee, and the other media personalities toe the party line. By this I mean they do not and will not break from the groupthink and ideological imperatives of the various Marxist-spawned movements. They are mouthpieces for and enforcers of ideological purity—true believers for the various intersecting Marxist-centric causes and belief systems, and mostly loyal members of the Democratic Party. There can be no disagreement or deviation from the party line. And for the most part, there is not.

Delgado and Stefancic remind us, like Marcuse before them, that, in the end, if a "peaceful transition" does not take place, given "the white establishment may resist an orderly progression toward power sharing, particularly in connection with upper-level and technical jobs, policies agencies, and government," what comes next, "[a]s happened in South Africa, the change may be convulsive and cataclysmic. If so, critical theorists and activists will need to provide criminal defense for resistance movements and activists and articulate theories and strategies for resistance. Or a third, intermediate regime may set in. . . . [W]hites may deploy neocolonial mechanisms, including token concessions and the creation of a host of light-skinned minority middle managers to stave off the transfer of power as long as possible."[77] This is a truly dangerous, unhinged, racist movement.

The group Black Lives Matter (BLM) is a product of the fusion of Marxism and CRT. In a 2015 video interview with Jared Ball of the Baltimore-based Real News Network, one of the three cofounders of BLM, Patrisse Cullors, declared that she and fellow founder Alicia Garza were Marxists. Cullors stated, in part: "I think of a lot of things, the first thing I think is that we actually do have an ideological frame; myself, and Alicia [Garza] in particular, are trained organizers, we are trained Marxists. We are super versed on ideological theories and I think that what we really try to do is build a movement that could be utilized by many, many black folk."[78] (The third of the cofounders is Opal Tometi.)

Meanwhile, BLM Marxist Khan-Cullors has acquired four homes worth several million dollars. She published a best-selling book and signed lucrative deals with Warner Bros. and other companies to promote her radical agenda.[79] Few Marxist revolutionaries and sympathizers live as they preach.

And there is ample evidence tying the BLM Global Network, the overarching organization, to violent Marxist-anarchist movements of the past. The Heritage Foundation's Mike Gonzalez notes that "Cullors trained for a decade as a radical organizer in the Labor/Community Strategy Center, established and run by Eric Mann, a former member of the Weather Underground, the 1960s radical faction identified by the FBI as a domestic terrorist group. The 'Weathermen' explained in their 1969 foundational statement that they were dedicated to 'the destruction of U.S. imperialism and the achievement of classless world: world communism.'"[80]

Gonzalez discovered a seminar in which Mann lectured attendees to ask themselves "am I making decisions to change the system? Am I being tied to the masses?" Moreover, Mann noted that "[t]he university is the place where Mao Zedong was radicalized, where Lenin and Fidel were radicalized, where Che was radicalized. The concept of the radical middle class of the colonized people, or in my case the radical middle class of the privileged people, is a model of a certain type of revolutionary." . . . "Take this country away from the white settler state, take this country away from imperialism and have an anti-racist, anti-imperialist and anti-fascist revolution."[81]

Scott Walter of the Capital Research Center explains: "If there were any question whether Black Lives Matter has ideological ties to the Communist terrorists of the 1960s, the story of

Susan Rosenberg should put that issue to bed. . . . BLM is ideologically tied—to the point of having [Susan] Rosenberg on the board of the central group—with trained Marxists with a history of extremism and violence. In fact, Rosenberg was a member of the May 19th Communist Organization (M19)."[82] Rosenberg had a long violent, criminal record as a Marxist revolutionary, for which she served sixteen years of a fifty-eight-year sentence, until her full pardon by Bill Clinton. Gonzalez notes that Rosenberg is "vice chair of the board of directors of Thousand Currents—the radical, grantmaking institution that until July [2020] sponsored the BLM Global Network. Rosenberg was also sought on federal charges that she aided the 1979 prison escape of Joanne Chesimard, a Communist now living in Cuba."[83]

Rosenberg and Mann, as well as Barack Obama's former associates, Bill Ayers and Bernardine Dohrn, were all associated with the Weather Underground. *Britannica* explains: "The Weather Underground, originally known as the Weathermen, evolved from the Third World Marxists, [and] was a faction within Students for a Democratic Society (SDS), the major national organization representing the burgeoning New Left in the late 1960s."[84]

Furthermore, as part of its earlier mission statement, since scrubbed from its website, BLM called for the dissolution of the nuclear family: "We disrupt the Western-prescribed nuclear family structure requirement for supporting each other as extended families and 'villages' that collectively care for one another, especially our children, to the degree that mothers, parents, and children are comfortable."[85] Neither the original mission statement nor its subsequent scrubbing was by accident. Marx believed that the nuclear family was a manifestation of bourgeois society. Like religion, the nuclear family interfered with the kind of social ideological brainwashing necessary to achieve the Marxist paradise. Thus, he attacked it and called for its destruction:

> Abolition of the family! Even the most radical flare up at this infamous proposal of the Communists.
>
> On what foundation is the present family, the bourgeois family, based? On capital, on private gain. In its completely developed form, this family exists only among the bourgeoisie. But this state of things finds its complement in the practical absence of the family among the proletarians, and in public prostitution.
>
> The bourgeois family will vanish as a matter of course when its complement vanishes, and both will vanish with the vanishing of capital.
>
> Do you charge us with wanting to stop the exploitation of children by their parents? To this crime we plead guilty.
>
> But, you say, we destroy the most hallowed of relations, when we replace home education by social.
>
> And your education! Is not that also social, and determined by the social conditions under which you educate, by the intervention direct or indirect, of society, by means of schools, &c.? The Communists have not invented the intervention of society in education; they do but seek to alter the character of that intervention, and to rescue education from the influence of the ruling class.
>
> The bourgeois clap-trap about the family and education, about the hallowed co-relation of parents and child, becomes all the more disgusting, the more, by the action of Modern Industry, all the family ties among the proletarians are torn asunder, and their children transformed into simple articles of commerce and instruments of labour.[86]

In the meantime, countless corporations, grant-making nonprofit groups, athletes, actors, and business executives, among others, provide tens of millions of dollars in financial support to BLM. Democratic Party mayors name streets and boulevards for the organization. And BLM is celebrated and even lionized throughout the culture and media, drawing support from countless individuals, especially young people.

As the Marxist–Critical Theory ideology and propaganda spread throughout academia, the media, and beyond, so do the number of movements associated with it. For example, another significant and growing movement is the "Latina/o Critical Race Theory" (LatCrit), which, as Lindsay Perez Huber, a "postdoctoral scholar" at UCLA writes, involves "experiences unique to the Latina/o community such as immigration, status, language, ethnicity, and culture. A LatCrit analysis has allowed researchers to develop the conceptual framework of racist nativism, a lens that highlights the intersection of racism and nativism. . . . The overarching theoretical frameworks . . . are CRT, and in particular, LatCrit. CRT in educational research unapologetically centers on the ways race, class, gender, sexuality and other forms of oppression manifest in the education experiences of People of Color. CRT draws from multiple disciplines to challenge the dominant ideologies such as meritocracy and colorblindness, which suggest educational institutions are neutral systems that function in the *same* ways for *all* students. This framework challenges these beliefs by learning and building from the knowledge of Communities of Color whose education experiences are marked by oppressive structures and practices. The efforts of revealing racism in education is a conscious move toward social and racial justice and empowerment among Communities of Color."[87]

To understand LatCrit, one must understand race and racism—that is, as with CRT generally, the nature of white supremacy and the white-dominant culture. "Understanding racism as a tool to subordinate People of Color reveals its intent as an ideological function of white supremacy. White supremacy can be understood as a system of racial domination and exploitation where power and resources are unequally distributed to privilege whites and oppress People of Color." Indeed, writes Huber, "One can be victimized by racism, despite the reality of whether or not any real differences exist. . . . [R]acism is defined as, *the assigning of values to real or imagined differences in order to justify white supremacy, to the beliefs of whites and at the expense of People of Color, and thereby defend the right of whites to dominance*."[88] (Italics in the original)

Furthermore, in defining racist nativism, Huber declares: "Historically, perceptions of the native have been directly tied to definitions of whiteness. Beliefs in white superiority and historical amnesia have erased the histories of the indigenous communities that occupied the U.S. prior to the first white European settlers. Whites have been historically and legally deemed the native 'founding fathers' of the U.S. With this important connection between nativism and whiteness in mind, racist nativism is defined as, *the assigning of values to real and imagined differences in order to justify the superiority of the native, who is perceived to be white, over that of the non-native, who is perceived to be People and Immigrants of Color, and thereby defend the native's right to dominance*."[89]

Stefancic asserts that Latino/a CRT has been around for half a century or so. Its "progenitor was Rodolfo Acuna," . . . "who was the first scholar to reformulate American history to take account of U.S. colonization of land formerly held by Mexico and how this colonization affected Mexicans living in those territories. His thesis has proven as powerful for Latinos as the potent theories of Derrick Bell have been in understanding the dynamics of race for blacks."[90]

Therefore, not only is the United States a white-dominant, systemically racist society oppressing all people of color, but the country's very existence is illegitimate due to its colonization of Mexico's land. Hence, the true natives are the indigenous Mexicans, not the whites who promote racist nativism.

Acuna's 1972 book, *Occupied America*, opens: "Mexicans—Chicanos—in the United States today are an oppressed people. They are citizens, but their citizenship is second-class at best. They are exploited and manipulated by those with more power. And, sadly, many believe that the only way to get along in Anglo-America is to become 'Americanized' themselves. Awareness of their history—of their contributions and struggles, of the fact that they were not the 'treacherous enemy' that Anglo-American histories have said they were—can restore pride and a sense of heritage to a people who have been oppressed for so long. In short, awareness can help them to liberate themselves."[91]

In other words, being the true natives, Mexicans and Chicanos ought not assimilate into an Anglo-American culture. The former are oppressed and the latter are colonialists.

But Acuna's dire assessment respecting the condition of the Mexican population in the United States cannot explain why "Mexico is the top origin country of the U.S. immigrant population. In 2018, roughly 11.2 million immigrants living in the U.S. were from there, accounting for 25% of all U.S. immigrants."[92] Why would millions of Mexican citizens leave their home country to migrate, both legally and illegally, to America, in some cases risking life and limb, only to be "exploited and manipulated"? The fact is that they are escaping oppression, poverty, crime, and corruption in their own countries for a better life in the United States.

In their book, *Navigating Borders—Critical Race Theory Research and Counter History of Undocumented Americans*, University of Arizona professor Ricardo Castro-Salazar and UK-Durham University professor Carl Bagley proclaim that "[s]cholars have repeatedly pointed out that U.S. people and their leaders tend to be 'chronic ignorers of history.' This amnesia becomes damaging when it forms the boundaries of inclusiveness in modern narratives of U.S. identity and citizenship. The quotidian narratives of history and current events in the United States overlook that 'America' encompasses two continents and includes Argentineans, Brazilians, Canadians, Colombians, Cubans, Dominicans, Guatemalans, Haitians, Jamaicans, Mexicans, Salvadorians, Venezuelans, and many other nations traveled by European explorers in the 1500s. In a proclivity for simplification and abbreviation, many U.S. people, *United Statesians*, . . . have forgotten that the United States is *of* America and not the other way around. The United States is located in Northern America but has shaped the realities of Central and South American nations."[93]

Thus, the argument goes, America is bigger than the United States, encompassing two continents, and the United States and its majority-white, European-linked population—namely, "United Statesians"—are the true trespassers. Indeed, "Mexican-origin Americans" have a greater claim to United States territory than "American Anglo-Protestants," according to Castro-Salazar and Bagley. They write: "Ironically, undocumented Americans of Mexican origin have a double American identity (United Statesian and Mexican) and possess a stronger historical connection with the American continent than the majority population in the U.S. People of Mexican origin, meaning those with a blend of indigenous and European heritage, lived in the lands that are now the Southwestern United States centuries before U.S. expansionism dispossessed Mexico of half of its territory. Those who perceive Mexican-origin Americans as a threat to American 'Anglo-Protestant identity' do not overlook this; they fear that 'No other immigrant group in U.S. history has asserted or could assert a historical claim to U.S. territory. Mexican and Mexican-Americans can and do make the claim.' "[94]

In applying CRT to the discussion about what Castro-Salazar and Bagley define as "undocumented Americans of Mexican origin," they argue that CRT holds that "all knowledge is historical, and, therefore, biased and subjective. Their Critical Theory of society rejected any claim to objective knowledge and focused on uncovering the oppressive mechanisms of society. The purpose was to understand such mechanisms in order to develop conditions that would allow the oppressed to free themselves."[95]

Therefore, illegal aliens are neither illegal nor aliens, and are actually the victims of "internal colonialism"—that is, "[t]he conquered group is dominated and controlled through various means, including violence and more subtle attacks on the subordinated group's culture, language, religion, and history."[96] Consequently, there is opposition and resistance to assimilation into the American culture by a host of racial and ethnic activists—the culture of Anglo-Protestant identity—or the white-dominant culture, for which they are taught to have complete and passionate contempt.

And what of Latino Americans who reject this ideological fanaticism? Again, echoing Marcuse and his "repressive tolerance" theory, Castro-Salazar and Bagley claim that "[t]he phenomenon becomes more complex when the colonized internalize the colonialist mentality and become part of the colonizing majority. In a pluralist capitalist democracy, those who have internalized the oppressor's mentality can become part of the colonizing structure and support many of its actions. . . ."[97] Thus, Mexican-Americans and other immigrants who assimilate into American society have been snookered by or sold out to the "colonizing white majority."

Castro-Salazar and Bagley declare: "Internal colonialism is a form of inegalitarian pluralism where different ethnicities and cultures coexist, but ethnic relations traditionally follow an assimilation model, like in the United States. It is also a form of racism where the dominant culture views the colonized ethnicities and cultures as alien and inferior, as in the case of Native-, African-, Asian-, and Mexican-Americans in the U.S. Internal colonialism exists in the United States with or without the intention of individuals and can be found in all dimensions of life. . . . Internal colonialism contradicts the notion of an integrated and democratic society where, some researchers argue, political and economic inequalities are not temporary, but necessary for the industrial, capitalist system. The dominant society does not see such contradiction, which perpetuates their privileges. . . ."[98]

Hence, according to Castro-Salazar and Bagley, assimilation and capitalism promote targeted oppression and inequality against minorities by the supposedly white-dominated society.

As with his embrace of CRT, soon after his swearing in, Biden signed five executive actions unilaterally changing immigration policy, all of which were sympathetic to, and supportive of the "Latina/o Critical Race Theory" (LatCrit) movement. Among other things, he ended construction of the border wall (later, continuing construction of a mere 13.5 miles), ended the Trump interior enforcement policies, instituted a hundred-day deportation moratorium, and proposed amnesty for individuals without legal status.[99] Moreover, Biden ended agreements the Trump administration had secured with Mexico and other Central American countries to send asylum seekers who arrived at the U.S.-Mexico border to one of three Central American countries. The result, as reported even by the Biden-supportive *Washington Post*: "[T]he new president began tearing down some of the guardrails [instituted by the Trump administration]. [Biden] issued five immigration executive orders on Inauguration Day alone and promised an immigration policy far more humane and welcoming than that of his predecessor. His administration also began allowing unaccompanied minors into the country, a marked departure from the Trump administration's approach. . . . The situation at the border—which Biden and his advisers steadfastly refuse to call a crisis—is the result of an administration that was forewarned of the coming surge, yet still ill-prepared and lacking the capacity to deal with it. Administration officials have been plagued by muddled messaging, sometimes making appeals that seem directed more at liberal activists than the migrants they need to dissuade from coming to the country."[100]

Biden and his transition team were warned early on by federal immigration officials that their initiatives would overwhelm the border and the immigration systems, but Biden ignored them. The *Post* report: "During the transition period, career officials at U.S. Customs and Border Protection tried to issue sober alarms to the Biden team about the likelihood of a crisis at the border that could quickly overwhelm the nation's capacity. Senior [Customs and Border Patrol] CBP officials delivered Zoom briefings to the Biden transition team that included modeling projections showing a steep increase in the arrival of unaccompanied minors if Trump's policies were suddenly lifted, according to one current and two former Department of Homeland Security officials."[101]

What was missing from this report was that Biden's decisions were in line with the LatCrit movement's view of immigration, to which he was appealing. Overwhelming the immigration system and border security forced significant numbers of CBP officials from their border enforcement duties and had the effect of creating an open, unmanned border. Untold thousands of immigrants were released into our country without even receiving court dates for asylum hearings and others had the coronavirus, among other diseases. Therefore, rather than defund CBP, a policy pushed by Marxists within the Democratic Party, and LatCrit activists, but which would not have received sufficient votes in Congress, the Biden administration simply changed the immigration and border dynamics by executive fiat.

Alas, as LatCrit preaches, there really is no such thing as United States sovereignty because America is bigger than just the United States and, besides, "United Statesians" are the real interlopers. Those crossing the border by the hundreds of thousands are the actual indigenous Americans. Moreover, the Democratic Party hopes to benefit from embracing the movement as it counts on wave after wave of illegal aliens, and subsequent grants of amnesty, as one of the ways in which it seeks a permanent hold on power. As Pew Research has reported, Latino voters favor the Democratic Party by a significant margin.[102]

Jim Clifton, chairman and CEO of Gallup, asks: "Here are questions every leader should be able to answer regardless of their politics: How many more people are coming to the southern border? And what is the plan? There are 33 countries in Latin America and the Caribbean. Roughly 450 million adults live in the region. Gallup asked them if they would like to move to another country permanently if they could. A whopping 27% said 'yes.' This means roughly 120 million would like to migrate somewhere. Gallup then asked them where they would like to move. Of those who want to leave their country *permanently*, 35%—or 42 million—said they want to go to the United States. Seekers of citizenship or asylum are watching to determine exactly when and how is the best time to make their move. In addition to finding a solution for the thousands of migrants currently at the border, let's include the bigger, harder question—what about all of those who would like to come? What is the message to them? What is the 10-year plan? 330 million U.S. citizens are wondering. So are 42 million Latin Americans."[103]

The plan is linked to the CT Marxist ideology—that is, the more migrants the better, continue to overwhelm and collapse the system, change the nation's politics, demographics, and citizenry, and ultimately transform the nature of the governing system. And by no means support or accept assimilation. After all, balkanization and tribalization are certain to destroy any country.

Another of the intersectional movements that have also grown into powerful political forces involves gender—Critical Gender Theory. As with other CT movements, at the heart of this movement is the claim that the dominant society and culture, which see gender through the lens of a biological, empirical, scientific, and normative fact, have been oppressing the LGBTQ+ communities, which see gender as a social construct—where the dominant beliefs are simply the viewpoints and traditions of the privileged status quo at a given point in time. Therefore, virtually all traditional gender and sexual binary distinctions and related moral beliefs are considered oppressive, bigoted, and unjust.

Moreover, a distinction has been developed over the last several decades between "sex" and "gender," which historically were interchangeable in understanding and use. But no more. As Scott Yenor, professor of political science at Boise State University, writes: "Many Americans today have accepted what seemed inconceivable just a generation ago: that gender is artificial, is socially constructed, and can be chosen freely by all individuals. This notion—that biological sex can be willfully separated from gender—originated in the arguments of influential radical feminists writing from the 1950s through the 1970s. The premises of their theories, in turn, have ushered in the new world of transgenderism. Yesterday's shocking theory has become today's accepted norm, with more changes to come. Yet whether this new world will prove to be fit for human flourishing remains to be seen." Yenor explains that nowadays, "[h]uman identity is not determined by one's biology, genes, or upbringing; it is a product of how people conceive of themselves. Human beings are, on this view, unsexed persons caught in a body of one sex or another without any need to follow previous gender scripts. 'No more vivid example exists,' writes the philosopher Roger Scruton, 'of the human determination to triumph over biological destiny, in the interests of a moral idea.'"[104]

Indeed, we are told, sex and gender orientation are more complicated than once thought. "'People often are unaware of the biological complexity of sex and gender,' says Dr. Eric Vilain, director of the Center for Gender-Based Biology at UCLA, where he studies the genetics of sexual development and sex differences. 'People tend to define sex in a binary way—either wholly male or wholly female—based on physical appearance or by which sex chromosomes an individual carries. But while sex and gender may seem dichotomous, there are in reality many intermediates.'"[105]

Academia, corporations, the media, and even the House of Representatives are adopting speech codes that eliminate pronoun distinctions between males and females. In the House "'He' or 'She' would become 'Member,' 'Delegate' or 'Resident Commissioner.' And 'father' and 'mother' would become 'parent' while 'brother' and 'sister' would be 'sibling.'"[106] Yet, Nancy Pelosi proudly and often reminds us, as do the media, that she is the first *female* speaker of the House.

ABC News reports that Facebook not only allows users to select from among "him," "her," or "their," but also from fifty-eight additional gender options: "Agender, Androgyne, Androgynous, Bigender, Cis, Cisgender, Cis Female, Cis Male, Cis Man, Cis Woman, Cisgender Female, Cisgender Male, Cisgender Man, Cisgender Woman, Female to Male, FTM, Gender Fluid, Gender Nonconforming, Gender Questioning, Gender Variant, Genderqueer, Intersex, Male to Female, MTF, Neither, Neutrois, Non-binary, Other, Pangender, Trans, Trans*, Trans Female, Trans* Female, Trans Male, Trans* Male, Trans Man, Trans* Man, Trans Person, Trans* Person, Trans Woman, Trans* Woman, Transfeminine, Transgender, Transgender Female, Transgender Male, Transgender Man, Transgender Person, Transgender Woman, Transmasculine, Transsexual, Transsexual Female, Transsexual Male, Transsexual Man, Transsexual Person, Transsexual Woman, and Two-Spirit."[107] And Facebook is hardly alone.

As with CRT and LatCrit, a few hours after his inauguration, Biden signed an executive order reinstating an Obama-era critical gender policy, which states, in part: "All persons should receive equal treatment under the law, no matter their gender identity or sexual orientation. These principles are reflected in the Constitution, which promises equal protection of the laws. These principles are also enshrined in our Nation's anti-discrimination laws, among them Title VII of the Civil Rights Act of 1964, as amended (42 U.S.C. 2000e et seq.)."[108]

But the Civil Rights Act of 1964 says nothing about "gender identity" or "sexual orientation." It prohibits discrimination in public accommodations and federally funded programs, and bans employment discrimination on the basis of race, color, religion, sex, or national origin. Therefore, it is already a violation of federal law to discriminate based on someone's sex.

In fact, "Biden is . . . explicitly laying out his administration's plans for instituting transgender ideology in every sphere of life from schools, locker rooms, and sports teams, to health care and homeless shelters," wrote *National Review*'s editors. Moreover, "[t]he executive order instructs 'the head of each agency' to review all existing regulations where a prohibition on 'sex discrimination' appears, and to apply the 'prohibitions on sex discrimination on the basis of gender identity or sexual orientation' from the Supreme Court's ruling last summer in *Bostock v. Clayton County*. This is overreach, plain and simple. In *Bostock*, the court explicitly restricted its decision to Title VII, stating that 'other policies and practices,' such as 'bathrooms, locker rooms, or anything else of the kind,' were 'questions for future cases.' By contrast, the executive order takes *Bostock*'s fallacious reasoning—that discrimination on the basis of 'gender identity' necessarily 'entails discrimination on the basis of sex'—and applies it to 'any other statute or regulation that prohibits sex discrimination.'"[109]

In addition, the Biden Education Department switched sides in two lawsuits before the Supreme Court, reversing the Trump administration's support for the female athletes—one in Connecticut and another in Idaho—where the female high school athletes sued to prevent biologically male athletes who identify as female from competing in girls' sports. Thus, Critical Gender Theory trumped both science and the integrity of female high school sports.

In another executive order, Biden "established a White House Gender Policy Council (Council) within the Executive Office of the President," with broad and far-reaching authority. It is granted sweeping power to "coordinate Federal Government efforts to advance gender equity and equality." Again, equality and equity are different things. The pursuit of equity, which is a result or end, often requires the unequal treatment of an individual or group to achieve. For example, the destruction of biological girls' high school sports to promote "equity" for biological males identifying as females. Nonetheless, the commission is directed to enforce the objectives of the critical gender theory movement as it applies to gender identity and sexual orientation.[110]

Do these Biden administration directives and actions apply to America's children? According to the Human Rights Campaign, yes. On its website, in a section titled "Transgender Children and Youth: Understanding the Basics," the group states:

> Children are not born knowing what it means to be a boy or a girl; they learn it from their parents, older children and others around them. This learning process begins early. As soon as a doctor or other healthcare provider declares—based on observing the newborn's external sex organs—'it's a boy' or 'it's a girl,' the world around a child begins to teach these lessons. Whether it's the sorting of blue clothes and pink clothes, 'boys' toys' and 'girls' toys' or telling young

> girls they're 'pretty' and boys they're 'strong.' It continues into puberty and adulthood as social expectations of masculine and feminine expression and behavior often become more rigid. But gender does not simply exist in those binary terms; gender is more of a spectrum, with all individuals expressing and identifying with varying degrees of both masculinity and femininity. Transgender people identify along this spectrum, but also identify as a gender that is different than the one they were assigned at birth."[111]

Michelle Cretella, M.D., and executive director of the American College of Pediatricians, a national organization of pediatricians and other health care professionals dedicated to the health and well-being of children, disagrees. "[T]ransgender ideology is not just infecting our laws. It is intruding into the lives of the most innocent among us—children—and with the apparent growing support of the professional medical community."[112] She adds: "Today's institutions that promote transition affirmation are pushing children to impersonate the opposite sex, sending many of them down the path of puberty blockers, sterilization, the removal of healthy body parts, and untold psychological damage."[113]

What does this have to do with Marxism? First, recall Marx's war on the nuclear family. As described by the Wiley Online Library, "Marxist feminism is a species of feminist theory and politics that takes its theoretical bearings from Marxism, notably the criticism of capitalism as a set of structures, practices, institutions, incentives, and sensibilities that promote the exploitation of labor, the alienation of human beings, and the debasement of freedom. For Marxist feminists, empowerment and equality for women cannot be achieved within the framework of capitalism. Marxist feminism is reluctant to treat 'women' as a stand-alone group with similar interests and aspirations. Marxist feminism thus distinguishes itself from other modes of feminist thought and politics by attending critically and systematically to the economic organization of societies, including stratification along the lines of class; by refusing to accord the category of 'women' separate and special status, without regard to class; by its commitment to the overthrow of capitalism; and by its allegiance to working-class and impoverished women."[114]

The International Socialism website explains, in part: "[T]he development of the forces and relations of production shaped, and continued to do so in different ways, the impact that biology had on the position of women and the development of women's oppression. This connection between productive forces and family structure is not mechanical—each new formation builds on what came before and is impacted also by battles between contending classes." . . . "Historical materialism emphasizes the particular historical circumstances in which the oppression of women, and later of trans people, emerged and developed. It allows us to look at the interplay between the biological and the social. The point is not to ask why trans people exist but to defend unconditionally their right to their gender identity."[115]

Laura Miles, author of the book *Transgender Resistance: Socialism and the Fight for Trans Liberation*, and contributor to the *Socialist Review*, "locates the origins of trans oppression in the enforcement of a greater rigidity of gender roles within the emergent nuclear family that arose around the time of another great transformation in productive forces—the industrial revolution. Women and children were pulled into the new factories alongside men, working in horrific conditions that resulted in a huge rise in infant mortality. The ruling class needed a reliable supply of future labor power, and some parts of the ruling class saw that this was under threat."[116]

Even if one does not accept a direct link or parallel to *classical*

Marxist historical materialism and class theory, as with other CT movements, it need not be. The movements are said to be developed from or tailored after Marxist ideology. Indeed, that was the basis of Marcuse's adaption.

I would be remiss if I did not at least touch on the fact that children are being drawn into these movements and being programmed. Writing in the *Washington Post*, Natalie Jesionka declares that "[i]n the year of Black Lives Matter and #MeToo, many parents are wondering when the right time is to talk to their children about social justice. Experts say it's never too early, and a new wave of tools and resources can help start the conversation. You can enroll in music class . . . that develops understanding of gender and personhood. A drag queen story time will soon be a television show. And there are more and more children's books that discuss intersectionality and broaden representation, plus flashcards and short videos that teach parent and toddler alike anti-racism ideas."[117] "Leigh Wilton and Jessica Sullivan, Skidmore College psychology professors who study race and social interaction, say that children develop implicit bias as early as 3 months old and at 4 years old are categorizing and developing stereotypes."[118]

With respect to Critical Gender Theory, Andrea Jones and Emilie Kao, in a Heritage Foundation essay titled "Sexual Ideology Indoctrination: The Equality Act's Impact on School Curriculum and Parental Rights," explain: "In recent years, activist groups have strengthened pressures on legislators and educators to require the teaching of radical Lesbian, Gay, Bisexual, and Transgender ideology in schools. They argue that inclusion and non-discrimination toward students who identify as gay or transgender require radical revision of curricula. Schools across the country and around the world have attempted to implement curricula that teach students the nonscientific belief that gender is fluid and subjective, and that traditional beliefs about marriage and family are rooted in bigotry."[119]

And the activism has reached into classrooms in an increasing number of states: "Around the country, five states and the District of Columbia have begun mandating SOGI [sexual orientation and gender identity] curricula in sex education and history, while 10 others have explicitly prohibited it. If Congress enacts a federal law ['The Equality Act'], it would usurp the states' authority on the issue and undermine parental rights."[120]

Jones and Kao point out that the powerful "Human Rights Campaign, a leading activist organization, already asserts that LGBT students 'have been denied equal access to educational opportunities in schools in every part of our nation' and explicitly draws comparisons to the Civil Rights Act's protections for characteristics such as race, sex, and national origin."[121]

I wish to make clear that I believe generally in the motto "Live and let live." That said, many of its activists are outspoken advocates of CT and are making escalating demands on the imposition of their beliefs on the rest of society and the culture, including in classrooms and respecting ever younger children, the United States armed forces, etc., by the force of government and law, if need be. As such, this is less about tolerance and more about indoctrination, obedience, and the widespread institution of an affirmative agenda. Moreover, the intersectional connection with other CT movements, and their Marxist roots, is undeniable.

As should be clear, the Critical Theory movement, born and developed by German Marxists, chief among them the late Herbert Marcuse, is more influential in the Oval Office, the halls of Congress, university and college classrooms, public schools, corporate boardrooms, the media, Big Tech, and the entertainment industry than the genius and works of Aristotle, Cicero, John Locke, Montesquieu, Adam Smith, John Adams, Thomas

Jefferson, James Madison, and so many others who contributed mightily to a civil and humane world. It is increasingly influential throughout the culture, too often at the cost of Judeo-Christian values and the lessons of the Age of the Enlightenment, which undergird the most tolerant, free, and beneficent societies—especially the United States. Instead, the intersectional network of a seemingly endless list of oppressed individuals and groups are obsessively committed to transforming and overthrowing the American republic and society—that is, the dominant culture and its supposedly repressive institutions—and are tearing this country apart. Of course, this is not to say that every individual or group associated with these movements or their professed purposes is knowingly part of such a rebellion or revolution. No doubt many are unfamiliar with the ultimate objectives and motivations of the fanatical leaders, organizers, and activists among them. Nonetheless, they are contributing to CT's extremely destructive and revolutionary purposes and ends.

CHAPTER FIVE

"CLIMATE CHANGE" FANATICISM

Capitalism has been explained in many ways by many brilliant scholars and philosophers. But a useful and concise definition, workable for the purposes of this chapter, is provided by economist George Reisman, professor emeritus of Economics at Pepperdine University and author.

Reisman explains in his book *Capitalism*: "Economic activity and the development of economic institutions do not take place in a vacuum. They are profoundly influenced by the fundamental philosophical convictions people hold. Specifically, the development of capitalist institutions and the elevation of the level of production to the standard it has reached over the last two centuries presuppose the acceptance of a *this-worldly, pro-reason philosophy*. Indeed, in their essential development, the institutions of capitalism and the economic progress that results represent the implementation of *man's right to life*. . . . Capitalism is the economic system that develops insofar as people are free to exercise their right to life and choose to exercise it. . . . [I]ts institutions represent, in effect, a self-expanded power of human reason to serve human life. The growing abundance of goods that results is the material means by which people further, fulfill, and enjoy their lives. The philosophical requirements of capitalism are identical with the philosophical requirements of the recognition and implementation of man's right to life."[1]

Moreover, as F. A. Hayek, economist, social theorist, philosopher, professor, and 1974 Nobel Prize winner in economics, explained in his book *The Fatal Conceit—The Errors of Socialism*, while people and institutions in capitalist economies apply reason to decision-making that affects them directly, "[t]o understand our civilization, one must appreciate that the extended order results not from human design or intention but spontaneously: it arose from unintentionally conforming to certain traditional and largely *moral* practices, many of which men tend to dislike, whose significance they usually fail to understand, whose validity they cannot prove, and which have nonetheless fairly rapidly spread by means of evolutionary selection. . . . This process is perhaps the least appreciated facet of human evolution. . . . The dispute between the market order and socialism would destroy much of present humankind and impoverish much of the rest. . . . [W]e generate and garner greater knowledge and wealth than could ever be obtained or utilized in a centrally-directed economy whose adherents claim to proceed strictly in accord with 'reason.' Thus socialist aims and programs are factually impossible to achieve or execute; and they also happen . . . to be logically impossible."[2]

Furthermore, Milton Friedman, economist, philosopher, professor, and 1976 Nobel Prize winner in economics, describes the inextricable link between economic and political freedom. "It is widely believed that politics and economics are separate and largely unconnected; that individual freedom is a political problem and material welfare an economic problem; and that any kind of political arrangements can be combined with any kind of economic arrangements. The chief contemporary manifestation of this idea is the advocacy of 'democratic socialism . . . ' " Friedman condemns such a view as a "delusion." "[T]here is an intimate connection between economics and politics, that only certain combinations of political economic arrangements are possible, and that in particular, a society which is socialistic cannot also be democratic, in the sense of guaranteeing individual freedom. Economic arrangements play a dual role in the promotion of a free society. On the one hand, freedom in economic arrangements is itself a component of freedom broadly understood, so economic freedom is an end in itself. In the second place, economic freedom is also an indispensable means towards the achievement of political freedom."[3] "Viewed as a means to the end of political freedom, economic arrangements are important because of their effect on the concentration or dispersion of power. The kind of economic organization that provides economic freedom directly, namely, competitive capitalism, also promotes political freedom because it separates economic power from political power and in this way enables the one to offset the other."[4] "History suggests that capitalism is a necessary condition of political freedom." It is, of course, also possible "to have economic arrangements that are fundamentally capitalist and political arrangements that are not free."[5]

In addition to the freedom Americans enjoy, albeit increasingly threatened by, among other things, the movements discussed in this book, capitalism has created a standard of living for the vast majority of the people unparalleled in any other society, ancient or present. It is important to take stock of the vast benefits to human life produced by this remarkable economic system. Indeed, the fact that we need reminding underscores its pervasiveness. In this regard, Reisman writes that the "industrialized civilization has produced the greatest abundance and variety of food in the history of the world, and has created the storage and transportation systems required to bring it to everyone. This same industrialized civilization has produced the greatest abundance of clothing and shoes, and of housing, in the history of the world. And while some people in countries may be hungry or homeless . . . it is certain that no one in the industrialized countries needs to be hungry or homeless. Industrial civilization has also produced the iron and steel pipe, the chemical purification and pumping systems, and the boilers, that enable everyone to have instant access to safe drinking water, hot or cold, every minute of the day. It has produced the sewage systems and the automobiles that have removed the filth of human and animal waste from the streets of cities and towns. It has produced the vaccines, anesthesias, antibiotics, and all the other 'wonder drugs' of modern times, along with all kinds of new and improved diagnostic and surgical equipment. It is such accomplishments in the foundations of public health and medicine, along with the improved nutrition, clothing, and shelter, that have put an end to plagues and radically reduced the incidence of almost every type of disease."[6]

Moreover, "[a]s the result of industrialized civilization," writes George Reisman, "not only do billions more people survive, but in the advanced countries, they do so on a level far exceeding that of kings and emperors in all previous ages—on a level that just a few generations ago would have been regarded as possible only in a world of science fiction. With the turn of a key, the push of a pedal, and the touch of a steering wheel, they drive along highways in wondrous machines at sixty miles an hour. With the flick of a switch, they light a room in the middle of darkness. With the touch of a button, they watch events taking place ten thousand miles away. With the touch of a few other buttons, they talk to other people across town or across the world. They even fly through the air at six hundred miles per hour, forty thousand feet up, watching movies and sipping martinis in air-conditioned comfort as they do so. In the United States, most people have all this, and spacious homes or apartments, carpeted heating, air conditioning, refrigerators, freezers, and gas or electric stoves, and also personal libraries of hundreds of books, records, compact disks, and tape recordings; they can have all this, as well as long life and good health—as the result of working forty hours a week."[7]

Conversely, the so-called environmental movement of the 1970s has devolved into another avenue to attack American constitutional republicanism and, of course, capitalism. From clean air and clear water, to global cooling/warming/climate change, the goal of many of the leading intellectuals behind this effort has been the introduction of Marxist thinking and objectives through the guise of environmentalism, as the Green New Deal, which promotes economic regression, radical egalitarianism, and autocratic rule. But the movement has expanded well beyond that, to include virtually every programmatic and agenda-driven goal of American Marxism, which has been embraced to one degree or another by the Democratic Party, among others. Moreover, the environmental movement has developed numerous areas of overlap with the other Marxist-centric ideologies and movements, such as Critical Race Theory via environmental justice, which declares the existence of environmental racism targeting minority communities. Some of the movement's masterminds insist that Marxism does not go far enough in establishing their degrowth utopianism as they imagine life in a perpetual state of nature, where productivity, growth, and material acquisition are toxic to the human spirit. Of course, in the end, it all involves a form of repression and autocracy.

At the core of this mind-numbing amalgamated Marxist-centric or Marxist-like crusade is the "degrowth movement." Mankind consumes and produces too much, and the blame resides with capitalism and America. Again, there are a variety of movements within movements targeting one or another approach, but there are basic tenets. The best way to explain this is to expose what certain of its leading advocates have to say.

In their essay, "What Is Degrowth—From an Activist Slogan to a Social Movement," leading degrowthers Federico Demaria, Francois Schneider, Filka Sekulova, and Joan Martin-Alier write that "[d]egrowth was launched in the beginning of the 21st century as a project of voluntary societal shrinking of production and consumption aimed at social and ecological sustainability. It quickly became a slogan against economic growth and developed into a social movement. . . . Unlike sustainable development, which is a concept based on false consensus, degrowth does not aspire to be adopted as a common goal by the United Nations, the OECD [Organisation for Economic Co-operation and Development] or the European Commission. The idea of 'socially sustainable degrowth,' or simply degrowth, was born as a proposal for radical change. The contemporary context of neo-liberal capitalism appears as a post-political condition, meaning a political formation that forecloses the political and prevents the politicization of particular demands. Within this context, degrowth is an attempt to re-politicize the debate on much needed socio-ecological transformation, affirming dissidence with the current world representations and search for alternative ones. . . . Degrowth . . . challenges the ideas of 'green growth' or 'green economy' and the associated belief in economic growth as a desirable path in political agendas. . . . Degrowth is not just an economic concept. [I]t is a frame constituted by a large array of concerns, goals, strategies and actions. As a result, degrowth has now become a confluence point where streams of critical ideas and political action converge."[8]

Hence, the goal is to reverse the massive economic progress resulting from, among other things, the Industrial Revolution, which created a huge, vibrant middle class and infinite technological, scientific, and medical advancements that have overwhelmingly improved the human condition.

The quartet continues: "Degrowth has evolved into an interpretative frame for a social movement, understood as the mechanism through which actors engage in a collective action. For instance, anti-car and anti-advertising activists, cyclists and pedestrian rights campaigners, partisans of organic agriculture, critics of urban sprawl, and promoters of solar energy and local currencies have started seeing degrowth as an appropriate common representative frame for their world view."[9]

The social movement envisioned by these utopians would drag America into a regressive, impoverished society with widespread economic and social dislocation—that is, a pre-industrialized environment where progress comes to an end, for that is the goal. Anti-car (mobility), anti-advertising (speech), anti–modern agricultural (abundant food), anti–fossil fuel (abundant energy), etc. One wonders, what of scientific and medical advances? How would they be developed and broadly applied for the benefit of the general population? Like Marxism generally, this movement is based on theories and abstractions that, when forcibly applied in the real world, particularly in a widely successful and advanced society, have a result that is disastrous for the population. Moreover, experience shows that for those among them who are famous, wealthy, and/or powerful, they will continue to luxuriate in a lifestyle created by capitalism.

"Degrowth is [also] an interpretative frame diagnosis that disparate social phenomena such as the social and environmental crises are related to economic growth," write the foursome. "Degrowth actors are thus 'signifying agents' engaged in the production of alternative and contentious meanings which differ from the ones defended by the mainstream. . . . The prognosis, usually characterized by a strong utopian dimension, seeks solutions and hypothesizes new social patterns. Beyond practical goals, this process opens new spaces and prospects for action. Strategies associated with the prognosis tend to be multiple. In terms of approaches, these can be alternatives building, opposition research, and in relation to capitalism, they can be 'anti-capitalist,' post-capitalist,' and 'despite capitalism.' "[10]

And there you have it. For many of the "environmental" intellectuals behind this amorphous yet widespread movement, the goal is to spawn myriad sub-movements aimed at taking down the capitalist system. As I explained in 2015 in *Plunder and Deceit*, among other things, "[t]he degrowthers seek to eliminate carbon sources of energy and redistribute wealth according to terms they consider equitable. They reject the traditional economic reality that acknowledges growth as improving living conditions generally but especially for the impoverished. They embrace 'less competition, large scale redistribution, sharing and reduction of excessive incomes and wealth.' Degrowthers want to engage in policies that will set 'a maximum income, or maximum wealth, to weaken envy as a motor of consumerism, and opening borders ("no-border") to reduce means to keep inequality between rich and poor countries.' And they demand reparations by supporting a 'concept of ecological debt, or the demand that the Global North pays for past and present colonial exploitation of the Global South.' "[11] The degrowthers also demand that government establish a living wage and reduce the workweek to twenty hours.[12]

Serge Latouche, a French emeritus professor of economics at

the University of Paris-Sud, is among the leading degrowthers. "In the 1970s, Serge Latouche spent several years in South Africa, where he conducted extensive research on traditional Marxism, where he formed his own ideology based on 'progresses and development.' He is among the pioneers of the degrowth theory."[13] Latouche emphasizes a utopian-type doctrine in which even Marxism fails to make the grade. In *Farewell to Growth*, he declared: "We do not dwell on a specific critique of capitalism because it seems to us that there is no point in stating the obvious. That critique was, for the most part, put forward by Karl Marx. And yet a critique of capitalism is not enough: we also need a critique of any growth society. And that is precisely what Marx fails to provide. A critique of the growth society implies a critique of capitalism, but the converse is not necessarily true. Capitalism, neo-liberal or otherwise, and productivist socialism are both variants on the same project for a growth society based upon the development of the productive forces, which will supposedly facilitate humanity's march in the direction of progress."[14]

In other words, even Marx's ideological approach, which does not reject the creation of wealth but attacks the methods of production and distribution, misses the mark. While eliminating capitalism and promoting redistribution and egalitarianism are important objectives, apparently vigorous economic production and materialism itself are the bigger problems.

Latouche writes that "[b]ecause it cannot integrate ecological constraints, the Marxist critique of modernity remains terribly ambiguous. The capitalist economy is criticized and denounced, but the growth of the forces it unleashes is described as 'productive' (even though they are as destructive as they are productive). Ultimately, growth, seen in terms of the production/jobs/consumption trio, is credited with every, or almost every, virtue, even though, when seen in terms of accumulation of capital, it is held responsible for every scourge. . . . De-growth is fundamentally anti-capitalist. Not so much because it denounces the contradictions and ecological and social limitations of capitalism as because it challenges its 'spirit.' . . . A generalized capitalism cannot but destroy the planet in the same way that it is destroying society and anything else that is collective."[15]

In this, of course, Latouche does point to a significant flaw in Marxism—that is, despite his attacks on capitalism, Marx does not abandon the growth and productivity goals inherent in capitalism. Meanwhile, for Latouche, the obvious absurdity of his radicalism is the claim or inference that economic regression can somehow occur without human regression, and that the populace will somehow willingly participate in creating its own economic and lifestyle degradation.

Latouche writes further: "More so than ever before, development is sacrificing populations and their concrete, local well-being on the altar of an abstract, deterritorialized well-being. The sacrifice is made to honor a mythical and disembodied people, and it works, of course, to the advantage of 'the developers' (transactional companies, politicians, technocrats and mafias). Growth is now a profitable business only if the costs are borne by nature, future generations, consumers' health, wage earners' working conditions and, above all, the countries of the South. That is why we have to abandon the idea of growth. . . . All modern regimes have been productivist: republics, dictatorships, authoritarian systems, no matter whether their governments were of the right or the left, and no matter whether they were liberal, socialist, populist, social-liberal, social-democratic, centrist, radical or communist. They all assumed that economic growth was the unquestionable cornerstone of their systems. The change of direction that is needed is not one that can be resolved merely by an election that brings in a new government or votes in a new majority. What is needed is much more radical: a cultural revolution, nothing more and nothing less, that re-establishes politics on a new basis. . . . The de-growth project is therefore a utopia, or in other words a source of hope and dreams. Far from representing a flight into fantasy, it is an attempt to explore the objective possibility of implementation."[16]

Latouche and his ilk refer to this as "concrete utopianism." Of course, there is nothing concrete about it. Indeed, he says no matter the governing regime, they are all "productivist." How large populations of people are to be fed, an immensely complex commercial enterprise from field to table, let alone have access to medical treatments and innovations, such as lifesaving vaccines and treatments, is left mostly unsaid. And when it is rarely addressed, it is done so in an abstract and even sophomoric way.

Nonetheless, try as Latouche might, the inspiration behind this eco-totalitarian movement is, for innumerable activists, undeniably Marxism. In his essay "Urban Sprawl, Climate Change, Oil Depletion, and Eco-Marxism," University of Miami political science professor George A. Gonzalez writes: "The U.S. urban zones are the most sprawled in the world. . . . Urban sprawl can only be fully comprehended within the political economy framework developed by Karl Marx. Marx's concepts of value and rent are indispensable to understanding the profligate use of fossil fuels—vis-à-vis urban sprawl—that has significantly contributed to oil depletion and to the recent global warming trend. This argument is consistent with the eco-Marxist contention that the writings of Marx and Frederick Engels contain a thorough ecological critique of capitalism."[17]

Thus, for Gonzalez, Marx's ideological writings provide a "thorough ecological critique of capitalism." For Latouche, they are utterly void of ecological considerations and adopt capitalist goals related to production and growth. Yet, for both the enemy is economic progress.

"Urban sprawl," writes Gonzalez, "was deployed in the United States during the 1930s as a means of reviving U.S. capitalism from the Great Depression. The sprawling of urban zones greatly increased the need for automobiles and other consumer durables. This use of urban sprawl to increase economic demand is consistent with Marx's argument that demand within capitalism is malleable and is geared toward increasing the consumption of goods and services produced through social labor. The exploitation of social labor is the basis of capitalist wealth."[18]

One wonders, what evil mastermind was behind the "deployment" of "urban sprawl." The large movement of individuals from farms to the cities, as well as the movement of immigrants to cities, was not about "deploying" people to save capitalism. People moved to population centers, thereby further increasing the population of cities, out of economic necessity—that is, to find jobs, to start businesses, to live among similar ethnic groups, and for scores of other self-interested and understandable reasons. It had nothing to do with "deploying" people and resources.

And there can be no doubt whatsoever that this movement has as its purpose to abolish or cripple the capitalist economic system and, by necessity, constitutional republicanism and its emphasis on individualism and private property rights. For example, Giorgos Kallis, an ecological economist from Greece and an ICREA research professor at ICTA–Universitat Autònoma de Barcelona, whose influence is considerable among the eco-radicals in the United States, explains in his book *In Defense of Degrowth* that "[s]ustainable degrowth is defined as an equitable downscaling of production and consumption that increases human well-being and enhances ecological conditions. [It] envision[s] a future wherein societies live within their ecological means, with localized economies, which distribute resources more equally through new forms of democratic institutions. . . . Material accumulation will no longer hold a central position in the cultural imaginary. The primacy given to efficiency will be substituted by a focus on sufficiency. The organizing principles will be simplicity, conviviality, and sharing. Innovation will no longer be directed to new technology for technology's sake but to new social and technological arrangements that will enable a convivial and frugal living."[19]

Again, one wonders, is Kallis fantasizing about some kind of 1960s national and international hippie commune? And yet, one also wonders how this "nirvana" will come to pass and, itself, be sustainable—that is, the very nature of the individual and mankind generally would require forced indoctrination, forced reeducation, forced relocation in many instances, etc. In other words, as Marx preached, the existing society must be abolished—its history, families, schools, and religions—which may well require a period of despotism, to cleanse society of existing norms and replace them with the Marxist paradise. The picture Kallis and other radicals paint is nothing like the inevitable, horrific nightmare their abstract dreams would unleash.

Kallis continues: "Sustainable degrowth denotes an intentional process of a smooth and 'prosperous way down,' through a range of social, environmental, and economic policies and institutions, orchestrated to guarantee that while production and consumption decline, human welfare improves and is more equally distributed. Various concrete and practical proposals are being debated for enabling such degrowth transitions. These include both policy-institutional changes *within* the current system—such as drastic changes to financial institutions, resource and pollution caps and sanctuaries, infrastructure moratoria, eco-taxes, work-sharing and reduced working hours, basic income and social security guaranteed for all—as well as ideas for creating new spaces outside of the system, such as eco-villages and co-housing, cooperative production and consumption, various systems of sharing, or community issued and regulated currencies, barter and non-money market exchanges. 'Exiting the economy,' to create new spaces of simplicity, sharing and conviviality, is the driving motto of degrowth."[20]

But Marxism dressed up as a green movement is still Marxism, at least in significant part. Moreover, "exiting the economy" would create not "sharing and conviviality," but need, poverty, indolence, and the overall decline of the civil society and the quality of life. One can envision how the *purposeful* shrinking of the economy would destroy "conviviality" and, in fact, create an explosive societal reaction by reducing the supply of even necessities (food, medicine, energy, clothing, housing, etc.) while increasing the demand for such basics (people chasing the availability of fewer necessities). Even where the shrinking of an economy is not purposeful but inevitable, such as in certain types of communist regimes (Venezuela and North Korea come to mind, and Cambodia of the recent past), it clearly is unmanageable once unbridled and the consequences for the people who live in these places, both in terms of human dignity and liberty, and even survivability, become horribly dire.

Kallis insists that "[e]scaping the capitalist economy and forming nowtopias is not an idyllistic ecologist call for a return to a bucolic past that has never existed. It is of course a romantic project, and this is fine, since a dose of romanticism is precisely what we need in this era of cold-blooded and self-destructive individualistic utilitarianism. Nowtopias are not just 'life style choices': they represent conscious 'life projects' for their participants, and are political actions, consciously and explicitly for some and unconsciously for others. But 'escaping the economy' is unlikely to become a massive movement on its own without an interlocked change at the political-institutional level that will make its flourishing possible. Institutions to limit the expansion of the economy and to open spaces for alternative life projects are a prerequisite for nowtopia."[21]

Indeed, even the *fact* of an economy is doubted by Kallis, among others. "[F]irst principle: the economy is an invention." "[W]hen and how did we come to think of an autonomous system out there called 'the economy'?"[22] And the economy is a political creation, not a spontaneous aggregation of untold commercial and financial interactions among a free people. "[T]he economy in the degrowth literature is political. It is not an independent system governed by the laws of supply and demand. The imaginary free market does not exist. . . . In ecological economics we do recognize the political nature of the economy. . . . Often though we reproduce the economistic distinction between an economy out there, with its own laws and processes, and a political process which distributes the fruits of this process or sets limits to it. . . ."[23]

Therefore, principles upon which America was founded, such as private property rights, the free flow of commerce, voluntary exchange, and the sanctity of the individual, and the establishment of a government around these principles, which is intended to undergird these principles and limit its own authority to molest or alter them, are dismissed.

In her book *Return of the Primitive—The Anti-Industrial Revolution*, published more than forty years ago, Ayn Rand presciently exposed the purpose of this movement: "The immediate goal is obvious: the destruction of the remnants of capitalism in today's mixed economy, and the establishment of a global dictatorship. The goal does not have to be inferred—many speeches and books on the subject state explicitly that the ecological crusade is a means to an end." Rand also noted that the movement demonstrated the failure of Marxism, writing that the new approach involved "the substitution of birds, bees and beauty—'nature's beauty'—for the pseudoscientific, super-technological paraphernalia of Marx's economic determinism. A more ludicrous shrinking of a movement's stature or a more obvious confession of intellectual bankruptcy could not be invented in fiction."[24]

"Instead of their old promises," writes Rand, "that collectivism would create universal abundance and their denunciations of capitalism for creating poverty, they are now *denouncing capitalism for creating abundance*. Instead of promising comfort and security for everyone, they are now denouncing people for being comfortable and secure. They are still struggling, however, to inculcate guilt and fear; these have always been their psychological tools. Only instead of exhorting you to feel guilty of exploiting the poor, they are now exhorting you to feel guilty of exploiting land, air and water. Instead of threatening you with bloody rebellion of the disinherited masses, they are now trying . . . to scare you out of your wits with thunderously vague threats of an unknowable, cosmic cataclysm, threats that cannot be checked, verified or proved."[25]

Rand hammered the "[t]he deeper significance of the ecological crusade," which she said "lies in the fact that it does expose a profound threat to mankind—though not in the sense its leaders allege. It exposes the ultimate motive of the collectivists—the naked essence of *hatred* for achievement, which means: hatred for reason, for man, for life." Rather than condemning the Industrial Revolution, Rand explains that it "was the great breakthrough that liberated man's mind from the weight of the ballast. The country made possible by the Industrial Revolution—The United States of America—achieved the magnificence which only free men can achieve, and demonstrated that reason is the means, the base, the precondition of man's survival."[26]

Rand's point, of course, is that freedom and capitalism are inextricably linked. And the Industrial Revolution is magnificent evidence of the capabilities of a free people.

She explained, "The enemies of reason—the mystics, the man-haters and life-haters, the seekers of the unearned and the unreal—have been gathering their forces for a counterattack, ever since. . . . The enemies of the Industrial Revolution—its displaced persons—were of the kind that had fought human progress for centuries. . . ." Today, "they are . . . reduced, like cornered animals, to baring their teeth and their souls, and to proclaiming that man has no right to exist. . . ."[27] In fact, the movement's refrain is a relentless condemnation of modern man's way of life—such as "man-made climate change."

Another of the movement's leading lights, Timothy W. Luke, a professor of political science at Virginia Polytechnic Institute and State University, and a Critical Theory advocate, writes in his essay "Climatologies as Social Critique: The Social Construction/Creation of Global Warming, Global Dimming, and Global Cooling," that due to mankind and capitalism, the planet has already been transformed—from nature to urbanature. "Global warming, dimming, and/or cooling are the unintended consequences of human organisms reshaping the earth's natural and artificial environments to support their survival. And, as the moves are made, human and natural life forms begin to inhabit a nature that, as habitat, is being recreated by the output of corporate labs, major industries, and big agribusiness. Products and their by-products infiltrate terrestrial ecologies through human actions, and this technonature congeals in a 'Second Creation,' or urbanaturalized environments, with a new atmosphere, changing oceans, different biodiversity, and remade land masses. And study of climate change must consider all these ramifications."[28]

In addition to Luke's use and abuse of the English language, which is pervasive throughout academia, he is describing human progress under capitalism as a hellish rebirth of the planet, away from nature. Indeed, he argues, the capitalist system is such a disaster that it is the impetus for communism.

"Climatology as social criticism maps how the unintended consequences of industrial capitalism are externalized as by-products of mass production and consumption, only to begin altering the earth's atmosphere. At one time, 'scientific socialism' presumed to foretell the workers of the world about the coming crisis of capitalism, out of which would come a more rational, just and equitable communist order. An intrinsic set of tendencies were believed to be creating the basis for full rationalization of the means of production as well as the opportunity to enact new forms of material equality, political deliberation, and psychological emancipation. Unalterable laws of surplus value would guarantee the advent and permanence of these outcomes as the chaotic dynamics of the market pushed the anarchy of exchange toward the order of communism."[29]

Rand deals with this, too, by observing that "in all the propaganda of the ecologists—amidst all their appeals to nature and pleas for 'harmony with nature'—there is no discussion of *man's* needs and the requirements of *his* survival. Man is treated as if he were an *unnatural* phenomenon. Man cannot survive in the kind of state of nature that ecologists envision—i.e., on the level of sea urchins or polar bears. In that sense, man is the weakest of the animals: he is born naked and unarmed, without fangs, claws, horns or 'instinctual' knowledge. Physically, he would fall an easy prey, not only to the higher animals, but also to the lowest bacteria: he is the most complex organism and, in a contest of brute force, extremely fragile and vulnerable. His only weapon—his basic means of survival is his mind."[30]

"It is not necessary to remind you," writes Rand, "of what human existence was like—for centuries and millennia—prior to the Industrial Revolution. That the ecologists ignore or evade it is so terrible a crime against humanity that it serves as their protection: no one believes that anyone can be capable of it. But, in this matter, it is not even necessary to look at history; take a look at the conditions of existence in the undeveloped countries, which means: on most of this earth, with the exception of the blessed island which is Western civilization."[31]

Luke acknowledges that while the eco-radical movement is not identical to Marx's model, it is not all that different, either. "While its scientific credibility clearly exceeds that of historical materialism, contemporary climatology, especially in its more engaged expressions as public policy, popular science, or economic forecasting, often strangely echoes, parallels, or reimagines postulates not unlike those of the materialist conception of history. While it clearly is not completely the same, it also is not entirely different."[32]

In *The Communist Manifesto* (1848), Marx and Engels state, in part: "The bourgeois cannot exist without constantly revolutionizing the instruments of production, and thereby the relations of production, and with them the whole relations of society. . . . Constant revolutionizing of production, uninterrupted disturbance of all social conditions, everlasting uncertainty and agitation, distinguish the bourgeois epoch from all earlier ones. All fixed, fast-frozen relations, with their train of ancient and venerable prejudices and opinions, are swept away; all newformed ones become antiquated before they can ossify. All that is solid melts into air, all that is holy is profaned, and man is at last compelled to face with sober sense his real conditions of life and his relations with his kind. The need of a constantly expanding market for its products chases the bourgeoisie over the whole surface of the globe. It must nestle everywhere, settle everywhere, establish connections everywhere."[33]

The condemnation of economic and technological progress by Marx, Engels, and their prodigy in this Marxist-oriented movement is not merely a demand to restrict technology but, as Rand asserts, "the demand to restrict man's mind. It is nature—

i.e., reality—that makes both these goals impossible to achieve. Technology can be destroyed, and the mind can be paralyzed, but neither can be restricted. Whether and whatever such restrictions are attempted, it is the mind—not the state—that withers away. Technology is applied science. The progress of theoretical science and technology—i.e., of human knowledge—is moved by such a complex and interconnected sum of the work of individual minds that no computer or committee could predict and prescribe its course. The discoveries in one branch of knowledge lead to unexpected discoveries in another; the achievements in one field open countless roads in all others. . . . [R]estrictions mean the attempt to regulate the unknown, to limit the unborn, to set rules for the undiscovered. . . . As to the notion that progress is unnecessary, that we know enough, that we can stop on the present level of technological development and maintain it, without going farther—ask yourself why mankind's history is full of the wreckage of civilizations that could not be maintained and vanished along with such knowledge as they had achieved; why men who do not move forward, fall back into the abyss of savagery."[34]

As you can see, it takes one Ayn Rand to tackle the entire academy of Marxist de-growthers. However, I would contribute a further observation to Rand's. Inasmuch as the purpose of this movement is to regress back to nature and a mere subsistence economy, where the communal psyche is anti-growth, anti-technology, anti-science, and anti-modernity, ironically the irrelevancy of higher education, graduate studies, and doctoral degrees, and the colleges and faculties themselves, particularly in the teaching of hard sciences, technology, engineering, and mathematics, are expendable. Illiberalism and its product, totalitarianism, do not require large educational edifices to enforce the impoverishment of man's mind and spirit, or to feed his hunger for knowledge and bare necessities.

Given the movement's Marxist inculcation, it is unsurprising that it "intersects" with the growing influence of Critical Race Theory and other such manifestations. Indeed, the early environmental movement has metastasized into a multi-headed Hydra with intersecting and overlapping revolutionary causes. For example, writing in *What Is Critical Environmental Justice?*, David Naguib Pellow, professor of environmental studies at the University of California, states: "[From] its earliest days, the Environmental Justice [EJ] movement articulated a transformative vision of what an environmentally and socially just and sustainable future might look like, at the local, regional, national, and global scales. . . . [D]uring the historic Environmental Justice Summit Conference in 1991, participants drafted what became known as the Principles of Environmental Justice, which not only embrace a synthesis of anti-racism and ecological sustainability but also support anti-militaristic, anti-imperialist, gender-justice politics. The Principles also recognize the inherent and cultural worth of nonhuman natures."[35]

Thus, the introduction of race, gender, pacifism, injustice, classism, and anti-Americanism generally under the nomenclature of environmental justice. Pellow continues: "The EJ movement is largely comprised of people from communities of color, indigenous communities, and working-class communities who are focused on combating environmental injustice, racism, and gender and class inequalities that are most visibly manifested in the disproportionate burden of environmental harm facing these populations. For the EJ movement, the battle for global sustainability cannot be won without addressing the ecological violence imposed on vulnerable human populations; thus social justice (that is, justice for humans) is inseparable from environmental protection. . . . While environmental justice is a vision of a possible future, environmental inequality (or environmental *in*justice) generally refers to a situation in which a particular social group is disproportionately affected by environmental hazards."[36]

Actually, the EJ movement is mostly led and driven by Marxist-oriented elitists, academics, and activists, like most of these movements, while enticing many unsuspecting followers. It is promoted and advocated throughout our colleges and universities, in the media, by activists and think tanks. Like Critical Race Theory, critical environmental justice studies are now prominent and growing. It means, as Pellow writes, "[b]uilding on the work of scholars across numerous fields that only periodically intersect (such as Environmental Justice Studies, Critical Race Theory, Critical Race Feminism, Ethnic Studies, Gender and Sexuality Studies, Political Ecology, Anti-Statist/Anarchist Theory, and Ecological Feminism). . . ."[37]

In essence, then, more "intersectionality"—that is, the combination of disparate causes and alleged victimizations under yet another radical, anti-capitalist umbrella united in their hatred for American society.

Pellow argues that the EJ framework is built on four pillars, including: "The first pillar . . . [which] involves the recognition that social inequality and oppression in all forms intersect, and that actors in the more-than-human world are subjects of oppression and frequently agents of social change. The fields of critical race theory, critical race feminism, gender and sexuality studies, queer theory, ecological feminism, disability studies, and critical animal studies all speak to the ways in which various social categories of difference work to place particular bodies at risk of exclusion, marginalization, erasure, discrimination, violence, destruction, and othering. These insights are important for building an understanding of the ways that intra-human inequality and oppressions function and how they intersect with human-nonhuman oppression."[38]

I must confess, it is difficult to keep up with the number and kind of alleged and proclaimed maladies supposedly unleashed by the most diverse, beneficent, tolerant, successful, and free nation ever established by mankind. But it would certainly seem that this movement has attracted them all. So much for clean air, clean water, and polar bears.

Skipping ahead, Pellow informs us that the third pillar "is the view that social inequalities—from racism to speciesism—are deeply embedded in society (rather than aberrations) and reinforced by state power, and that therefore the current social order stands as a fundamental obstacle to social and environmental justice. The logical conclusion of that observation is that social change movements may be better off thinking and acting beyond human supremacy and beyond the state as targets of reform and reliable partners. . . ."[39]

Therefore, it must follow that the current society must be fundamentally transformed into an egalitarian nirvana. Is the state to be abolished altogether? Is this transformation achieved by force, repression, and educational brainwashing? And what of the constitutional limitations placed between the individual and government in order to protect the individual—that is, how is this revolution manifested?

"Most of human history," Pellow writes, "has been marked by the absence of states, suggesting that the modern condition of state dominance is anything but natural or inevitable. My view, and the view of a growing number of scholars, is that states are social institutions that tend to lean toward practices and relationships that are authoritarian, coercive, racist, patriarchal, exclusionary, militaristic, and anti-ecological."[40]

This is a strange formulation. Of course, "most of human history" has been plagued by uncivil societies, where governments have rejected the view enunciated in our Declaration of Independence—"We hold these truths to be self-evident, that all men are created equal, that they are endowed by their Creator with certain unalienable Rights, that among these are Life, Liberty and the pursuit of Happiness.—That to secure these rights, Governments are instituted among Men, deriving their just powers from the consent of the governed . . ."[41] The law of the jungle, resulting from the collapse of norms, traditions, customs, law, and order, breeds the kind of hellish existence Pellow would unleash on mankind.

"The fourth pillar . . . centers on a concept I call *indispensability*. . . . A Critical EJ Studies perspective . . . counter[s] the ideology of a white supremacy and human dominionism, and articulating the perspective that excluded, marginalized, and othered populations, beings, and things—both human and more-than-human—must be viewed not as expendable but rather as *indispensable* to our collective futures. This is what I term *racial indispensability* (when referring to people of color) and *socioecological indispensability* (when referring to broader communities within and across the human/more-than-human spectrum). . . . CEJ extends the work of Ethnic Studies scholars and activists who argue that, in this society, people of color are constructed as and rendered expendable. Building on those ideas and challenging the ideology of white supremacy and human dominionism, CEJ articulates the perspective that excluded, marginalized, and othered populations, beings and things—both human and more-than-human—must be viewed as *indispensable* to our collective futures. . . ."[42]

Pellow broadly proclaims that a white supremacist–dominant society and human dominance of nature overall, which includes ruling over other species (such as animals, insects, etc.), highlight the indispensability of marginalized people. Notice here, and throughout these movements, individual human beings are treated in conformity with the Marxist model—broken into classes of oppressed groups based on an endless list of victimizations and stereotypes.

Pellow continues, "In addition to building on Environmental Justice Studies, Critical EJ Studies draws inspiration from a number of other important fields, such as Critical Race Theory and Ethnic Studies, Critical Race Feminism and Gender and Sexuality

Studies, and Anti-Statists/Anarchist Theory, which have done an enormous service by producing rigorous conceptual and grounded understandings of how social inequality, oppression, privilege, hierarchy, and authoritarian institutions and practices shape the lives of human beings. These scholars have explored and revealed myriad ways in which gender, race, sexuality, citizenship, social class, and ability reflect and are reflective on how social structures function in society. . . . They show how the domination of those persons without privilege is accomplished through practices, policymaking, and discourses on a daily basis. Thus these fields are invaluable to strengthening [EJS], which is, at its root, an area of inquiry concerned with inequality, domination, and liberation."[43]

Of course, Pellow cannot explain why, in an open society, where people are mobile and free to escape the kind of systemic racial hatred and multiplicity of abuses he conceptualizes, they choose not to leave the United States. There are many low- or no-growth economies throughout the world, where nature dominates the people, and where the majority populations are nonwhite. The reason, of course, is that for many if not most in these countries, life is very difficult if not hellish. In fact, he cannot explain why millions of people from countries where the majority populations are nonwhite and the economic system is other than capitalistic risk their health and lives to escape their societies and migrate to the United States. Nonetheless, Pellow is hardly alone in his ideological fiction and fanaticism, which is fast traveling throughout, and rolling over, American institutions.

On July 18, 2014, a large number of delegates from radical groups throughout the world gathered to issue a joint proclamation called the Margarita Declaration on Climate Change. It is revealing that their proclamation leads with a quote from Venezuela's late Marxist dictator, Hugo Chávez: "Let us go to the future, let us bring it and sow it here." Of course, thanks to Chávez and his successor, Nicolás Maduro, the Venezuelan economy and society are devastated, the people are dying of starvation and seeking refuge in the United States and other countries, there is a complete breakdown in health care and basic public services, and the government is a violent police state that represses any and all dissonant voices. Indeed, the proclamation reads like a modern version of Marx's *Communist Manifesto*, laced with environmental declarations and platitudes. While it is insipid and absurd on so many levels, it is also dangerously appealing and increasingly acceptable as a matter of national and international policy. The declaration states, in part:

> It is necessary to reach an alternative development model based on the principles of living in harmony with nature, guided by absolute and ecological sustainability limits, and the capacity of Mother Earth as well; a fair, egalitarian model that constructs sustainable economies that moves us away from energy models based on fossil fuels and hazardous energies, that guarantees and recognizes the respect to Mother Earth, the rights of women, children, adolescents, gender diversity, the impoverished, the vulnerable minority groups and the original indigenous peoples—A fair and egalitarian model that fosters the peaceful coexistence of our peoples. We likewise want a society where the right of Mother Earth prevails over neoliberal policies, economic globalization and patriarchy, because without Mother Earth life does not exist.[44]

Nothing says bombast and narcissism like a gathering of self-righteous Marxists working together to construct a statement of purpose, to include every possible group and cause in their coalition, and to treat "Mother Earth" as if she is some kind wallflower or victim. The result: an incoherent and nonsensical mission statement. Nonetheless, the movement is for real and it threatens our way of life. Hayek explains in *The Fatal Conceit* that this is "a morality [that] pretends to be able to do something that it cannot possibly do, e.g., to fulfill a knowledge generating and organizational function that is impossible under its own rules and norms, then this impossibility itself provides a decisive rational criticism of that moral system. It is important to confront these consequences, for the notion that, in the last resort, the whole debate is a matter of value judgments and not of facts has prevented professional students of the market order from stressing forcibly enough that socialism cannot possibly do what it promises."[45]

The Declaration continues:

> The main sources for climate crisis are the political and economic systems commercializing and reifying nature and life, thus impoverishing spirituality and imposing consumerism and developmentalism that generate unequal regimes and exploitation of resources. This global crisis is exacerbated by unsustainable practices of exploitation and consumption by the developed countries and the elites of the developing countries. We demand the leaders in the North not continue such wicked practices that destroy the planet and demand the leaders in the South not follow the development models in place in the North which lead to this civilizing crisis. We urge them to construct an alternative path to achieve fair, egalitarian and sustainable societies and fair economies. For such purposes, it is required that the developed countries meet their moral and legal obligations, especially vis-à-vis vulnerable and marginalized countries and communities by lifting barriers such as intellectual property rights which prevent the attainment

> of the preservation of life over the planet and the salvation of human species. We likewise urge them to comply with the financial contribution and the transfer of safe and locally suitable technologies free from barriers such as intellectual property rights, strengthen capacities and embrace the principles set forth in the Climate Change Convention and in the Rio Earth Summit, especially as to the common but differentiated responsibilities and respective capabilities, and the principles of precaution and gender equality.[46]

I am reminded of what Thomas Sowell wrote in his book *The Quest for Cosmic Justice* about such widely overstated, generalized, and untested "visions": "V. I. Lenin represented one of the purest examples of a man who operated on the basis of a vision and its categories, which superseded the world of flesh-and-blood human beings or the realities within which they lived out their lives. Only tactically or strategically did the nature of the world beyond the vision matter, as a means to the end of fulfilling that vision. . . . Lenin's preoccupation with visions was demonstrated not only by his failure to enter the world of the working class, in whose name he spoke, but also his failure to ever set foot in Soviet Central Asia—a vast area larger than Western Europe, and one in which the doctrinaire and devastating schemes of Lenin and his successors would be imposed by force for nearly three-quarters of a century."[47] Sowell added that "[v]isions are inescapable because the limits of our own direct knowledge are inescapable. The crucial question is whether visions provide a basis for theories to be tested or for dogmas to be proclaimed and imposed. Much of the history of the twentieth century has been a history of the tyranny of visions as dogmas. Previous centuries saw the despotisms of monarchs or of military conquerors, but the twentieth century has seen the rise of ruling individuals and parties whose passport to power was their successful marketing of visions. Almost by definition, this was the marketing of the *promises* of visions, since performance could not be judged before achieving the power to put the vision into action. . . . The prevalence and power of a vision is shown, not by what its evidence of logic can prove, but precisely by its *exemption* from any need to provide evidence or logic—by the number of things that can be successfully asserted because they fit the vision, without having to meet the test of fitting the facts."[48]

As if leading an international Marxist revolution, the radicals at the convention went on to demand "the change of the production and consumption patterns taking into account the historic responsibilities of the emissions from nations and corporations and their cumulative nature, thus recognizing that the carbon atmospheric space is finite and needs to be equally distributed amongst the countries and their peoples. The historically unequal overconsumption of the global emissions budget managed by mainstream corporations and economic systems has contributed to cause inequalities in terms of the capacities of the countries. Some key indicators to measure such disparity would be the national per capita emission of greenhouse effect gases since 1850, the distribution and size of the wealth and national income, and the technological resources owned by a country. Such indicators may be used to determine the fair portion of effort corresponding to each country . . . the needs for sustainable development, the losses and damages caused by climate change and the need of technology transfer and financial support are recognized." And what would a revolution be without a Star Chamber. "We demand the implementation of a Justice, Ethics and Moral Court on Climate Change, where humanity at large may file complaints against crimes related to this topic."[49]

The Margarita Declaration on Climate Change then proceeds to declare "a great world social movement," a "people's movement" that requires an anticapitalist economic transformation, a change in thinking, reeducation, and indoctrination, the "eradication" of fossil fuels, and much more:

> We must organize ourselves to guarantee life on the planet through a great world social movement. A change of attitude for a conscience of power keeping the peoples united becomes necessary. As organized peoples we can push for the transformation of the system.
>
> The structural causes for climate change are linked to the current capitalist hegemonic system. Fighting the climate change involves changing the system. The change of the system must provide for a transformation of the economic, political, social and cultural systems at local, national, regional and global levels. Education is a right of the peoples, a continuous process of fair, free, and transversal comprehensive training. Education is one of the fundamental driving forces for transformation and construction in diversity of the new women and men, for the Good Living and the respect of life and Mother Earth. Education should be oriented to reflect value, create, raise awareness, coexist, participate and act. When we speak of education to face the climate change, we speak of the main roots of such change and the historic and current responsibilities. We also speak of poverty, inequality and vulnerability of the peoples, especially the indigenous peoples and other historically excluded and victimized groups.

The colossal incoherence and imbecility of this movement cannot be overstated. Nonetheless, it stridently marches on with appeal and force.

The declaration continues:

We propose the following actions to change the system:

- Transformation of the power relations and the decision-making systems for the construction of an anti-patriarchal people's power.
- Transformation of food production systems into agro-ecological systems, thus ensuring food sovereignty and security and valuing knowledge, innovations, ancestral and traditional practices.
- Transformation of the energy production systems, eradicating dirty energies respecting the right of the peoples to fight poverty and keeping fair transition as a guiding principle.
- Transformation of the energy consumption patterns through education, regulations to large energy consumers and empowerment of the people over community-scaled systems of renewable energies production under control of the communities.
- Implementation of participative government of territory and city planning systems, thus ensuring fair and sustainable access to land and to urban services, as well as other means that are necessary to face the Climate Change impacts.
- Shifting from an energy and materials profligate system to a cyclic system that emphasizes the eradication of the unsustainable exploitation of nature and promotes reduction, reutilization, and recycling of residues.
- Ensuring financing by the developed countries to developing countries for such transformations, and for com-

pensation and rehabilitation of the impacts of Climate Change. Financing must not be conditional, and the management of the funds supplied shall be in the hands of the Peoples.

- Creation of accessible mechanisms for the protection of the displaced people and the defenders of environmental rights.[50]

Two of the traditional attacks on capitalism, productivity, and economic growth have revolved around the claimed depletion of natural resources and carbon dioxide emissions, both of which, among other things, are said to lead to climate change. With respect to the former, George Reisman explains that mankind has not come close to even scratching the surface of the earth's resources. He writes: "What is true of the earth is equally true of every other planetary body in the universe. Insofar as the universe consists of matter, it consists of nothing but chemical elements, and thus of nothing but natural resources."[51] "Because the earth is literally nothing but an immense solid ball of chemical elements and because man's intelligence and initiative in the last two centuries were relatively free to operate and had the incentive to operate, it should not be surprising that the supply of useable, accessible minerals today vastly exceeds the supply that man is economically capable of exploiting."[52] "[T]he portion of nature that represents wealth should be understood as a tiny fraction that began as virtually zero and even though it has since been multiplied by several hundredfold, is still virtually zero when one considers how small is the portion of the mass of the earth, let alone the universe, that is subject to man's control, and how far man is from understanding all aspects and potential uses of what has become subject to his control."[53]

A common theme and, therefore, significant problem respecting too many social activists and self-proclaimed revolutionaries is their utter ignorance about matters in which they are passionately, if not violently, committed. "Conservationism regards the existing supply of economically useable natural resources as nature-given," writes Reisman, "rather than as the product of human intelligence and its corollary, capital accumulation. It does not see that what nature provides is, for all practical purposes, an infinite supply of matter and energy, which human intelligence can progressively master, in the process creating a steadily increasing supply of economically useable natural resources. . . . Having no conception of the role of human intelligence in the creation of economically useable natural resources, and confusing the present supply with all the natural resources present in nature, the conservationists naively believe that every act of production that consumes natural resources is an act of impoverishment, using up an allegedly priceless, irreplaceable treasure of nature. On this basis, they conclude that the pursuit of self-interest by individuals under economic freedom leads to the wanton consumption of mankind's irreplaceable natural heritage, with no regard for the needs of future generations."[54]

Nevertheless, ignorance is apparently no excuse for altering beliefs. Reisman writes that "[o]nce having arrived at the existence of this altogether illusory problem, the product of nothing more than their own ignorance of the productive process, the conservationists further conclude that what is necessary to solve this alleged problem is government intervention designed to 'conserve' natural resources by restricting or prohibiting in various ways mankind's use of them."[55]

Respecting the second issue, carbon dioxide emissions and climate change generally, it must be first unequivocally stated that carbon dioxide is not, never has been, and never can be a pollutant. Moreover, during the last half century, "scientists" and "experts" have asserted with certainty that the earth was facing a cooling period, then a warming period, and now simply and more broadly put, climate change, thereby covering all possibilities with no future need for clarification or correction. The main culprit, we are told, is carbon dioxide resulting primarily from the use of fossil fuels. Of course, as any elementary school science teacher explains to her students, carbon dioxide is oxygen to plants, and in turn plants generate oxygen for the rest of us.

As for carbon dioxide emissions and the impact on the atmosphere, earth, and climate, the debate even among scientists and experts rages on, despite efforts to intimidate skeptics, shut them down, and dismiss them as "deniers." However, suffice to say there is simply no consensus. For example, as recently as September 23, 2019, "A global network of more than 500 knowledgeable and experienced scientists and professionals in climate and related fields" signed a letter to the United Nations secretary-general insisting that "[c]limate science should be less political, while climate policies should be more scientific. Scientists should openly address the uncertainties and exaggerations in their predictions of global warming, while politicians should dispassionately count the real benefits as well as the imagined costs of adaptation to global warming, and the real costs as well as the imagined benefits of mitigation."[56]

The letter goes on to say that "[t]he general-circulation models of climate on which international policy is at present founded are unfit for their purpose. Therefore, it is cruel as well as imprudent to advocate the squandering of trillions of dollars on the basis of results from such immature models. Current climate policies pointlessly and grievously undermine the economic system, putting lives at risk in countries denied access to affordable, reliable electrical energy. We urge you to follow a climate policy based on sound science, realistic economics and genuine concern for those harmed by costly but unnecessary attempts at mitigation."[57] The signatories explain that "natural as well as anthropogenic factors cause warming, warming is far slower than predicted, climate policy relies on inadequate models, CO2 is plant food, the basis of all life on Earth, global warming has not increased natural disasters, and climate policy must respect scientific and economic realities."[58]

Indeed, there are so many scientists and experts who question or reject the climate change movement that it is impossible to list them all here. Nonetheless, a few examples suffice.

Ian Plimer, emeritus professor of earth sciences at University of Melbourne, and professor of mining geology at the University of Adelaide, explains: "The theory of human-induced global warming is not science because research is based on a pre-ordained condition, huge bodies of evidence are ignored, and the analytical procedures are treated as evidence. Furthermore, climate 'science' is sustained by government research grants. Funds are not available to investigate theories that are not in accord with government ideology."[59] Of alternative energy sources, such as wind and solar, Plimer writes that "[t]he 'alternative' energy systems such as wind and solar are environmentally disastrous. They cause loss of ecosystems, destruction of wildlife, sterilization of the land, inordinate costs that may not be retrieved during the life of the system, and the emission of huge amounts of CO2 during construction. Furthermore, both wind and solar power are inefficient. They can't provide 24/7 base-load power and need backup by coal-burning carbon dioxide–emitting electricity generating plants."[60]

Plimer condemns the entire movement: "Climate change catastrophism is the biggest scientific fraud that has ever occurred. Much climate 'science' is political ideology dressed up as science. There are times in history when the popular consensus is demonstrably wrong and we live in such a time. Cheap energy is fundamental for employment, living in the modern world, and for bringing the Third World out of poverty. . . . Furthermore, the education system has been captured by activists, and the young are inculcated with environmental, political, and economic ideology. During their education, these same young people are not given the basic critical and analytical methods to evaluate ideology that has been presented as fact. . . ."[61]

Patrick J. Michaels was director of the Center for the Study of Science at the Cato Institute, past president of the American Association of State Climatologists, program chair for the Committee on Applied Climatology of the American Meteorological Society, and research professor of environmental sciences at University of Virginia for thirty years. He contends that climate models are failing: "In its most basic form, science consists of statements of hypotheses that are retained by critical tests against observations. Without such testing, or without a testable hypothesis, [philosopher] Karl Popper stated that what may be called 'science' is, in fact, 'pseudo-science.' A corollary is that a theory which purports to explain everything in its universe of subject matter is, in fact, untestable and therefore is pseudo-science. In climate, perhaps it is charitable to refer to untested (or untestable) climate model projections as 'climate studies' rather than 'climate science.' "[62]

Richard S. Lindzen, atmospheric physicist, and former professor of meteorology at Massachusetts Institute of Technology (1983–2013), states that "[g]lobal warming is about politics and power rather than science. In science, there is an attempt to clarify; in global warming, language is misused in order to confuse and mislead the public. The misuse of language extends to the use of climate models. Advocates of policies allegedly addressing global warming use models not to predict but rather to justify the claim that catastrophe is possible. As they understand, proving something to be impossible is itself almost impossible."[63]

Robert M. Carter, emeritus fellow and science policy adviser at the Institute of Public Affairs, science adviser at the Science and Public Policy Institute; chief science adviser for the International Climate Science Coalition, and former professor and head of the

School of Earth Sciences at James Cook University, writes: "It needs to be recognized that the theoretical hazard of dangerous human-caused warming is but one small part of a much wider climate hazard that all scientists will agree upon, which is the dangerous weather and climate events that Nature intermittently presents us with—and always will. It is clear from the many and continuing climate-related disasters that occur around the world that the governments of even advanced, wealthy countries are often inadequately prepared for such disasters. We need to do better, and squandering money to give Earth the benefit of the doubt based upon an unjustifiable assumption that dangerous warming will shortly resume is exactly the wrong type of 'picking winners' approach."[64]

Carter makes a point that no serious person should dispute: "The reality is that no scientist on the planet can tell you with credible probability whether the climate in 2030 will be cooler or warmer than today. In such circumstances the only rational conclusion to draw is that we need to be prepared to react to either warming or cooling over the next several decades, and also to severe weather events, depending upon what Nature chooses to serve up to us. A primary government duty of care is to protect the citizenry and the environment from the ravages of natural climate-related events. What is needed is not unnecessary and penal measures against CO2 emissions, but instead a prudent and cost-effective policy of preparation for, and adaptive response to, all climate events and hazards."[65]

Rather than giving politicians, bureaucrats, media, advocates, and activists pause, these experts and innumerable others are demeaned and dismissed, as they dare to challenge an ideologically driven movement that targets America's economic system, and presses on more aggressively than ever. For example, as if lifting the language directly from the Margarita Declaration on Climate Change in authoring her congressional resolution for a "Green New Deal," Representative Alexandria Ocasio-Cortez and dozens of her Democrat colleagues drafted an equally ludicrous, Marxist-centric bill. I have included most of it here, because to summarize the bill would diminish a true understanding of its dangerousness. It states, in part:

> *Whereas* climate change, pollution, and environmental destruction have exacerbated systemic racial, regional, social, environmental, and economic injustices (referred to in this preamble as "systemic injustices") by disproportionately affecting indigenous communities, communities of color, migrant communities, deindustrialized communities, depopulated rural communities, the poor, low-income workers, women, the elderly, the unhoused, people with disabilities, and youth (referred to in this preamble as "frontline and vulnerable communities");
>
> . . . *Resolved*, That it is the sense of the House of Representatives that—
>
> (1) it is the duty of the Federal Government to create a Green New Deal—
>
> (A) to achieve net-zero greenhouse gas emissions through a fair and just transition for all communities and workers;
>
> (B) to create millions of good, high-wage jobs and ensure prosperity and economic security for all people of the United States;
>
> (C) to invest in the infrastructure and industry of the United States to sustainably meet the challenges of the 21st century;
>
> (D) to secure for all people of the United States for generations to come—
>
> (i) clean air and water;
>
> (ii) climate and community resiliency;

(iii) healthy food;

(iv) access to nature; and

(v) a sustainable environment; and

(E) to promote justice and equity by stopping current, preventing future, and repairing historic oppression of indigenous communities, communities of color, migrant communities, deindustrialized communities, depopulated rural communities, the poor, low-income workers, women, the elderly, the unhoused, people with disabilities, and youth (referred to in this resolution as "frontline and vulnerable communities");

(2) the goals described in subparagraphs of paragraph (1) above (referred to in this resolution as the "Green New Deal goals") should be accomplished through a 10-year national mobilization (referred to in this resolution as the "Green New Deal mobilization") that will require the following goals and projects—

(A) building resiliency against climate change-related disasters, such as extreme weather, including by leveraging funding and providing investments for community-defined projects and strategies;

(B) repairing and upgrading the infrastructure in the United States, including—

(i) by eliminating pollution and greenhouse gas emissions as much as technologically feasible;

(ii) by guaranteeing universal access to clean water;

(iii) by reducing the risks posed by flooding and other climate impacts; and

(iv) by ensuring that any infrastructure bill considered by Congress addresses climate change;

(C) meeting 100 percent of the power demand in the United States through clean, renewable, and zero-emission energy sources, including—

(i) by dramatically expanding and upgrading existing renewable power sources; and

(ii) by deploying new capacity;

(D) building or upgrading to energy-efficient, distributed, and "smart" power grids, and working to ensure affordable access to electricity;

(E) upgrading all existing buildings in the United States and building new buildings to achieve maximal energy efficiency, water efficiency, safety, affordability, comfort, and durability, including through electrification;

(F) spurring massive growth in clean manufacturing in the United States and removing pollution and greenhouse gas emissions from manufacturing and industry as much as is technologically feasible, including by expanding renewable energy manufacturing and investing in existing manufacturing and industry;

(G) working collaboratively with farmers and ranchers in the United States to eliminate pollution and greenhouse gas emissions from the agricultural sector as much as is technologically feasible, including—

(i) by supporting family farming;

(ii) by investing in sustainable farming and land use practices that increase soil health; and

(iii) by building a more sustainable food system that ensures universal access to healthy food;

(H) overhauling transportation systems in the United States to eliminate pollution and greenhouse gas emissions from the transportation sector as much as is technologically feasible, including through investment in—

(i) zero-emission vehicle infrastructure and manufacturing;

(ii) clean, affordable, and accessible public transportation; and

(iii) high-speed rail;

(I) mitigating and managing the long-term adverse health, economic, and other effects of pollution and climate change, including by providing funding for community-defined projects and strategies;

(J) removing greenhouse gases from the atmosphere and reducing pollution, including by restoring natural ecosystems through proven low-tech solutions that increase soil carbon storage, such as preservation and afforestation;

(K) restoring and protecting threatened, endangered, and fragile ecosystems through locally appropriate and science-based projects that enhance biodiversity and support climate resiliency;

(L) cleaning up existing hazardous waste and abandoned sites to promote economic development and sustainability;

(M) identifying other emission and pollution sources and creating solutions to eliminate them; and

(N) promoting the international exchange of technology, expertise, products, funding, and services, with the aim of making the United States the international leader on climate action, and to help other countries achieve a Green New Deal;

(3) a Green New Deal must be developed through transparent and inclusive consultation, collaboration, and partnership with frontline and vulnerable communities, labor unions, worker cooperatives, civil society groups, academia, and businesses; and

(4) to achieve the Green New Deal goals and mobilization, a Green New Deal will require the following goals and projects—

(A) providing and leveraging, in a way that ensures that the public receives appropriate ownership stakes and returns on investment, adequate capital (including through community grants, public banks, and other public financing), technical expertise, supporting policies, and other forms of assistance to communities, organizations, Federal, State, and local government agencies, and businesses working on the Green New Deal mobilization;

(B) ensuring that the Federal Government takes into account the complete environmental and social costs and impacts of emissions through—

(i) existing laws;

(ii) new policies and programs; and

(iii) ensuring that frontline and vulnerable communities shall not be adversely affected;

(C) providing resources, training, and high-quality education, including higher education, to all people of the United States, with a focus on frontline and vulnerable communities, so those communities may be full and equal participants in the Green New Deal mobilization;

(D) making public investments in the research and development of new clean and renewable energy technologies and industries;

(E) directing investments to spur economic development, deepen and diversify industry in local and regional economies, and build wealth and community ownership, while prioritizing high-quality job creation and economic, social, and environmental benefits in frontline and vulnerable communities that may otherwise struggle with the transition away from greenhouse gas intensive industries;

(F) ensuring the use of democratic and participatory processes that are inclusive of and led by frontline and vulnerable communities and workers to plan, implement, and administer the Green New Deal mobilization at the local level;

(G) ensuring that the Green New Deal mobilization creates high-quality union jobs that pay prevailing wages, hires local workers, offers training and advancement opportunities, and guarantees wage and benefit parity for workers affected by the transition;

(H) guaranteeing a job with a family-sustaining wage, adequate family and medical leave, paid vacations, and retirement security to all people of the United States;

(I) strengthening and protecting the right of all workers to organize, unionize, and collectively bargain free of coercion, intimidation, and harassment;

> (J) strengthening and enforcing labor, workplace health and safety, antidiscrimination, and wage and hour standards across all employers, industries, and sectors;
>
> (K) enacting and enforcing trade rules, procurement standards, and border adjustments with strong labor and environmental protections—
>
> (i) to stop the transfer of jobs and pollution overseas; and
>
> (ii) to grow domestic manufacturing in the United States;
>
> (L) ensuring that public lands, waters, and oceans are protected and that eminent domain is not abused;
>
> (M) obtaining the free, prior, and informed consent of indigenous people for all decisions that affect indigenous people and their traditional territories, honoring all treaties and agreements with indigenous people, and protecting and enforcing the sovereignty and land rights of indigenous people;
>
> (N) ensuring a commercial environment where every businessperson is free from unfair competition and domination by domestic or international monopolies; and
>
> (O) providing all people of the United States with—
>
> (i) high-quality health care;
>
> (ii) affordable, safe, and adequate housing;
>
> (iii) economic security; and
>
> (iv) access to clean water, clean air, healthy and affordable food, and nature.[66]

Milton Ezrati at *Forbes* rounded up some of the cost estimates for this proposal. Here are figures for just some of its goals: "The proposed expansion of renewables to provide 100% of the nation's power needs would, according to respected physicist Christopher Clark, cost about $2 trillion or approximately $200 billion a year for ten years. The Deal's desire to build a 'smart power grid' for the entire country, would, according to the Electric Power Institute, cost some $400 billion or $40 billion a year for ten years; according to several sources, AOC's aspiration to 'draw down greenhouse gases' would cost upwards of $11 trillion or about $110 billion a year for ten years."[67] Moreover, "the Deal's goal to upgrade every home and industrial building in the country to state-of-the-art safety and energy efficiency would run some $2.5 trillion over ten years or about $250 billion a year. This figure may well be understated. Consider that there are 136 million dwellings in the United States. An upgrade of each would conservatively cost $10,000 a unit on average or near $1.4 trillion, and this does not even include the industrial and commercial structures. Nor does it include upkeep."[68] In addition, "the Green New Deal also aspires to provide jobs guarantees at a 'living wage.' A government assessment of a similar proposal by Sen. Cory Booker (D-NJ) puts the cost of such a program at $543 billion in its first year. Though the costs thereafter would fall, the cumulative expense over ten years would come to some $2.5 trillion. The goal of developing a universal, single payer health-care system would, according to an MIT-Amherst study of a similar plan put forward by Senator Bernie Sanders, come to about $1.4 trillion a year."[69]

"Just these six of AOC's long list of aspirations," states Ezrati, "would then roughly cost some $2.5 trillion a year. Since Washington's 2018 budget put spending at $4.5 trillion, the Deal would effectively increase federal spending by a touch over half again. That is a hefty price tag, considerably more than the estimated $700 billion a year that would emerge from AOC's proposal to raise the maximum tax rate to 70%."[70]

The Heritage Foundation's Kevin Dayaratna and Nicolas Loris note that "according to the Heritage Energy Model, as a result of the taxes and carbon-based regulations, by 2040 one can expect: a peak employment shortfall of over 1.4 million jobs; a total income loss of more than $40,000 for a family of four; an aggregate gross domestic product loss of over $3.9 trillion; and, increases in household electricity expenditures averaging approximately 12 to 14 percent. Unquestionably, these projections from the Heritage Energy Model significantly underestimate the costs of the Green New Deal's energy components. As Ocasio-Cortez's Frequently Asked Questions sheet notes, the carbon tax is only one of many policy tools Green New Deal advocates hope to implement."[71]

And the American Action Forum, headed by former Congressional Budget Office director Douglas Holtz-Eakin, concludes that the Green New Deal may cost up to $93 trillion over ten years—between $8.3 trillion and $12.3 trillion to eliminate, at least theoretically, carbon emissions from the power and transportation sectors, and between $42.8 trillion and $80.6 trillion for its massive social and economic undertakings.[72]

Apart from the crushing financial costs of these preposterous and perilous undertakings, and the horrendous economic dislocations that would follow, I continue to return to the fact that it would require us to abandon such foundational principles as limited government, private property rights, and the capitalist economic system, and require the assembly of an even more massive bureaucracy with immense regulatory control and police powers. Decision making would be further centralized in Washington, DC, and politicians would wield enormous authority over the individual and citizenry generally. Furthermore, imagine the brownouts, blackouts, fuel shortages, scarcity of basic necessities, etc. Of course, basic human liberties, free will, mobility, etc. would eventually fade and then vanish, as the Marxist vision is pursued in earnest.

Even so, Joe Biden and the Democratic Party are all in. One of Biden's first acts after his inauguration was signing an executive order returning the United States to the Paris Agreement of 2015. Of course, such an agreement should be handled as a treaty, given the far-reaching impact this kind of an international agreement will have on American society. But rather than risk losing a vote in the Senate, where treaties require the support of two-thirds (67) of the senators, Biden, like President Barack Obama before him, simply issued an edict.

Among other things, the agreement commits signatories to "[a]cknowledg[e] that climate change is a common concern of humankind, [and therefore] Parties should, when taking action to address climate change, respect, promote and consider their respective obligations on human rights, the right to health, the rights of indigenous peoples, local communities, migrants, children, persons with disabilities and people in vulnerable situations and the right to development, as well as gender equality, empowerment of women and intergenerational equity."[73] One of the signatories to this agreement is Communist China, which is currently running concentration camps, where more than 1 million Uyghurs and other minorities are being enslaved, tortured, and raped, and where Uyghur women are sterilized and prisoners are summarily executed.[74]

Indeed, on January 19, 2021, the Trump administration formally accused China of committing "genocide and crimes against humanity" in its oppression of Uyghur Muslims in its Xinjiang region.[75] However, on February 16, 2021, when asked about China's conduct during a CNN town hall, Biden said, in part: "If you know anything about Chinese history, it has always been, the time when China has been victimized by the outer world is when they haven't been unified at home. So the central, well, vastly overstated, the central principle of [China's president] Xi Jinping is that there must be a united, tightly controlled China. And he uses his rationale for the things he does based on that." He later added, shockingly: "Culturally there are different norms that each country and their leaders are expected to follow."[76]

Thus, all the talk and proclamations about equality, human rights, indigenous peoples, empowerment of women, as well as the right to health care, jobs, and the like in the Paris Agreement, the Green New Deal, the claims of Critical Race Theory and intersectionality, etc., are essentially ignored when a Democrat administration is faced with a brutal regime like China. Meanwhile, Biden obligates the United States to global economic and financial conditions set by international governments and bureaucrats under the rubric of climate change, without any formal input from our representatives in Congress, which will very likely negatively affect our quality of life, and which countries like China have no intention of adhering to.

In fact, literally a few hours after he was sworn in as president, Biden also signed an executive order shutting down further construction of the Keystone XL pipeline. Among other things, his fiat repeated the propaganda of some of the most hyped charges of the extreme climate-change propagandists: "Climate change has had a growing effect on the U.S. economy, with climate-related costs increasing over the last 4 years. Extreme weather events and other climate-related effects have harmed the health, safety, and security of the American people and have increased the urgency for combatting climate change and accelerating the transition toward a clean energy economy. The world must be put on a sustainable climate pathway to protect Americans and the domestic economy from harmful climate impacts, and to create well-paying union jobs as part of a climate solution. . . . That crisis must be met with action on a scale and at a speed commensurate with the need to avoid setting the world on a dangerous, potentially catastrophic climate trajectory. . . ."[77] Of course, the use of fossil fuels has actually reduced carbon dioxide levels. It is cheaper and cleaner than coal. And pipelines are far more efficient than transporting fuel by truck and railcar. Regardless, Biden destroyed the pipeline and thousands of union jobs with it.

But Biden was not done. On January 27, 2021, he issued another executive order that, in part, provides, as the White House explained:

> [T]hat, in implementing [the order]—and building on—the Paris Agreement's objectives, the United States will exercise its leadership to promote a significant increase in global ambition. It makes clear that both significant short-term global emission reductions and net zero global emissions by mid-century—or before—are required to avoid setting the world on a dangerous, potentially catastrophic, climate trajectory.
>
> Among numerous other steps aimed at prioritizing climate in U.S. foreign policy and national security, the order directs the Director of National Intelligence to prepare a National Intelligence Estimate on the security implications of climate change, the State Department to prepare a transmittal package to the Senate for the Kigali Amendment to the Montreal Protocol, and all agencies to develop strategies for integrating climate considerations into their international work. . . .
>
> The order also calls for the establishment of a Civilian Climate Corps Initiative to put a new generation of Americans to work conserving and restoring public lands and waters, increasing reforestation, increasing carbon sequestration in the agricultural sector, protecting biodiversity, improving access to recreation, and addressing the changing climate.
>
> The order formalizes President Biden's commitment to

> make environmental justice a part of the mission of every agency by directing federal agencies to develop programs, policies, and activities to address the disproportionate health, environmental, economic, and climate impacts on disadvantaged communities.
>
> The order establishes a White House Environmental Justice Interagency Council and a White House Environmental Justice Advisory Council to prioritize environmental justice and ensure a whole-of-government approach to addressing current and historical environmental injustices, including strengthening environmental justice monitoring and enforcement through new or strengthened offices at the Environmental Protection Agency, Department of Justice, and Department of Health and Human Services. . . .
>
> The order directs the Secretary of the Interior to pause on entering into new oil and natural gas leases on public lands or offshore waters to the extent possible, launch a rigorous review of all existing leasing and permitting practices related to fossil fuel development on public lands and waters, and identify steps that can be taken to double renewable energy production from offshore wind by 2030.[78]

Biden's executive order bypassed Congress and instituted by edict the foundation of the Green New Deal Movement's radical agenda.

In addition to striking blow after blow against the capitalist engine of the American economy, Biden next sought to seize for the federal government unprecedented authority over the private economy by expending unimaginable sums of money and plunging the nation into inconceivable debt, redirecting trillions of dollars in private sector resources to his political priorities, and imposing unprecedented regulatory controls on American industry, not only to take initial steps to fulfill the demands of the degrowth activists and their Green New Deal, but to rearrange major aspects of American society and daily life.[79]

On March 31, 2021, Biden announced a $2.5 trillion plan (on top of $1.9 trillion already spent on a so-called COVID-19 relief bill, only 9 percent of which was actually related to COVID-19[80]), that includes: "$10 Billion to Create a 'Civilian Climate Corp'; $20 Billion to 'Advance Racial Equity and Environmental Justice'; $175 Billion in Subsidies for Electric Vehicles; $213 Billion to Build/Retrofit 2 Million Houses & Buildings; $100 Billion for New Public Schools and Making School Lunches 'Greener'; $12 Billion for Community Colleges; Billions to Eliminate 'Racial and Gender Inequities' in STEM; $100 Billion to Expand Broadband Internet (and Government Control of It); and, $25 Billion for Government Childcare Programs." Only $621 billion of the multi-trillion-dollar proposal actually goes to "transportation infrastructure and resilience."[81] And, says Biden, there is more to come. Indeed, the revolution can never end. The radical site *Mother Jones* reported: "The Democratic Party's left flank has argued that the [$2.5 trillion] plan doesn't spend nearly enough to address the crises the country faces. Rep. Pramila Jayapal (D-Wash.), chair of the Congressional Progressive Caucus, said the package 'should be substantially larger,' noting Biden had committed to $2 trillion in climate investment alone as a candidate."[82] And they are ready with something called the THRIVE Act—the Transform, Heal, and Renew by Investing in a Vibrant Economy.[83] The cost: $10 *trillion*![84]

And after all of this, when it comes to energy, the public will suffer. America's largest state, California, has been an incubator for far-left environmental experiments. During the summer of 2020, California's climate policies resulted in a widespread blackout. Millions of its citizens had their electrical power cut off in the midst of a heat wave. Michael Shellenberger at *Forbes* explains: "[T]he underlying reasons that California . . . experience[ed] rolling black-outs for the second time in less than a year stem[s] from the state's climate policies. . . ." . . . "California saw its electricity prices rise six times more than the rest of the United States from 2011 to 2019, due to its huge expansion of renewables. . . ."[85]

"Even though the cost of solar panels declined dramatically from 2011 and 2019," writes Shellenberger, "their unreliable and weather-dependent nature meant that they imposed large new costs in the form of storage and transmissions to keep electricity reliable. California's solar panels and farms were all turning off as the blackouts began, with no help available from the states to the East already in nightfall. . . . The two blackouts in less than a year are strong evidence that the tens of billions that Californians have spent on renewables come with high human, economic, and environmental costs."[86]

In February 2021, Texas experienced a disastrous energy crisis during a severe winter storm. The Institute for Energy Research (IER) reports that "Texas's current energy problem is reminiscent of California's problems last summer—another state with a renewable energy mandate. . . . These recent experiences prove that during extreme weather, solar panels and wind turbines are of little value to the electric grid, especially when investment flows to them because of subsidies and mandates at the expense of grid reliability and resilience."[87]

IER described how Texas's growing reliance on renewables was catastrophic. "Wind turbines at times . . . generated over half of the Texas power *generation*. As wind generation dropped off and demand surged, fossil-fuel generation increased and covered the supply gap. Between the mornings of Feb. 7 and Feb. 11, wind as a share of the state's electricity fell to 8 percent from 42 percent, according to the Energy Information Administration. Gas-fired plants produced 43,800 MW of power Sunday night and coal plants chipped in 10,800 MW—about two to three times what they usually generate at their peak on any given winter day. Between 12 a.m. on Feb. 8 and Feb. 16, wind power plunged 93 percent while coal increased 47 percent and gas 450 percent. Nuclear dropped 26 percent due to a reactor shutting off because the sensor could not relay that the system was stable—a safety feature. . . . [T]he state's electricity grid that depends increasingly on subsidized, intermittent wind and solar energy needs backup power to handle surges in demand. Natural gas helps but reliable coal and nuclear power are also needed."[88]

IER issued this warning: "Energy security and resilience is the opposite of what . . . Biden and other politicians want for our future when they advocate for a 'green new deal' or something similar by indicating that the United States should stop consuming hydrocarbons and use only carbon free sources. They want electricity to be almost entirely generated by renewable energy and for all sectors of the economy to be supplied solely by electricity. This means if cars and trucks and other vehicles become all electric, the increased electric demand will be supplied mainly by renewable energy, which will also need to replace the retiring hydrocarbon capacity—capacity that would last for decades if it was not forced to prematurely shutter, and which supplies 62 percent of our electricity."[89]

And Biden issued an executive order in January requiring the Interior Department to develop a so-called 30 by 30 conservation plan, in which the Interior Department, working with the Agricultural and Commerce Departments, is to protect "at least 30 percent of our lands and waters by 2030" as a first step to an even more aggressive conservation policy. The left-wing Internet site

Vox characterized this initiative as "a game-changing approach to nature conservation." While details are sparse, you can imagine the kind of power that is likely to be used against private-property owners and publicly available and used areas of the country. In fact, Vox celebrates the plan as "monumental," explaining that it "redefines what 'conservation' means"; "indigenous rights and sovereignty are front and center"; "farms, ranches, and other working lands will contribute to the 30 percent"; "it will increase access to nature in low-income communities"; and "the initiative also seeks to generate a lot of jobs."[90]

Of course, given the desires of this Marxist-oriented movement, the anti–private property disposition of the federal bureaucracy, the endless overreach of successive administrations, and federalization of land and water use decisions, this has all the markings of an economic and property-rights catastrophe.

Unfortunately, true science, experience, and knowledge are not hallmarks of the anticapitalist degrowth zealots. As I explained in *Plunder and Deceit*, their Marxist-oriented mind-set "has . . . developed into a pseudo-religion and public policy obsession. In fact, the degrowthers insist their ideology reaches far beyond the environment or even its odium for capitalism and is an all-encompassing lifestyle and governing philosophy."[91] And their influence reaches directly into the Oval Office and the halls of Congress, where the American economic marvel is quickly unraveling before our eyes.

CHAPTER SIX

PROPAGANDA, CENSORSHIP, AND SUBVERSION

My purpose here is not to restate in truncated form what I wrote at length in *Unfreedom of the Press*. Nonetheless, some initial and limited overlap is necessary to explain how the media are now well suited as propagandists for an anti-American, pro-Marxist agenda—from Critical Race Theory and the 1619 Project to the degrowth movement and its war on capitalism.

Writing in *Jacobin* magazine, a self-described socialist publication, Steven Sherman notes that Marx "was a journalist more or less all of his adult life. He started writing for the *Rheinische Zeitung* in 1842, and founded his own paper in 1848. His work for the [*New York*] *Tribune* came about because he'd met an American newspaper editor, Charles Dana (who would later go on to edit the *New York Sun*) in Cologne in 1848, and a few years later Dana asked Marx to contribute some articles to the *New York Tribune* on the situation in Germany. I think that Marx and Engels viewed the *Tribune* as a way to publicize their views and to influence debate with a large number of readers. . . ."[1]

In an interview with James Ledbetter, the editor of *Dispatches for the New York Tribune*, a 2008 book of Marx's articles for the *Tribune*, Ledbetter explains that "the basic Marx approach to his *New York Tribune* column was to take an event that was in the news—an election, an uprising, the second Opium War, the outbreak of the American Civil War—and sift through it until he could boil it down to some fundamental questions of politics or economics. And then on those questions he would make his judgment. In this sense, Marx's journalism does resemble some of the writing that is published today in journals of opinion, and it's not hard to see a direct line between Marx's journalistic writing and the kind of tendentious writing on public affairs that characterized much political journalism (especially in Europe) in the twentieth century."[2]

Thus, Marx approached journalism as modern journalists do today—that is, he was unencumbered by a commitment to actual news reporting. Instead, his reporting would shape the news around his own opinions and ideology.

"After 1848, Marx learned the power of counterrevolution," writes Ledbetter, "and began to believe that existing systems of government and economy could not be overthrown until a relatively informed and organized proletariat could be mobilized to do so. As became clear with every passing year, in many nations such organization was decades away, if it existed at all."[3]

In short, Marx understood the power of mass communication and the need to control it and shape it to frame events and opinions. In other words, the purpose was to propagandize, not inform.

"[R]eading through Marx's *Tribune* dispatches, you can't help but see an urgency, an excitement—almost an impatience—in his portrayals of some insurrections and crises in Europe and India. At times he wrote as if this particular rise in corn prices, or this little dust-up with authorities in Greece, was going to be *the* spark that would ignite revolution. And it's not as if one can fault Marx for feeling that way; after all, during this period crowned heads of Europe were toppling and certainly at least liberal revolutions seemed likely in a number of settings. But there are times when his discipline of thought appears to leave him, and he is also prone to the tautology that revolution can only occur when the masses are ready, but we can't know for certain if the masses are ready until they create a revolution."[4]

Ledbetter explains that Marx was indeed a revolutionary advocating his ideology of material historicism, but he was, first and foremost, a journalist. "Marx today is taught as an economic theorist; as a political thinker; and to some degree as a historian and philosopher. Each category is valid; each is also incomplete. The historical record, however, at least suggests another category: that Marx should be thought of as a professional writer, as a journalist. The Penguin Classics volume I've edited is but a sample; overall Marx produced, with help from Engels, nearly five hundred articles for the *Tribune*, which together amass nearly seven volumes of the two men's fifty-volume collected works. I think we come closer to understanding the importance of rhetoric in Marx's work if we think of him as a journalist."[5]

The fact is modern journalists, from the *New York Times* and *Washington Post* to CNN and MSNBC, and most other news platforms, have much in common with Marx-the-journalist, as will become evident. They have abandoned the traditional role of a reporter for that of social activist—driving most of the same major issues and agendas as the various Marxist movements in the United States. The transition did not happen overnight, but has been building for the better part of a century.

Indeed, more than a half century ago, the late Richard M. Weaver, professor of English at the University of Chicago, and referenced earlier in the book, had already commented on the beginning of the end of genuine journalism in America. In his book *Ideas Have Consequences*, he wrote that the modern press is actually a highly negative force in our society. He was not opposed to a free press, of course, but he was repelled by what it had become. Weaver opined, "[F]or Plato, truth was a living thing, never wholly captured by men even in animated discourse and its purest form, certainly, never brought to paper. In our day it would seem that a contrary presumption has grown up. The more firmly an utterance is stereotyped, the more likely it is to win credit. It is assumed that engines as expensive and as powerful as the modern printing press will naturally be placed in the hands of men of knowledge. Faith in the printed word has raised journalism to the rank of oracles; yet how could there be a better description of them than these line from the *Phaedrus*: 'They will appear to be omniscient and will generally know nothing; they will be tiresome, having the reputation of knowledge without the reality?' "[6]

"If the realization of truth is the product of a meeting of minds," wrote Weaver, "we may be skeptical of the physical ability of the mechanism to propagate it as long as that propagation is limited to the printing and distribution of stories which give 'one unvarying answer.' And this circumstance brings up at once the question of the intention of the rulers of the press. There is much to indicate that modern publication wishes to minimize discussion. Despite many artful pretensions to the contrary, it does not want an exchange of views, save perhaps on academic matters. Instead, it encourages men to read in the hope that they will absorb."[7]

In this, Weaver is condemning the nature of media as organized propaganda involving individuals who are not particularly bright or knowledgeable about the matters on which they write or speak, but are propagandists for particular viewpoints.

Weaver argued that "[t]here is another circumstance which raises grave doubts about the contribution of journalism to the public weal. Newspapers are under strong pressure to distort in the interest of holding attention. . . . It is an inescapable fact that newspapers thrive on friction and conflict. One has only to survey the headlines of some popular journal, often presented symbolically in red, to note the *kind* of thing which is considered news. Behind the big story there nearly always lies a battle of some sort. Conflict, after all, is the essence of drama, and it is a truism that newspapers deliberately start and prolong quarrels; by allegation, by artful quotation, by the accentuation of unimportant differences, they create antagonism where none was felt to exist before. And this is profitable practically, for the opportunity to dramatize a fight is an opportunity for news. Journalism, on the whole, is glad to see a quarrel start and sorry to see it end. In the more sensational publications this spirit of passion and violence, manifested in a certain recklessness of diction, with vivid verbs and fortissimo adjectives, creeps into the very language. By the attention it gives their misdeeds it makes criminals heroic and politicians large than life. . . ."[8]

I would go a step further—the press not only starts and prolongs quarrels, but thrives today on the exploitation of issues and agendas that serve the purposes of the various Marxist movements, and in doing so inflames and divides the entire nation along ideological lines.

"In reviewing the persistent tendency of the newspapers to corrupt, I shall cite a passage from [author] James Fenimore Cooper," writes Weaver. "Though Cooper lived before the advent of yellow journalism, he seems to have stated the essential situation with a truth and eloquence impossible to improve on when he said in The American Democrat: 'As the press of this country now exists, it would seem to be expressly devised by the great agent of mischief, to depress and destroy all that is good, and to elevate and advance all that is evil in the nation. The little truth that is urged, is usually urged coarsely, weakened and rendered vicious, by personalities; while those who live by falsehoods, fallacies, enmities, partialities and the schemes of the designing, find the press the very instrument that the devils would invent to effect their designs.'"[9]

Weaver and Cooper were highlighting what would become the media's use of targeted, personal attacks on individuals and subjects that defy or resist the trajectory of events and movements for which journalists have become committed and open advocates. This is seen every day with, for example, the relentless polemical characterizations of individuals and groups as climate change deniers, Trump deplorables, white supremacists, etc.

Weaver observes, "The constant stream of sensation, eulogized as lively propagation of what the public wants to hear, discourages the pulling-together of events from past time into a whole for contemplation. Thus, absence of reflection keeps the individual from being aware of his former selves, and it is highly questionable whether anyone can be a member of a metaphysical community who does not preserve such memory. Upon the presence of the past in the present depends all conduct and direct knowledge. There can be little doubt that this condition of the mind is a large factor in the low political morality of the age."[10]

Of course, the whole of Marxist thought is the cleansing of history for the purification of future existence—that is, all that came before must be rejected and destroyed, by violent revolution if necessary, to make way for the Marxist society.

As will become clear, a combination of propaganda, pseudo-events, social activism, and targeted, personal attacks has replaced traditional journalism. Moreover, it actively promotes the various causes and movements of the American Marxist.

Edward Bernays, considered the father of modern propaganda, wrote in his 1928 book, *Propaganda*, that "propaganda is a consistent, enduring effort to create or shape events to influence the relations of the public to an enterprise, idea or group. . . . So vast are the numbers of minds which can be regimented, and so tenacious are they when regimented, that a group at times offers an irresistible pressure before which legislators, editors, and teachers are helpless."[11]

Bernays explained: "The minority [including elites and activists] has discovered a powerful help in influencing majorities. It has been found possible so to mold the mind of the masses that they will throw their newly gained strength in the desired direction. In the present structure of society, this practice is inevitable. Whatever of social importance is done today, whether in politics, finance, manufacturing, agriculture, charity, education, or other fields, must be done with the help of propaganda. Propaganda is the executive arm of the invisible government."[12]

Richard Gunderman at phys.org points out that "[w]hat Bernays' writings furnish is not a principle or tradition by which to evaluate the appropriateness of propaganda, but simply a means for shaping public opinion for any purpose whatsoever, whether beneficial to human beings or not. This observation led Supreme Court Justice Felix Frankfurter to warn President Franklin Roosevelt against allowing Bernays to play a leadership role in World War II, describing him and his colleagues as 'professional poisoners of the public mind, exploiters of foolishness, fanaticism, and self-interest.' "[13]

In his 1927 book, *Propaganda Technique in the World War*, Harold Dwight Lasswell describes propaganda as a tool used by the press and others, cloaked as learning and wisdom. "Propaganda is a concession to the rationality of the modern world. A literate world, a reading world, a schooled world prefers to thrive on argument and news. It is sophisticated to the extent of using print; and he that takes to print shall live or perish by the Press. All the apparatus of diffused erudition popularizes the symbols and forms of pseudo-rational appeal; the wolf of propaganda does not hesitate to masquerade in the sheepskin. All the voluble men of the day—writers, reporters, editors, preachers, lecturers, teachers, politicians—are drawn into the service of propaganda to amplify a master voice. All is conducted with the decorum and the trappings of intelligence, for this is a rational epoch, and demands its raw meat cooked and garnished by adroit and skillful chefs."[14]

The late political theorist Hannah Arendt wrote in her book *The Origins of Totalitarianism* that "while it is true that the masses are obsessed by a desire to escape from reality because in their essential homelessness, they can no longer bear its accidental, incomprehensible aspects, it is also true that their longing for fiction has some connection with those capacities of the human mind whose structural consistency is superior to mere occurrence. The masses' escape from reality is a verdict against the world in which they are forced to live and in which they cannot exist, since coincidence has become its supreme master and human beings need the constant transformation of chaotic and accidental conditions into a man-made pattern of relative consistency. The revolt of the masses against 'realism,' common sense, and all 'the plausibilities of the world' . . . was the result of their atomization, of their loss of social status along with which they lost the whole sector of communal relationships in whose framework common sense makes sense. In their situation of spiritual and social homelessness, a measured insight into the interdependence of the arbitrary and the planned, the accidental and the necessary, could no longer operate. Totalitarian propaganda can outrageously insult common sense only where common sense has lost its validity. Before the alternative of facing the anarchic growth and total arbitrariness of decay or bowing down before the most rigid, fantastically fictitious consistency of an ideology, the masses probably will always choose the latter and be ready to pay for it with individual sacrifices—and this not because they are stupid or wicked, but because in the general disaster this escape grants them a minimum of self-respect."[15]

In other words, people in a culture or society in decline, which ceases to be a unifying and civil society, and where the just social order unravels, are highly susceptible to believing and following dangerous fictions, even if they lead to their own demise.

"Before they seize power and establish a world according to their doctrines," wrote Arendt, "totalitarian movements conjure up a lying world of consistency which is more adequate to the needs of the human mind than reality itself; in which, through sheer imagination, uprooted masses can feel at home and are spared the never-ending shocks which real life and real experiences deal to human beings and their expectations. The force possessed by totalitarian propaganda—before the movements have the power to drop iron curtains to prevent anyone's disturbing, by the slightest reality, the gruesome quiet of an entirely imaginary world—lies in its ability to shut the masses off from the real world. The only signs which the real world still offers to the understanding of the unintegrated and disintegrating masses—whom every new stroke of ill luck makes more gullible—are, so to speak, its lacunae, the questions it does not care to discuss publicly, or the rumors it does not dare to contradict. . . ."[16]

As I explained in *Ameritopia*, Utopianism [which would include totalitarianism] . . . finds a receptive audience among the society's disenchanted, disaffected, dissatisfied, and maladjusted who are unwilling or unable to assume responsibility for their own real or perceived conditions but instead blame their surroundings, 'the system,' and others. They are lured by the false hopes and promises of utopian transformation and the criticisms of the existing society, to which their connection is tentative or nonexistent. Improving the malcontents' lot becomes linked to the utopian cause. Moreover, disparaging and diminishing the successful and accomplished becomes an essential tactic. . . . By exploiting human frailties, frustrations, jealousies, and inequities, a sense of meaning and self-worth is created in the malcontent's otherwise unhappy and directionless life. Simply put, equality in misery—that is, equality of result or conformity—is advanced as a just, fair, and virtuous undertaking. Liberty, therefore, is inherently immoral, except where it avails equality."[17]

In addition to propaganda, or perhaps a form of propaganda, is what the late Daniel J. Boorstin, a librarian of the United States Congress and professor of history at the University Chicago, labeled "pseudo-events"—that is, staged press events. Boorstin explained: "In a totalitarian society, where people are flooded by purposeful lies, the real facts are of course misrepresented, but the representation itself is not ambiguous. The propaganda lie is asserted as if it were true. Its object is to lead people to believe that the truth is simpler, more intelligible, than it really is. . . . Propaganda oversimplifies experience, pseudo-events overcomplicate it."[18]

Boorstin notices how the media cleverly use pseudo-events to promote causes and agendas. He explained that "[a]t first it may seem strange that the rise of pseudo-events has coincided with the growth of the professional ethic which obliges newsmen to omit editorializing and personal judgments from their news accounts. But now it is in the making of pseudo-events that newsmen find ample scope for their individuality and creative imagination."[19]

Indeed, we are inundated by pseudo-events rather than actual news—that is, an unreality of the journalist's making. For example, for literally several years, our nation was fed relentless "news" stories about President Donald Trump's having colluded with Russia to win his election in 2016. This spurred congressional hearings, a criminal investigation, and endless stories piled upon endless stories. Pulitzer Prizes were awarded for utterly false news reports. It was perhaps the greatest media hoax in journalistic history.

As Boorstin observes, "In a democratic society like ours—and more especially in a highly literate, wealthy, competitive, and technologically advanced society—the people can be flooded by pseudo-events. For us, freedom of speech and the press and of broadcasting includes freedom to create pseudo-events. Competing politicians, competing newsmen, and competing news media contest in this creation. They vie with one another in offering attractive, 'informative' accounts and images of the world. They are free to speculate on the facts, to bring new facts into being, to demand answers to their own contrived questions. Our 'free market place of ideas' is a place where people are confronted by competing pseudo-events and are allowed to judge among them. When we speak of 'informing' the people this is what we really mean."[20]

Thus, we seem to live in two worlds simultaneously: the fictional world that the media have created for us, and the real world of our daily existence that has little or no relationship to pseudo-events. Yet for many, the former can be alluring. "The American citizen," wrote Boorstin, "thus lives in a world where fantasy is more real than reality, where the image has more dignity than its original. We hardly dare face our bewilderment because our ambiguous experience is so pleasantly iridescent, and the solace of belief in contrived reality is so thoroughly real. We have become eager accessories to the great hoaxes of the age. These are the hoaxes we play on ourselves."[21]

The repetition, force, and pervasiveness of pseudo-events create a seductive appeal, making it more difficult to discern news and real events from the concocted. And the fake often becomes more appealing than the factual. "Pseudo-events from their very nature tend to be more interesting and more attractive than spontaneous events. Therefore, in American public life today pseudo-events tend to drive all other kinds of events out of our consciousness, or at least to overshadow them. Earnest, well-informed citizens seldom notice that their experience of spontaneous events is buried by pseudo-events. Yet nowadays, the more industriously they work at 'informing' themselves the more this tends to be true."[22]

In fact, pseudo-events, like propaganda, which are intended to deceive, control, and direct the people, are critical to promoting Marxist and totalitarian movements. Conversely, they are thoroughly destructive of a free, open, and democratic society. Boorstin explains that "[i]n nineteenth-century America the most extreme modernism held that man was made by his environment. In twentieth-century America, without abandoning belief that we are made by our environment, we also believe our environment can be made almost wholly by us. . . . But to what end? How surprising if men who make their environment and fill experience with whatever they please could not also make their God! . . ."[23]

More recently, journalism professors and others have invented another rationale for insinuating "social activism" into reporting. They call it "public (or community) journalism." As with American Marxism generally, and education in particular, the social activist journalists who now populate the vast majority of America's newsrooms are John Dewey followers. Most of them consciously, some of them unknowingly. Some among them openly admit it, others pretend otherwise. Among other things, Dewey asserted: "When . . . I say that the first object of a renascent liberalism is education, I mean that its task is to aid in producing habits of mind and character, the intellectual and moral patterns, that are somewhere near even with the actual movements of events. It is, I repeat, the split between the latter as they have externally occurred and the ways of desiring, thinking, and of putting emotion and purpose into execution that is the basic cause of present confusion in mind and paralysis in action. The educational task cannot be accomplished merely by working upon men's minds, without action that effects actual change in situations. The idea that dispositions and attitudes can be altered by merely 'moral' means conceived of as something that goes on wholly inside of persons is itself one of the old patterns that has to be changed. Thought, desire and purpose exist in a constant give and take of interaction with environing conditions. But resolute thought is the first step in that change of action that will itself carry further the needed change in patterns of mind and character."[24]

Thus, Dewey argues that "the habit of the mind" and certain ways of thinking, combined with social activism, must be indoctrinated into the public psyche. In other words, the public must be indoctrinated with the social activist mind-set.

Dewey continued: "In short, liberalism must now become radical, meaning by 'radical' perception of the necessity of thoroughgoing changes in the set-up of institutions and corresponding activity to bring the changes to pass. For the gulf between what the actual situation makes possible and the actual state itself is so great that it cannot be bridged by piecemeal policies undertaken *ad hoc*. . . . If radicalism be defined as perception of need for radical change, then today any liberalism which is not also radicalism is irrelevant and doomed."[25]

Hence, radical steps must be taken, if and as necessary, to drive ideological ambitions into action throughout society. No half-measures or half-steps. As Dewey clearly knew, Marx was also intolerant of half-measures. He condemned socialism as a bastardization of his ideology, making the "workers' paradise" an impossibility.

And this is what animates and motivates the Dewey adherents in the press, which now accounts for most newsrooms. Michael

Schudson, professor at University of California, San Diego, writes: "Public journalism, like reforms of the Progressive Era, advances an unresolved blend of empowering the people and entrusting elites and experts with public responsibility. The Progressives supported both the initiative and referendum, which gave power to the people, and city manager government, which shifted power to professionals. The Progressives praised both direct primaries, giving power to the people, and a merit-based civil service, giving power to the educationally qualified. What all these reforms, both populist and elitist, shared was antipathy to political parties and to conventional partisanship. They also shared something like public journalism's ethical emphasis on proceduralism: advocate democracy without advocating particular policy solutions."[26]

Yet journalists assure us that such an approach is not about taking political sides or ideological positions, but problem solving and serving the community. This is nonsense. For example, in a 2016 article for *Stanford Magazine*, Theodore L. Glasser, professor of communications at Stanford University, reveals himself. He writes, in part: "In his remarkably provocative commencement address, documentarian Ken Burns called on members of the Stanford Class of 2016 to put aside their political differences and work together to defeat Donald Trump. Without mentioning him by name, Burns portrayed Trump as unequivocally unqualified for the presidency. In an indictment we might expect from the leftist filmmaker Michael Moore, the politically mainstream Burns dismissed Trump as an 'infantile, bullying man'; a 'person who easily lies'; a candidate 'who has never demonstrated any interest in anyone or anything but himself and his own enrichment.' While Burns said he has for decades 'diligently practiced and rigorously maintained a conscious neutrality' in his work, 'avoiding the advocacy' of many of his colleagues, he now believes that 'there comes a time when I—and you—can no longer remain neutral, silent. We must speak up—and speak out.' Burns singled out journalists, 'torn between a nagging responsibility to good journalism and the big ratings a media circus always delivers,' for failing 'to expose this charlatan.' "[27]

Glasser, writing approvingly, states: "But does Burns really want journalists to speak up and speak out, to abandon, at least in their dealings with Trump, their commitment to neutrality? Is he rejecting the ideal of the detached and disinterested reporter? Does he envision a press no longer steeped in the virtues of impartiality and objectivity? Does he plan to produce his own account of Trump-the-charlatan, something akin to the work of legendary CBS documentarian Edward R. Murrow, whom he mentioned approvingly; something, say, in the spirit of Murrow's exposé of Wisconsin senator Joseph McCarthy, the charlatan of the 1950s? Yes, I hope, to all of the above."[28]

And Glasser is hardly alone in this deceit.

Davis Merritt, author of *Public Journalism and Public Life*, declares: "Because we are unavoidably participants and because our profession is dependent on democracy's continuing success, we need to develop a working philosophy of participation in helping public life go well. I call it *the fair-minded participant*. Adopting that philosophy does not mean abandoning good judgment, fairness, balance, accuracy or truth. It does, however, mean employing those virtues on the field of play, not from the far-removed press box; not as a contestant, but as a fair-minded participant whose presence is necessary in order for outcomes to be determined fairly; that is, under the agreed-on rules, by the contestants. . . . The tradition that says journalists should not deal in the realm of values creates yet another disconnect between us (and our product) and citizens at large."[29]

And how does Merritt's fair-minded participation play out on the pages of his newspaper? Here is an example where on December 8, 2015, writing for his Kansas newspaper, Merritt proclaimed: "Donald Trump has not received a single vote and has zero delegates to the Republican National Convention, so time remains to head off what theoretically could be a candidate disaster for the GOP and a governing disaster for America. But that's a lot less time than the nation had in August when his bizarre presidential campaign took wings out of a huge, raucous rally in Mobile, Ala."[30]

Of course, Trump would go on to win the presidency. But, again, Merritt is a partisan whose idea of public journalism is the promotion of his ideological bias. Indeed, he makes no bones about his hatred for Trump. "The persistence of Trump's reckless, bullying, superficial, no-apologies, often truth-free campaign has mainline Republicans terrified. To most of them, a candidate as radical as Trump would surely result in the loss of another presidential race (see Barry Goldwater and George McGovern) and likely the loss of the Senate."[31]

Merritt admonishes that objective or impartial reporting, or at least its pursuit, is too sterile for the public journalism crowd. In truth, their view of improving democracy and solving community problems is, in fact, more about the promotion of their political agenda. Nonetheless, Merritt and his colleagues self-servingly insist on the openness and earnestness of their approach. In fact, they seem to view themselves, self-righteously, as Good Samaritans: "My primary purpose is not to try to describe or encourage a particular device or set of practices," explains Merritt. "To do so would, in itself, limit the possibilities. My objective is to stimulate thoughtful, serious discussion both inside and outside the profession about journalism's true place in democracy. The aim is not to provide, even if I could, immediate and specific answers. Journalism and public life did not reach their points of present decline quickly, and they will not recover quickly. Those specific answers will have to be found over time and through earnest experimentation."[32]

Another of the public journalism preachers is Jay Rosen, professor of journalism at New York University. He argues that "the newspaper of the future will have to rethink its relationship to all the institutions that nourish public life, from libraries to university to cafes. It will have to do more than 'cover' these institutions when they happen to make news. It will have to do more than print their advertisements. The newspaper must see that its own health is dependent on the health of dozens of other agencies which pull people out of their private worlds. For the greater pull of the public life, the greater the need for the newspaper. *Empty streets are bad for editors*, despite the wealth of crime news they may generate. The emptier the streets, the emptier the newspaper will seem to the readers barricaded in the private homes. . . ."[33]

Like the others, Rosen insists that journalism is dying not because of its failure to approach the news in an objective and impartial way, but because of its failure to relate to the common man through social activism. Indeed, Rosen condescendingly lectures that "[i]f the public is assumed to be 'out there,' more or less intact, then the job of the press is easy to state: to inform people about what goes on in their name and their midst. But suppose the public leads a more broken existence. At times it may be alert and engaged, but just as often it struggles against other pressures—including itself—that can win out in the end. Inattention to public matters is perhaps the simplest of these, atomization of society one of the more intricate. Money speaks louder than the public, problems overwhelm it, fatigue sets in, attention falters, cynicism swells. A public that leads this more fragile kind of existence suggests a different task for the press: not just to inform a public that may or may not emerge, but to improve the changes that will emerge. John Dewey, an early hero of mine, had suggested something like this in his 1927 book, *The Public and Its Problems*."[34]

With Dewey as his hero, Rosen has spent years teaching his journalism students, and promoting to seminarians, his ideological approach to reporting. Cloaked in the nomenclature of "public" or "community" journalism, said to be without specific rules or form, and urging the abandonment of traditional journalism, "public journalism" has contributed mightily to justifying the near complete and extensive politicization of the newsroom—where social activism in support of various American Marxist movements has engulfed the former profession of journalism, and substituted slanted and biased opinion for news.

And Rosen, like Glasser, Merritt, and most of the rest of the media, is further exposed by his open contempt for Trump. Indeed, Trump, as their target, has done more to reveal this radical movement than any other individual possibly could. Writing in the *Washington Post* during the 2016 presidential election, Rosen asserted: "Imagine a candidate who wants to *increase* public confusion about where he stands on things so that voters give up on trying to stay informed and instead vote with raw emotion. Under these conditions, does asking 'Where do you stand, sir?' serve the goals of journalism, or does it enlist the interviewer in the candidate's chaotic plan? I know what you're thinking, journalists: 'What do you want us to do? Stop covering a major party candidate for president? That would be irresponsible.' True. But this reaction short-circuits intelligent debate. Beneath every common practice in election coverage there are premises about how candidates will behave. I want you to ask: Do these still apply? Trump isn't behaving like a normal candidate; he's acting like an unbound one. In response, journalists have to become less predictable themselves. They have to come up with novel responses.

They have to do things they have never done. They may even have to shock us."[35]

"They may need to collaborate," writes Rosen, "across news brands in ways they have never known. They may have to call Trump out with a forcefulness unseen before. They may have to risk the breakdown of decorum in interviews and endure excruciating awkwardness. Hardest of all, they will have to explain to the public that Trump is a special case, and normal rules do not apply."[36]

Clearly, Rosen's instruction was aggressively and relentlessly pursued. Conversely, in reporting on the candidacy of Joe Biden's presidential campaign and now presidency, the "public journalism" troop has demonstrated a dramatic turnaround and utter disinterest—even a disciplined incuriosity—in its coverage. The media today serve as a Praetorian Guard around Biden and his extremely radical agenda, where serious and substantive scrutiny are mostly nonexistent.

Martin Linsky at the *American Prospect*, a self-described "progressive" advocacy magazine and website, cut to the chase: "For one thing, the [public journalism] movement took the cloak of detachment off the emperor. Some press icons finally acknowledged what politicians and bureaucrats and interest groups and citizens have long understood—namely, that the media are players in the game of public affairs, not disinterested observers. What they do and how they do it has consequences, whether they want to take responsibility for them or not. . . . Rosen dissects the myth of journalistic detachment. Every story, every decision about what to cover, is based on some (usually unspoken) assumption about how the world is supposed to work. Rosen is surely right when he says that all forms of political journalism rest on a mental picture of how politics and democracy should function. There is nothing detached about it. (It must also be the case that assessments of the state of American democracy, including his own, similarly rest on a mental picture of democratic ideals.) A story about income inequality, for example, is only a story if there exists in the newsroom a perspective that inequality is bad. That a campaign looks more like a sporting event than an Oxford-Cambridge debate is a cause for hand-wringing only if you think that campaigns were once—or at least should now be—decorous."[37]

The combination of propaganda, pseudo-news, and social activism in America's newsrooms has resulted in the disastrous state of the modern press. No longer are there discernable, traditional, or professional standards applied to the reporting of news. Indeed, journalism, such as it is, has come full circle, returning to the approach applied by Marx himself. Again, as Ledbetter explained earlier: "Marx's journalism does resemble some of the writing that is published today in journals of opinion, and it's not hard to see a direct line between Marx's journalistic writing and the kind of tendentious writing on public affairs that characterized much political journalism (especially in Europe) in the twentieth century."[38] Moreover, Marx's influence goes well beyond his opinion journalism: the American media have become special pleaders for the Marxist ideology, or at least advocates for those who apply it to numerous aspects of society.

But the story does not end here. In fact, it gets worse. The next step is the logical progression away from an open and free society, where indoctrination and activism are key to controlling thought and outcomes, ultimately to repression—that is, the silencing of opposition on contrary voices in pursuit of ideological purity. And that involves targeting and canceling people who refuse to relent.

In his book *Rules for Radicals*, Saul Alinsky, well-known Marxist community organizer, wrote: "A reformation means that masses of our people have reached the point of disillusionment with past ways and values. They don't know what will work but they do know that the prevailing system is self-defeating, frustrating, and hopeless. They don't act for change but won't strongly oppose those who do. The time is then ripe for revolution. . . . Remember: once you organize people around something as commonly agreed upon as pollution, then an organized people are on the move. From there it's a short and natural step to political pollution, to Pentagon pollution."[39]

The media have played a huge role in dispiriting the public and undermining American institutions, traditions, and institutions. And by Alinsky's measure, the revolution is now upon us. Among other things, his tactics must now be deployed, and they include "[p]ick[ing] the target, freez[ing] it, personaliz[ing] it, and polariz[ing] it." Alinsky continued: "In conflict tactics there are certain rules that the organizer should always regard as universalities. One is that the opposition must be singled out as the target and 'frozen.' . . . Obviously there is no point to tactics unless one has a target upon which to center the attacks. . . . With this focus comes a polarization. As we have indicated before, all issues must be polarized if action is to follow."[40]

On January 2, 2019, Chuck Todd, the host of NBC's *Meet the Press*, provided a stark example of things to come. He openly issued a declaration to the nation that incorporated and combined all the worst practices and tactics discussed earlier. And it should have rattled every person who cares about freedom of speech and the legitimate competition of ideas as bulwarks of our country. Todd announced:

> This morning, we're going to do something we don't often get to do, dive in on one topic. It's obviously extraordinarily difficult to do this, as the end of this year has proven, in the era of Trump. But we're going to take an in-

> depth look, regardless of that, at a literally Earth-changing subject that doesn't get talked about this thoroughly on television news, at least, climate change. But just as important as what we are going to do this hour is what we're not going to do. We're not going to debate climate change, the existence of it. The Earth is getting hotter. And human activity is a major cause, period. We're not going to give time to climate deniers. The science is settled, even if political opinion is not. And we're not going to confuse weather with climate. A heat wave is not more evidence that climate change exists than a blizzard means that it doesn't, unless the blizzard hits Miami. We do have a panel of experts with us today to help us understand the science and consequences of climate change and, yes, ideas to break the political paralysis over it.[41]

There are literally hundreds, if not thousands, of experts and scholars who have challenged the view that the earth is warming, or that it is warming due to man's activities, or that it may be warming but not to the extent that alarmists are claiming, or that it is warming to some extent but due to the sun or matters out of our control, etc., Todd dismisses them all as "deniers" and refuses them a national platform from which they can share their informed knowledge with the public or engage in debate on the subject. Of course, Todd does so even though he has no expertise. He is motivated by his allegiance to the climate change movement and insists on fronting for it. Obviously, he is not alone. In fact, you would be hard-pressed to find experts and scientists who challenge the climate change narrative appearing on television news programs or providing input in published news stories. But the story lines and guests promoting it are endless.[42]

The identical situation applies to Critical Race Theory and

related movements. As Zach Goldberg demonstrated in *Tablet* magazine: "Countless articles have been published . . . often under the guise of straight news reporting, in which journalists take for granted the legitimacy of novel theories about race and identity. Such articles illustrate a prevailing new political morality on questions of race and justice that has taken power at the [*New York*] *Times* and the [*Washington*] *Post*—a worldview sometimes abbreviated as 'wokeness' that combines the sensibilities of highly educated and hyper-liberal white professionals with elements of Black nationalism and academic critical race theory."[43]

"For some Americans," writes Goldberg, "all of this is surely good news. For them, the rapid proliferation of articles employing the tropes of critical race theory to ascribe racial guilt in the American system represents a reckoning with white supremacy and inequality that is long overdue. There are many possible objections to this line of argument: To start, there's the fact that dividing a diverse, multiethnic society into oppressed and oppressor categories on the basis of skin color has, as a matter of historical precedent, more often led to sectarian bloodshed than enhanced justice and equity. What's more, the narratives promoting this new system of racial division are both factually fraudulent—built on false or misleading premises and assumptions—and deeply hostile to any attempts at factual correction. If one points out, for instance, that accounts of white supremacy as an all-powerful force in American society tend to discount that some nonwhite groups like Nigerian Americans, Indian Americans, and East Asian Americans all have more income equity than the average white person, this itself is invalidated as a racist microaggression. The media has actively promoted a theory of racism that misrepresents facts about the world while stigmatizing any effort to criticize those facts as racist."[44]

Consequently, the media have joined the critical race activists, once dismissed as advocates for a radical and fringe movement, and the horrendous racism and demonization they represent and espouse, in enthusiastically advocating for their Marxist-centric transmutation of American society.

While Goldberg acknowledges inequities in American society, he also is repulsed by the "steamrolling on suppressing inconvenient facts" by those who seek to transform our country. "What the data presented . . . suggests is that editorial decisions made over the past decade at some of the most powerful media outlets in the world about what kind of language to use and what kind of stories merited coverage when it came to race—whatever the intention and level of forethought behind such decisions—has stoked a revival of racial consciousness among their readers. Intentionally or not, by introducing and then constantly repeating a set of key words and concepts, publications like *The New York Times* have helped normalize among their readership the belief that 'color' is the defining attribute of other human beings. For those who adopt this singular focus on race, a racialized view of the world becomes baseline test of political loyalty. It requires adherents to overlook the immense diversity among so-called 'People of Color' and 'People Not-of-Color' (i.e., whoever is being lumped together as 'white' according to the prevailing ideological fashion). In doing so, it has made stereotypes socially acceptable, if not laudable."[45]

Of course, the *Times*' propaganda is intentional. As discussed earlier, it is the same media corporation aggressively promoting the discredited 1619 Project, which is being broadly distributed throughout the country's public school system and, as discussed, has as its purpose brainwashing students to believe that America, from its birth, was and is an irredeemably racist and oppressive society.

Goldberg explains that "[t]he same media institutions that have promoted revisionist identitarianism and the radical transformation of American society along racial lines, could instead have focused their attention and influence on improving the *quality* of life for *all*."[46]

Not surprisingly, CNN is all in. "CNN's [CEO] Jeff Zucker announced the expansion of its beat covering race, with plans for several new positions. Delano Massey will lead the beat, and the network is creating new positions for a senior editor, senior writer and breaking and trends writer. This team will break news and cover the stories and conversations around race,' Zucker wrote in a memo. 'The struggles, progress, and triumphs. The systemic racism that the majority of Americans now acknowledge exists. The latest polls and studies and data. How race is intertwined with inequality in business, politics, sports, media, housing, healthcare, and education. Lack of representation in leadership roles in so many industries. The still-present signals and symbols of racism. Voices who provide solutions, inspiration, and leadership. Black, White, Latino, Asian American, Native American, Multiracial, and all races.' "[47]

Gone are the days when the Rev. Martin Luther King Jr. declared: "I have a dream that my four little children will one day live in a nation where they will not be judged by the color of their skin, but by the content of their character."[48]

Having laid the foundation for revolutionary change in multiple areas of our society and culture, the banning, canceling, and silencing have begun in earnest. Repression, not engagement; compliance, not speech; conformity, not independence; and subjugation, not liberty, are all hallmarks of American Marxism.

Writing in the *City Journal*, Robert Henderson explains in his essay "Tell Only Lies" that "[i]t is no longer enough to be ideologically pure by current standards. One must always have held the proper beliefs. Of course, such tortuous moral standards can only lead to lying. In a recent paper titled 'Keeping Your Mouth

Shut: Spiraling Self-Censorship in the United States,' political scientists James L. Gibson and Joseph L. Sutherland reveal that self-censorship among Americans has soared. In the 1950s, at the height of McCarthyism, 13.4 percent of Americans reported that they 'felt less free to speak their mind than they used to.' In 1987, the figure reached 20 percent. By 2019, 40 percent of Americans reported that they did not feel free to speak their minds."[49]

"What are the consequences of this continuous self-censorship?" asks Henderson. He notes that "in his book *The Great Terror*, the British historian Robert Conquest suggests one possible answer. In a passage about Soviet show trials, Conquest was troubled by something: Why did innocent people falsely confess to appalling crimes, even when most Soviet citizens themselves did not believe these people when they confessed? Conquest offers a chilling answer: Soviet citizens grew so used to lying that expressing one more falsehood was no big deal. People grew conditioned to accept the ever-changing standards, and even affirm support for them."[50] Moreover, Henderson notes that "management expert Jerry B. Harvey . . . describes situations in which individuals disagree with an idea but acquiesce out of a perception that others agree with it. If honesty becomes unfashionable, we operate under the assumption that others hold certain opinions, which, in fact, they do not."[51]

Henderson warns: "As the rules of the game keep shifting, and individuals lose jobs or prominence because of things that they have said in the past, we will all become more adept at expressing falsehoods. It is likely that such a system will select for individuals predisposed to being comfortable with deception. Over time, only liars will speak openly."[52]

America's colleges and universities are among the most intolerant environments for administrators, faculty, and students alike who dare to cross any of the various intersecting Marxist movements that dominate on campus. Indeed, academic freedom and free speech, once considered foundations of higher education, are no more.

The intolerance and cancel culture have spread to outright discrimination in hiring, promotion, grants, and publication of professors and graduate students who do not abide the ideology demanded by the campus revolutionaries. A March 1, 2021, study by Eric Kaufmann of the Center for the Study of Partisanship and Ideology found, among other things:

"Over 4 in 10 US and Canadian academics would not hire a Trump supporter . . . ; only 1 in 10 academics support firing controversial professors, nonetheless, while most do not back cancellation, many are not opposed to it, remaining non-committal; right-leaning academics experience a high level of institutional authoritarianism and peer pressure; in the US, over a third of conservative academics and PhD students have been threatened with disciplinary action for their views, while 70% of conservative academics report a hostile departmental climate for their beliefs; in the social sciences and humanities, over 9 in 10 Trump-supporting academics . . . say they would not feel comfortable expressing their views to a colleague; more than half of North American and British conservative academics admit self-censoring in research and teaching; younger academics and PhD students, especially in the United States, are significantly more willing than older academics to support dismissing controversial scholars from their posts, indicating that the problem of progressive authoritarianism is likely to get worse in the coming years; [and] a hostile climate plays a part in deterring conservative graduate students from pursuing careers in academia. . . ."[53]

A large study of student attitudes toward free speech in 2017 by the Foundation for Individual Rights in Education found, in part: "46 percent of students recognize that hate speech is protected by the First Amendment, and 48 percent of students think the First Amendment should not protect hate speech . . . ; 58 percent of college students think it's important to be part of a campus community where they are not exposed to intolerant or offensive ideas . . . ; in class, 30 percent of students have self-censored because they thought their words would be offensive to others; a majority of students (54 percent) report self-censoring in the classroom at some point since the beginning of college."[54]

Unfortunately, taxpayer-funded elementary and secondary public schools have not escaped the politicization of thought and learning. In fact, they are now the target of such authoritarian efforts.

Diane Ravitch, a historian, education policy expert, and professor at New York University, in 2004 wrote in her book *The Language Police*: "Like others who are involved in education . . . I had always assumed that textbooks were based on careful research and designed to help children learn something valuable. I thought that tests were designed to assess whether they had learned it. What I did not realize was that educational materials are now governed by an intricate set of rules to screen out language and topics that might be considered controversial or offensive. Some of this censorship is trivial, some is ludicrous, and some is breathtaking in its power to dumb down what children learn in school. Initially these practices began with the intention of identifying and excluding any conscious or implicit statements of bias against African Americans, other racial or ethnic minorities, and females, whether in tests or textbooks, especially any statements that demeaned members of these groups. These efforts were entirely reasonable and justified. However, what began with admirable intentions evolved into a surprisingly broad and increasingly bizarre policy of censorship that has gone far beyond its original scope and now excises from tests and textbooks words, images, passages, and ideas that no reasonable person would consider biased in the usual meaning of the term."[55]

As Ravitch rightly declares: "Censorship distorts the literature curriculum, substituting political judgments for aesthetic ones. Because of the bias and social content guidelines, editors of literature anthologies must pay more attention to having the correct count of gender groups and ethnic groups among their characters, authors, and illustrations than they do to the literary quality of the selections. . . ."[56]

Today, matters are far worse. Children in classrooms throughout America are being indoctrinated with Critical Race Theory (CRT), white children are taught that they were born privileged and advantaged, and students study lessons prepared by the disgraceful *New York Times* 1619 Project; Black Lives Matter, an openly Marxist and often violent organization that actively seeks the elimination of capitalism and the American governing system, is celebrated.[57]

Moreover, in school district after school district, teachers are being trained to confront their white privilege and taught to refocus their knowledge of history to accommodate CRT. One need only scan the Internet for endless examples. Students and teachers are being forced to spend time on other intersectional ideologies and their politics, including gender identity and gender rights.[58]

Consequently, in many areas of the country, and growing, American history, the civil society, and for many, familial ethnicities, ancestries, and religious faith are being dishonored and degraded. Education is being infused with a Marxist-oriented, extremely divisive, racist and intersectional ideology, where teachers and students alike are compelled to participate in and embrace their own indoctrination.[59]

And there is more. The One UN Climate Change Learning

Partnership, also known as UN CC:Learn, is "a collaborative initiative of 36 multilateral organizations working together to help countries build the knowledge and skills they need to take action on climate change," including "better climate literacy and other crucial skills to tackle this challenge." It produces learning materials and advice encouraging schools to indoctrinate children into the climate change movement.[60] For example, in one instructional guide titled "Why Should Schools Teach Climate Education," the organization states: "Climate change education provides an important window into individual and societal responsibility. As educators, schools not only have an interest in teaching subjects that will prepare students for careers and earn them good test scores, but to teach them to be mindful citizens. Teaching on climate change means teaching on topics like environmental stewardship and collective responsibility—teaching students that they and those around them have a responsibility to something larger than themselves. *How do their actions affect the environment? How do changes in the environment then affect others? Why should they care about recycling or sustainability?*"[61]

The guidance continues in its promotion of globalism, communalism, and activism: "Climate change asks us to consider the world beyond ourselves. More than that, it asks that we consider a time beyond the present. Incorporating the topic into school curriculum only stands to bring students closer to their communities. Civic engagement, one of the most important lessons schools impart on their students, can be taught through student engagement with local institutions. *How are their communities working to be more sustainable? What policies are governments putting in place, and how might students push for more?* It is not enough to simply teach students about the science behind climate change; students also need to learn how institutions and individuals deal with problems of this scale, and how they fit into that larger picture. As long as schools have a responsibility to teach global citizenship and community stewardship, they have reason to teach about climate change."[62]

The ideological indoctrination and, conversely, censorship have spread well beyond formal educational institutions and the subjects of race and climate change to corporate America. *New York Post* business columnist Charles Gasparino, writing about "How corporations surrendered to hard-left wokeness," explains that "[c]ompanies used to be in business to make money, sell stuff and employ people. They were run by executives who were proudly capitalist and believed in the country's founding principles. No longer, it seems. Big businesses' support of green-energy legislation, various social-justice edicts and the silencing of right-wingers on Twitter have become so routine it's almost not news anymore." Gasparino adds: "[T]he left-wing forces have assembled to transform corporate America into something resembling the progressive wing of the Democratic Party. The left might hate capitalism, but it has been busy implementing capitalist tools to bend big business to its will."[63]

And Gasparino notes that it is working: "[M]ost shareholder votes now involve progressive edicts under the guise of so-called Environmental Social Governance investing. ESG, as it is known on Wall Street, is a way to measure everything from a firm's compliance with green-energy initiatives to its embrace of causes such as Black Lives Matter." Moreover, "[t]he average retail investors in mutual funds have no say or vote in this vast transformation even as their money is being used for political purposes. The fund is responding to the vocal minority that figured out how the game is played."[64]

Indeed, a reign of ideological terror has spread throughout our society and culture, canceling and banning people (professors, teachers, writers, actors, executives, reporters, etc.), historic figures, monuments, movies, television shows, radio broadcasts, books, cartoons, toys, other products, product names and brands, and even words.[65] Even President Trump was banned from Twitter, Facebook, and alternative social media communication platforms. The list is so long and growing so fast as to make an up-to-date compilation impossible.

So egregiously threatening to our country is this noxious and widespread war on free speech and liberty, and so quickly is it transforming American society, that on July 7, 2020, 150 mostly left-wing authors penned a public letter in *Harper's Magazine*, titled "A Letter on Justice and Open Debate." Although the signatories, among them Noam Chomsky, share many if not most of the goals of the various Marxist-oriented movements, and some have influenced the thinking of certain of its most radical activists, they apparently also realize that unleashed tyranny is difficult if not impossible to manage and may inevitably devour many of its architects, proponents, and admirers—witness the aftermath of the French Revolution, the Russian Revolution, and China's communist revolution. Their letter states, in part:

> The free exchange of information and ideas, the lifeblood of a liberal society, is daily becoming more constricted. While we have come to expect this on the radical right, censoriousness is also spreading more widely in our culture: an intolerance of opposing views, a vogue for public shaming and ostracism, and the tendency to dissolve complex policy issues in a blinding moral certainty. We uphold the value of robust and even caustic counter-speech from all quarters. But it is now all too common to hear calls for swift and severe retribution in response to perceived transgressions of speech and thought. More troubling still, institutional leaders, in a spirit of panicked damage control, are

> delivering hasty and disproportionate punishments instead of considered reforms. Editors are fired for running controversial pieces; books are withdrawn for alleged inauthenticity; journalists are barred from writing on certain topics; professors are investigated for quoting works of literature in class; a researcher is fired for circulating a peer-reviewed academic study; and the heads of organizations are ousted for what are sometimes just clumsy mistakes. Whatever the arguments around each particular incident, the result has been to steadily narrow the boundaries of what can be said without the threat of reprisal. We are already paying the price in greater risk aversion among writers, artists, and journalists who fear for their livelihoods if they depart from the consensus, or even lack sufficient zeal in agreement.
>
> This stifling atmosphere will ultimately harm the most vital causes of our time. The restriction of debate, whether by a repressive government or an intolerant society, invariably hurts those who lack power and makes everyone less capable of democratic participation. The way to defeat bad ideas is by exposure, argument, and persuasion, not by trying to silence or wish them away. We refuse any false choice between justice and freedom, which cannot exist without each other. As writers we need a culture that leaves us room for experimentation, risk taking, and even mistakes. We need to preserve the possibility of good-faith disagreement without dire professional consequences. If we won't defend the very thing on which our work depends, we shouldn't expect the public or the state to defend it for us.[66]

One wonders how many of the signatories have supported Marxist movements like Black Lives Matter. Nonetheless, their letter has fallen on deaf ears. Indeed, since July 7, 2020, speech has come under an even more aggressive withering attack. For example, Big Tech—including Google, Amazon, Facebook, Apple, and Twitter—are censoring and banning at will, using one pretext after another. Again, the instances are so numerous and mounting by the day that listing them here is undoable. Nonetheless, some prominent examples are illustrative.

First, as reported by the Media Research Center (MRC), "[d]uring one of several Senate hearings into Big Tech bias [in 2020], even the CEOs of Facebook and Twitter could not name a single high-profile leftist person or entity that had been censored on their platforms when asked." Moreover, "[h]eavily censored themes included anything related to the election, COVID-19 and the response to it and statements released by President Donald Trump. However, Big Tech even found reasons to censor conservatives over things as innocuous as a children's book celebrating women's suffrage."[67]

MRC assembled a 2020 top ten list demonstrating the various "offenses" that caused them to sanction free speech:

1. Big Tech shuts down *New York Post*'s bombshell reporting on Hunter Biden

2. Twitter censors Trump tweet about mail-in voting in unprecedented manner

3. Candace Owens's Facebook page is demonetized and suppressed

4. YouTube removes COVID video featuring Trump advisor Dr. Scott Atlas

5. Facebook demonetizes [the satirical site] The Babylon Bee page over Monty Python joke

6. Twitter removes all instances of Joe Biden meme

7. Instagram removes FBI crime statistics, calling them "hate speech"

8. YouTube removes video featuring man who reversed his transgender surgery

9. YouTube suspends and demonetizes conservative news network One America News (OAN)

10. Instagram bans ads for Senator Marsha Blackburn's children's book

On January 31, 2021, Project Veritas released a video it received from a Facebook insider where CEO Mark Zuckerberg and other top executives discussed the company's "wide-ranging powers to censor political speech and promote partisan objectives."[68]

> In the January 7 video, Zuckerberg is seen accusing then-President Trump of subverting the republic.
>
> "It's so important that our political leaders lead by example, make sure we put the nation first here, and what we've seen is that the president [Trump] has been doing the opposite of that. . . . The president [Trump] intends to use his remaining time in office to undermine the peaceful and lawful transition of power."
>
> "His [Trump's] decision to use his platform to condone rather than condemn the actions of his supporters in the Capitol I think has rightly bothered and disturbed people in the US and around the world."
>
> Zuckerberg also insinuated that Capitol protesters received better treatment than Black Lives Matter protest-

ers. "I know this is just a very difficult moment for a lot of us here, and especially our black colleagues. It was troubling to see how people in this [Capitol] mob were treated compared to the stark contrast we saw during protests earlier this [past] year."

Guy Rosen, Facebook's vice president of integrity, described how the platform targets speech it deems dangerous. "We have a system that is able to freeze commenting on threads in cases where our systems are detecting that there may be a thread that has hate speech or violence . . . these are all things we've built over the past three-four years as part of our investments into the integrity space our efforts to protect the election."

Zuckerberg praised Biden and his political agenda. "I thought President Biden's inaugural address was very good."

"In his first day, President Biden already issued a number of Executive Orders on areas that we as a company care quite deeply about and have for some time," Zuckerberg said.

Zuckerberg continued, "Areas like immigration, preserving DACA, ending restrictions on travel from Muslim-majority countries, as well as other Executive Orders on climate and advancing racial justice and equity. I think these were all important and positive steps."

In the same January 21 meeting, Facebook's head of global affairs, Nick Clegg, addressed the international backlash that resulted from then-President Trump's suspension from the platform. "There has been quite a lot of disquiet expressed by many leaders around the world, from the President of Mexico to Alexei Navalny in Russia, and Chancellor Angela Merkel and others saying, 'well this shows that private companies have got too much power . . .' we agree with that." "Ideally, we wouldn't be making these decisions on our own, we would be making these decisions in line with our own conformity, with democratically agreed rules and principles. At the moment, those democratically agreed rules don't exist. We still have to make decisions in real-time."

Facebook's vice president of civil rights, Roy Austin, said that the company's products should reflect their views on race.

"I wonder whether or not we can use Oculus to help a white police officer to understand what it feels like to be a young black man who's stopped and searched and arrested by the police. . . . I want every major decision to run through a civil rights lens."[69]

One reason given by Big Tech executives for censoring and banning speech on the Internet is the rise of "hate crimes." However, a report prepared for and provided to Congress by the Commerce Department's National Telecommunications and Information Administration (NTIA) in January—"The Role of Telecommunications in Hate Crimes"—but, incredibly, withheld from the public, concludes that the Internet did not lead to more hate crimes and that Big Tech is operating perilously like a tyrannical oligarch.

A copy of the report, which was provided to Breitbart News, emphatically concludes that "[t]he evidence does not show that during the last decade, a time of expansive growth of electronic communications, particularly on the Internet and mobile devices as well as social media, there has been a rise in hate crime incidents." The NTIA's report also issues a sharp warning: "We caution that efforts to control or monitor online speech, even for the worthy goal of reducing crime, present serious First Amendment concerns and run counter to our nation's dedication to free expression. . . ."[70]

The NTIA strongly admonishes Big Tech against its tyrannical practices: "[T]ech leaders have recognized that relying on human teams alone to review content will not be enough and that artificial intelligence will have to play a significant role. That said, there are, of course, significant policy and practical limitations to reliance on automated content moderation. Interestingly, much of this technology is being developed from approaches pioneered by the Chinese Communist Party to stifle political discussion and dissent.

The report goes on: "Given that all the major social media platforms have rules against hate speech and, in fact, employ sophisticated algorithmic artificial intelligence (AI) approaches to enforce these often vague and contradictory rules in a manner also used by tyrannous regimes, it is appropriate to ask what they gain from it. Certainly, as this Report shows, the platforms have no reasonable expectation that their censorship will end hate crimes or even diminish it, as no empirical evidence exists linking increased hate speech with hate crimes. Further, this censorship poses real dangers to our political system. Under the hate speech prohibitions and other censorship rules, the platforms have removed content that many consider seriously engaged with pressing political and social issues."[71]

No doubt, the NTIA will be ignored. That is the nature of ideologically driven decision making. In fact, at a Senate hearing in November 2020, the Democrats on the committee demanded that Big Tech do more, and faster, to silence speech on their platforms.[72]

Big Tech also went to extraordinary lengths to try to destroy a small, entrepreneurial company, Parler, which was quickly gaining a following of millions of citizens who mostly did not share the ideological bias, political partisanship, and censorship practices of these huge multibillion-dollar global companies. As the *Pittsburgh Post-Gazette* put it: "The social media site Parler has been suspended from Google's and Apple's app stores, and Amazon has stopped providing the company with cloud services, effectively killing the service and prompting Parler to launch a federal lawsuit against the tech giant. . . . The killing of Parler amounts to a chilling assault on speech. . . . Social media, like much of the news media, has become a wedge between Americans who are decamping to different platforms along ideological lines in the tens of thousands in the wake of the bans. That cannot be a good thing for the country."[73]

Parler has fought its way back, but the collusive and monopolistic acts of Big Tech to destroy an independent platform were an extraordinary act of tyranny, and many in the media, unlike the *Post-Gazette*, were either silent or supportive of Big Tech's action, constantly referring to Parler as a platform for right-wingers, white supremacists, violent conspirators, and the like, all of which was untrue.

Big Tech's ideological and political preferences can also be established by examining the political donations of their executives and employees, and which candidates and party they subsidize and invest in. The picture could not be clearer. The Center for Responsive Politics reports that "[e]mployees at big tech giants, including Alphabet (Google's parent), Amazon, Facebook, Apple and Microsoft, donated millions to various Democrats' campaigns in the 2020 election cycle. Employees at the five companies shelled out a combined $12.3 million to Biden's campaign and millions more to Democrats in high-profile Senate contests, such as recently elected Jon Ossoff (D-Ga.) and Raphael Warnock (D-Ga.). Employees of big tech firms ranked among the top donors to each of those Democrats. With most donations coming from company employees, Alphabet contributed around $21 million to Democrats in the 2020 election cycle, with Amazon contributing around $9.4 million. Facebook, Microsoft and Apple contributed about $6 million, $12.7 million and $6.6 million to Democrats, respectively. The majority of each of the big tech firm's contributions went to Democratic candidates, and excluding Microsoft, the Biden campaign was the top recipient with Ossoff and Warnock ranking in the top 10. Microsoft's top recipient for contributions was the Senate Majority PAC, the super PAC affiliated with Democratic Senate leader Chuck Schumer. The Democratic National Committee ranked in the top three recipients for all of the companies."[74]

CNBC reported: "Of current CEOs at large-cap tech companies, Netflix's Reed Hastings opened his wallet the widest. Hastings and his wife, Patty Quillin, donated more than $5 million. The biggest chunk went to the Senate Majority PAC, a group backing Democratic candidates in the closest races, like in Maine, Texas and Iowa. . . . Between funds to campaigns and outside groups, employees from internet companies committed 98% of their contributions to Democrats, according to the Center for Responsive Politics."[75]

And then there is the incestuous relationship between the Biden administration and Big Tech, in which Biden rewarded Big Tech companies by hiring at least fourteen current and former executives from Apple, Google, Amazon, Twitter, and Facebook to serve in his transition team and administration.[76]

The Democratic Party, not merely its surrogates, is playing a major and direct role in promoting censorship and repression. In November 2020, Rep. Alexandria Ocasio-Cortez (D-NY) posted on Twitter: "Is anyone archiving these Trump sycophants for when they try to downplay or deny their complicity in the future? I foresee decent probability of many deleted Tweets, writings, photos in the future." Encouraged by her declaration, a group called the Trump Accountability Project was formed. The group declared: "Remember what they did. We should not allow the following groups of people to profit from their experience: Those who elected him. Those who staffed his government. Those who funded him."[77]

Indeed, there was much talk on social media and the media generally about blacklisting Trump administration officials and Trump supporters, and preventing them from finding work in the private sector. Former first lady Michelle Obama posted a statement on Twitter after rioters overran the Capitol Building, demanding that Trump be banned from all social platforms for life. Needless to say, there were numerous others in public office or public positions who did the same. And Big Tech complied.

Perhaps the most chilling and blatant example of the war on speech is a February 22, 2021, letter sent from two senior California House Democrats, Anna Eshoo and Jerry McNerney, to the chief executives of AT&T, Verizon, Roku, Amazon, Apple, Comcast, Charter, DISH, Cox, Altice, Hulu, and Alphabet, demanding to know why Fox News (Fox), One American News Network (OANN), and Newsmax are carried on these corporations' platforms. The companies received essentially the same letter. The congresspeople include a long list of sources, which are mostly partisan "studies" and articles. I will focus on the letter sent to AT&T.

The congresspeople wrote: "Misinformation on TV has led to our current polluted information environment that radicalizes individuals to commit seditious acts and rejects public health best practices, among other issues in our public discourse. Experts have noted that the right-wing media ecosystem is 'much more susceptible . . . to disinformation, lies, and half-truths.' Right-wing media outlets, like Newsmax, One America News Network, and Fox News all aired misinformation about the November 2020 elections. . . . Fox News . . . has spent years spewing misinformation about American politics.

"These same networks also have been key vectors of spreading misinformation related to the pandemic. A media watchdog found over 250 cases of COVID-19 misinformation on Fox News in just a five-day period, and economists demonstrated that Fox News had a demonstrable impact on non-compliance with public health guidelines. . . ."[78]

The congresspeople failed to mention that the "media watchdog" is the notoriously dishonest Media Matters, a radical, left-wing, pro-Democrat site. The *Daily Caller* found that they "did not provide the methodology used to establish each instance of what it identified as Fox News misinformation for independent review." It further concluded that the report itself was filled with "misinformation."[79]

The congresspeople demanded that AT&T and the other companies provide them, in about two weeks' time, the following information—in part:

> What moral or ethical principles (including those related to journalistic integrity, violence, medical information, and public health) do you apply in deciding which channels to carry or when to take adverse actions against a channel?
>
> Do you require, through contracts or otherwise, that the channels you carry abide by any content guidelines? If so, please provide a copy of the guidelines.
>
> What steps did you take prior to, on, and following the November 3, 2020, elections and the January 6, 2021,

> attacks to monitor, respond to, and reduce the spread of disinformation, including encouragement or incitement of violence by channels your company disseminates to millions of Americans? Please describe each step that you took and when it was taken.
>
> Have you ever taken any actions against a channel for using your platform to disseminate any disinformation? If yes, please describe each action and when it was taken.
>
> Are you planning to continue carrying Fox News, Newsmax, and OANN . . . both now and beyond any contract renewal date? If so, why?[80]

This is an extraordinarily appalling letter, intended to intimidate and threaten targeted center-right broadcast and media organizations, for the sole purpose of silencing their speech. And virtually none of the other media and news organizations wrote or spoke against it. The reason: they agree with it. Even more, many news groups, journalists, and opinion writers were the first to propose de-platforming Fox, OANN, and Newsmax and are campaigning for government regulators and these platform companies to shut them down—as with Parler; which brings me back to the American media, where I started this chapter.

The intersectional movements that form the core of American Marxism are largely supported by the Democratic Party and promoted by the media. Of this there can no longer be any doubt. Therefore, speech, debate, and challenges to Marxist-centric ideas are not tolerated. The purpose is societal and economic transformation; the means are social advocacy and activism. Opposition must be denounced, besmirched, and crushed.

In fact, it is now obvious that the letter to these various corporations resulted from media demands for de-platforming Fox, OANN, and Newsmax, which preceded the letter's date. On January 8, 2021, CNN's Oliver Darcy wrote: "[W]hat about TV companies that provide platforms to networks such as Newsmax, One America News—and, yes, Fox News? Somehow, these companies have escaped scrutiny and entirely dodged this conversation. That should not be the case anymore. After Wednesday's [January 6, 2021] incident of domestic terrorism on Capitol Hill, it is time TV carriers face questions for lending their platforms to dishonest companies that profit off of disinformation and conspiracy theories. After all, it was the very lies that Fox, Newsmax, and OAN spread that helped prime President Trump's supporters into not believing the truth: that he lost an honest and fair election.[81]

"Yes, Sean Hannity and Tucker Carlson and Mark Levin and others are responsible for the lies they peddle to their audiences. But the TV companies that beam them into millions of homes around the country also bear some responsibility. And yet we rarely, if ever, talk about them."[82]

Notice Darcy's Alinsky tactics as he attempts to smear the cable networks and certain television hosts, including me: "Pick the target, freeze it, personalize it, and polarize it."[83] Neither the networks nor the hosts he mentions had anything whatsoever to do with the storming of the Capitol Building.

New York Times columnist Nicholas Kristof picked up where Darcy left off, Alinsky tactics and all, and joined the de-platforming campaign. He wrote: "We can't impeach Fox or put [Tucker] Carlson or Sean Hannity on trial in the Senate, but there are steps we can take—imperfect, inadequate ones, resting on slippery slopes—to create accountability not only for Trump but also for fellow travelers at Fox, OANN, Newsmax and so on."[84]

Thus, Kristof demanded from his *Times* soapbox that "we"—the Marxist-like mob—must hold these nonconforming media outlets and hosts to account; that is, they must be silenced.

Kristof continues: "That can mean pressure on advertisers to avoid underwriting extremists (of any political bent), but the Fox News business model depends not so much on advertising as on cable subscription fees. So, a second step is to call on cable companies to drop Fox News from basic cable TV packages."[85]

In fact, Kristof's second step was obviously lifted from Media Matters.

Next, Kristof frames his perverse tyrannical screed as protecting the consumer from having to fund Fox and, further, having to supposedly subsidize his biased and stereotypical description of its viewers as racist, violent, and anti-government. "The issue here is that if you're like many Americans, you: A) don't watch Fox News, and B) still subsidize Fox News. If you buy a basic cable package, you're forced to pay about $20 a year for Fox News. You may deplore bigots and promoters of insurrection, but you help pay their salaries."[86]

Kristof then cites Angelo Carusone, the radical ideologue and bigot who leads Media Matters, as an authority for his hit job against nonconforming media. "Carusone . . . says that Fox News relies on unusually generous cable fees—more than twice what CNN receives and five times what MSNBC commands. So, Media Matters started a campaign . . . for people to ask cable carriers to drop Fox News from their packages. 'Given all the damage that Fox News has caused and the threat that it remains, they absolutely should unbundle Fox News,' Carusone told me. 'It's not a news channel. It's a propaganda operation mixed with political smut. If people want that, they should be forced to pay for it the way that they pay for Cinemax.' "[87]

Margaret Sullivan (*Washington Post*), Max Boot (*Washington Post*), Brian Stelter (CNN), Anand Giridharadas (MSNBC), and numerous other reporters and columnists piled on with the same or similar propaganda and demands. And congressional Democrats, using their governmental pedestals and authority, seek to oblige them.

From our schools and entertainment, to the media and government, we are witnessing the onslaught of repressive actions, including threats, censorship, and character assassination, and the demand for more of it. Marx would approve.

In fact, banning people, speech, words, broadcasts, and social media access; and redefining language, history, knowledge, and science—all of which are occurring or pursued in our current culture and environment—are the trademarks of totalitarianism. So, too, is the routine and unchallenged abuse of power, and undermining of republicanism and constitutionalism by President Biden, who legislates via executive orders, thereby bypassing Congress and the constitution's checks and balances, to institute fundamental change to American society without input from the people's representatives in Congress or the people themselves. Or the efforts of Democratic Party congressional leaders, such as Speaker Pelosi and Senate Majority Leader Schumer, to baldly threaten the independence of the judiciary in order to influence the outcome of legal decisions and to further their ideological and political agenda; and the collusive actions by the Democratic leadership in both elected branches of the federal government to radically alter the electoral process throughout the country to ensure the Democratic Party rarely if ever loses its power to rule. Plus, with the smallest majority in the House in decades, and a tied Senate at 50–50 senators, they seek to stack the Senate with several additional Democrat seats and eliminate the filibuster rule, the purpose of which is to impose radical changes on the nation without broad support from representatives of other parts of the country.

Yet it is the opponents of this tyranny who are labeled, often successfully, as the offenders of civil liberties and human rights, obstructers of progress, and foes of the people by the *actual* offenders, for the latter have already devoured most of the instrumentalities of the state and the culture, and dominate the narrative.

In his book *Doubletalk: The Language of Communism*, Harry Hodgkinson wrote: "Language was to Marx the 'direct reality' of thought; 'ideas do not exist divorced from' it. And for [Joseph] Stalin 'the reality of thought manifests itself in language.' Words are tools as well as weapons, each fashioned for a precise function. . . . The language of Communism . . . is not so much a means of explaining to an unbeliever what Communism means, but an armory of weapons and tools intended to produce support or dissolve opposition to Communist policies on the part of people either hostile or indifferent to them. The meaning of a Communist word is not what you think it says, but what effect it is intended to produce."[88]

Moreover, writes Hodgkinson, "[t]o Communists, a majority has no particular sanctity and is called upon to do, not what it wishes, but 'its duty before the court of history.' Choice between parties is a 'drab formality' of *Bourgeois Democracy*. . . . Democracy is generally used with a qualifying adjective. . . ."[89]

Hence Marxist senator Bernie Sanders uses the qualifying adjective *Democratic* Socialist. Even so, as Sanders knows, "to the Communist [such a phrase] is no more than an essential stage on the road to Communism."[90]

The wave of repression sweeping our nation is not unlike the earliest days of the French, Russian, and Chinese revolutions, among others. All were promoted as popular movements and people's revolutions, intended to establish Rousseauian communalism or Marxist egalitarianism. But that is where the similarity ends. These revolutions were sold as liberation movements, where the masses or the proletariat would rise up against the governing tyranny and corrupt society. They became genocidal police states. Of course, unlike these other governments and societies, America is a constitutional, representative republic, not a monarchy or other form of dictatorship. There is no widespread dissatisfaction in the country. In fact, most Americans are patriotic and revere the country. But the forces of false liberation today are led by fanatical ideologues and activists, who are the real purveyors of tyranny and even totalitarianism. They use propaganda, sabotage, and subversion in an effort to demoralize, destabilize, and ultimately, destroy the existing society and culture. It is they who are repressing the liberties of their fellow citizens through what is loosely called "the cancel culture." It is they who demand conformity of thought by banning differing views from social media; it is they who use the false narrative of "oppressors and oppressed" to stigmatize those they claim as part of "the white-dominant culture" and silence the voices of fellow citizens; it is they who are banning words, books, products, movies, and historical symbols; it is they who are destroying the careers of doubters and boycotting the businesses of nonconformists; it is they who are undermining academic freedom and intellectual curiosity through fear and intimidation; it is they who are distorting American history and brainwashing students; it is they who demand the deplatforming of cable news networks and the muzzling of hosts; and it is they who are using and promoting racism, sexism, ageism, etc., as weapons of disunity and rebellion while claiming to want to end them. Even worse, they are using America's freedom to destroy freedom and the Constitution to destroy the Constitution. And as their poison spreads throughout the culture, the intent is to sow doubt about the country, dispirit the citizenry, and soften the public's innate and reasoned resistance—to the point of acquiescence—to the tyranny of the Marxist-inspired and related domestic movements.

CHAPTER SEVEN

WE CHOOSE LIBERTY!

I am often asked on radio what are "we" going to do about recovering our country. Too often, what is meant is—what is someone else going to do to save America. That mind-set is simply unacceptable. If we are to rally to the defense of our own liberty and unalienable rights, then each of us, in our own roles and ways, must become personally and directly involved as citizen activists, in our own fate and the fate of our country. The time has come to reclaim what is ours—the American republic—from those who seek to destroy it. If we expect others to rescue our nation for us, as we go about our daily lives as mere observers to what is transpiring, or close our eyes and ears to current events, we will lose this struggle. And yes, it is a struggle.

We have allowed the American Marxists to define who we are as a people. They defame us, slander our ancestors and history, and trash our founding documents and principles. They are mostly reprobates who hate the country in which they live, and have contributed nothing to its betterment. Indeed, they live off the sweat and toil of others, while they pursue a destructive and diabolical course for our nation, undermining and sabotaging virtually every institution in our society. Their ideology and worldview are based on the arguments and beliefs of a man, Karl Marx, whose writings are responsible for the enslavement, impoverishment, torture, and death of untold millions. This is a hard fact, despite the predictable protestations from some in our society who embrace and advance Marxism's core ideas but attempt to disassociate themselves from responsibility for its inevitable outcomes. These are the "useful idiots" who occupy influential or leadership positions in the Democratic Party, media, academia, the culture, etc.

But we must take solace and find strength in the sacrifice and bravery of *our* early revolutionaries—Joseph Warren, Samuel Adams, John Hancock, Paul Revere, and Thomas Paine, to name a few; and become energized and inspirited by the wisdom and genius of George Washington, Thomas Jefferson, John Adams, James Madison, Benjamin Franklin, and many others. While they have been smeared and degraded by American Marxists and their ilk, we must continue to celebrate them, be invigorated by them, and remember that together they defeated the most powerful military force on earth and founded the greatest and most extraordinary nation in the history of mankind.

Indeed, future generations of patriots, at tremendous sacrifice, fought the Civil War to end slavery, something no other country had ever done, costing hundreds of thousands of lives on fields and in towns throughout America. At Gettysburg alone, there were 51,000 casualties. But there were other battles with terrible casualties—Chickamauga, Spotsylvania, the Wilderness, Chancellorsville, Shiloh, Stones River, Antietam, Bull Run (twice), Fort Donelson, Fredericksburg, Port Hudson, Cold Harbor, Petersburg, Gaines's Mill, Missionary Ridge, Atlanta, Seven Pines, Nashville, and many more.

Last century, millions of Americans fought, and hundreds of thousands died, in two world wars. In World War I, some 4,000,000 American soldiers were mobilized to fight Germany, Austria-Hungary, Bulgaria, and the Ottoman Empire, and over 116,000 Americans perished—at the battles of Somme, Verdun, Passchendaele, Gallipoli, Tannenberg, and several others. In World War II, more than 16,000,000 American soldiers fought the German Nazis, Japan, and Italy, and over 400,000 lost their lives—at the battles of Sicily, Anzio, the Atlantic, Normandy, Operation Dragoon, the Bulge, Iwo Jima, Guadalcanal, Tarawa, Saipan, Okinawa, and many more.

During the Cold War with the Soviet Union, American soldiers fought the spread of communism, including in Korea, where the Soviet- and Chinese-backed communists in the northern part of the Korean Peninsula invaded the south. Over 5,700,000 Americans were engaged in the war, and nearly 34,000 lost their lives. Almost 3,000,000 Americans served in uniform in the Vietnam War, which was intended to prevent, again, the Soviet- and Chinese-backed communists in the northern part of that country from taking over the south. Over 58,000 American soldiers lost their lives. And there have been many battles since, including but not limited to Iraq and Afghanistan, and the war on terrorism.

Contrary to the American Marxists' slurs that America is an imperial and colonizing force, our soldiers are noble warriors who have fought and died, and still do, to protect and liberate the oppressed from one end of the world to the other—and regardless of the religion, skin color, ethnicity, or race of the victimized. And unlike some of our enemies, we do not seek to conquer other countries for the purpose of occupation and territorial expansion.

In America, one generation after another has been willing to sacrifice everything, and so many have paid the ultimate price, in defense of this magnificent country and its founding principles from foreign enemies. They believed that America and her principles were worth fighting and dying for. And for many of us, our family members were and are among them.

Yet the American Marxist has recently succeeded, through the bureaucracy and Democratic Party policies, in imposing the Critical Race Theory (CRT) and Critical Gender Theory agendas on our armed forces.[1] Soldiers are now forced to participate in training that reinforces these ideologies. They have even reached into West Point, where cadets are brainwashed about "white rage."[2] And the Pentagon has also declared climate change a national security priority, meaning it is as grave a threat to our survival as such enemies as Communist China, North Korea, Iran, and Russia.[3] Meanwhile, successive Democratic administrations have denied our military services the funds needed to maintain top readiness and have strained their budgets, while enemy states, especially Communist China, are preparing for war.

On the home front, most of us have always viewed our police as selfless and brave guardians of the law, who protect us from criminals and keep the peace. We look up to them and appreciate them. They are highly trained professionals and their job is extremely dangerous, given the level of violent criminality that exists in too many areas of our country. The National Law Enforcement Memorial Fund reports that "since the first known line-of-duty death in 1786, more than 22,000 U.S. law enforcement officers have been killed in the line of duty. . . . [In 2018 alone], there have been 58,866 assaults against law enforcement officers . . . , resulting in 18,005 injuries."[4]

And on 9/11 every year, we honor those officers, along with firefighters, emergency personnel, and others, who lost their lives in infinite heroic acts to save the poor souls in the Twin Towers and the Pentagon who were slaughtered by al-Qaeda terrorists. These incredible men and women have not changed. They are the same patriotic and self-sacrificing Americans today as they were on that day and are on other days.

Yet what has changed in recent years, with the rise of American Marxism and Marxist-anarchist groups like Antifa and Black Lives Matter, is that law enforcement at all levels has come under brutal assault. Suddenly, they can do no good. They must be constrained and retrained, and policing itself must be "reimagined." We are told police officers are "systemically racists," targeting African Americans and other minorities for disparate treatment, despite indisputable statistics and overwhelming evidence to the contrary.[5] Of course, the relentless degrading and weakening of police forces, unremitting media disinformation about law enforcement, the ideological and political exploitation of certain videotaped encounters, and the slashing of police budgets by major-city Democratic politicians destabilize communities and the public's faith in policing, thereby undermining the rule of law and, ultimately, the civil society. If your goal is to "fundamentally transform" America[6]—that is, abolish our history, traditions, and ultimately our republic—then you must subvert support for the police. After all, without law enforcement the civil society collapses.

Indeed, as the Law Enforcement Legal Defense Fund reports, "across major US cities, tangible de-policing occurred June 2020 through February 2021 after anti-police protests, officials' statements, and policy decisions, and as arrests and searches plummeted—homicides soared in the months since the George Floyd incident. . . . Last year [2020], the United States tallied over 20,000 murders—the highest total since 1995 and 4,000 more killings than in 2019. Preliminary FBI data for 2020 points to a 25% surge in murders—the largest single year increase since the agency began publishing uniform data in 1960."[7] Police officers are leaving and retiring in droves.[8] And major cities are depopulating as people are now leaving in unprecedented numbers due, in significant part, to the increase in crime.[9]

Especially pernicious is the American Marxist's control over our public school and college classrooms, with the full support and active role of the two national teachers' unions—the National Education Association (NEA)[10] and the American Federation of Teachers (AFT)[11]—where your children and grandchildren are being taught to hate our country and are brainwashed with racist propaganda. If this persists, it will most assuredly lead to the nation's downfall. As the Heritage Foundation reports: "The dissemination of curricular content and instruction based on CRT [Critical Race Theory] in K–12 schools is second only in scope to the presence of CRT in post-secondary instruction, where CRT originated. The spread within college- and university-level syllabi and journal articles took place over the course of many decades throughout the 20th century, while the effects on K–12 schools in such areas as social studies, history, and civics have, by comparison, become visible more recently."[12]

Without your knowledge, let alone consent, "[d]istricts around the country have integrated CRT into school curricula. Both of the nation's largest teacher unions support the Black Lives Matter organization, with the National Education Association specifically calling for the use of Black Lives Matter curricular materials in K–12 schools. This curriculum is 'committed' to ideas such as a 'queer-affirming network,' which have nothing to do with rigorous instructional content, and promotes racially charged essays such as 'Open Secrets in First-Grade Math: Teaching about White Supremacy on American Currency.' As of 2018, officials in at least 20 large school districts, including Los Angeles and Washington, DC, were promoting Black Lives Matter curricular content and the organization's 'Week of Action.' According to an *Education Week* survey in June 2020, 81 percent of teachers, principals, and district leaders 'support the Black Lives Matter movement . . . ' "[13]

In fact, "[s]ome school systems have applied action civics to teaching disruptive protests."[14] Moreover, this Marxist-based ideology has spread to private schools, including private religious schools.[15]

However, this poison was first spread in our colleges and universities, where it reigns supreme and, as such, little is left there of academic freedom and free speech. Those pursuing degrees in education have been especially targeted. Jay Schalin of the James G. Martin Center for Academic Renewal explains: "[T]he 'long march' through the education schools has been successful; the most influential thinkers in our education schools are political radicals [Marxists] intent on transforming the nation to a collectivist, utopian vision."[16] . . . "The radical ideas are hard to escape in education schools. The higher one goes up the educational hierarchy, the more likely he or she is to have had a lengthy exposure to extremist ideas—and the less likely to reject them. To rise to a position of influence in education, one must make it through a minefield of graduate education courses that are intended to indoctrinate the gullible and weed out the recalcitrant."[17]

And not to be left out or behind, America's corporatists are all in. In fact, there are too many corporations committed to the various Marxist–Critical Theory movements, and the human resources, training, and hiring-related practices promoting them, to list here. Lily Zheng, an author and diversity, equity, and inclusion consultant, writing in *Harvard Business Review*, tells us: "Corporate Social Justice is not a feel-good approach that allows everyone to be heard, and by nature it won't result in initiatives that will make everyone happy. The first step that many companies have taken by publicly supporting Black Lives Matter through public statements and donations is an example of that: a commitment to taking a stance, even if it alienates certain populations of consumers, employees, and corporate partners. The company must decide that it is okay with losing business from certain groups (say, white supremacists or police departments), since taking money from those groups would run counter to its Corporate Social Justice strategy."[18]

These corporations are also currying favor and colluding with the Democratic Party by using their financial muscle to help create a one-party political machine.[19] Their recent joint war on the Georgia Republican legislature is one of many examples.[20]

Furthermore, social media, including Facebook/Instagram, Twitter, Google/YouTube, which were once thought to be the antidote to corporate media's oligopolist role as propagandists for the Democratic Party and mouthpieces for "social activism" and "progressivism," and embraced as open, public places for communication, turned out to be an autocratic ruse. A hard lesson has been learned, particularly in the last year, that Big Tech is, in fact, an oligopoly of its own, in which a few billionaires censor, suspend, ban, and edit the postings, videos, and comments that offend or challenge the orthodoxy of the Democratic Party, the various Marxist movements, the coronavirus pandemic authoritarians, etc. Facebook billionaire Mark Zuckerberg even contributed hundreds of millions of dollars in grants during the last election to increase turnout in Democratic Party strongholds in key battleground states.[21]

What can be done about these assaults on our liberty, families, and country? Of course, I do not have all the answers. To begin with, I warned years ago, in *Liberty and Tyranny*, that we "must become more engaged in public matters. . . . This will require a new generation . . . of activists, larger in number, shrewder, and more articulate than before, who seek to blunt the Statist's counterrevolution."[22] We must seize every opportunity to take back our institutions by running for office, seeking appointed office, and populating professions—including academia, journalism, and business—with patriots who can make a difference. We must take it upon ourselves to teach our children and grandchildren about the magnificence of our country, constitution, and capitalism, and the evils of Marxism and the people and organizations that promote it. We must explain to them why it is important to support and respect our police and armed forces, who protect us from criminals and foreign enemies.

Given the urgency of the moment, however, even this is not nearly enough. Indeed, the fate of our country rests in *your* hands and in *you* becoming strong and vocal activists for our nation and our liberty. Even though, at times, our future seems bleak, we must not now or ever surrender to this enemy from within.

Lest we forget, on December 19, 1776, as the Revolutionary War looked lost, and the morale of George Washington's army had reached bottom, Thomas Paine wrote *The American Crisis, No. 1*, which opened with:

> THESE are the times that try men's souls. The summer soldier and the sunshine patriot will, in this crisis, shrink from the service of their country; but he that stands by it now, deserves the love and thanks of man and woman. Tyranny, like hell, is not easily conquered; yet we have this consolation with us, that the harder the conflict, the more glorious the triumph. What we obtain too cheap, we esteem too lightly: it is dearness only that gives every thing its value. Heaven knows how to put a proper price upon its goods; and it would be strange indeed if so celestial an article as FREEDOM should not be highly rated.[23]

And Paine called for all Americans to join the fight against tyranny:

> I call not upon a few, but upon all: not on this state or that state, but on every state: up and help us; lay your shoulders to the wheel; better have too much force than too little, when so great an object is at stake. Let it be told to the future world, that in the depth of winter, when nothing but hope and virtue could survive, that the city and the country, alarmed at one common danger, came forth to meet and to repulse it.[24]

On the night of December 25, 1776, Washington ordered Paine's words read to his exhausted troops before the Battle of Trenton, which, of course, they went on to win. Paine's pamphlet not only energized Washington's men but quickly spread throughout the colonies, rousing and galvanizing the people.

Our challenge today is just as crucial and urgent, and in many ways, more complicated. We did not ask for this confrontation, but it is here. And, in truth, like the early days of the Revolutionary War, we are losing. Unfortunately, most of the country has been caught flat-footed and remains unengaged. What must be understood is that the various Marxist-associated movements are constantly agitating, pressuring, threatening, overtaking, and even rioting to accomplish their ends, for which there is no effective or sustained counter-pressure or agitation—that is, pushback. That must change today.

This is a call for action!

The time to act is now. Each of us must take time out of our daily lives to help save our country. We must be tactical and nimble in our responses to American Marxism and its multiple movements. And we must organize, rally, boycott, protest, speak, write, and more—and, where appropriate, we must use the Marxist's strategies and tactics against him. In other words, we must become the new "community activists." But unlike the Marxists, our cause is *patriotism*.

Here are some of the important strategies we must use:

BOYCOTT, DIVESTMENT, SANCTIONS (BDS)

No doubt the Boycott, Divestment, and Sanctions or BDS movement sounds familiar, as it has been used to try to economically destroy the state of Israel by its extremist enemies. The operational elements of this movement, however, can be adopted by American patriots against corporations, other organizations, donors, etc., who are funding or otherwise supporting Marxist movements in our country.

BOYCOTTS involve withdrawing support for corporate media, Big Tech, other corporations, Hollywood, sporting, cultural, and academic institutions engaged in promoting American Marxism and its various movements.

DIVESTMENT campaigns pressure banks, corporations, local and state governments, religious institutions, pension funds, etc. to withdraw investments in and support for the various Marxist movements.

SANCTIONS campaigns pressure local and state governments to end taxpayer subsidies and other forms of support for institutions with ties to various Marxist movements and policies; and ban the teaching and indoctrination of Critical Race Theory (CRT), Critical Gender Theory, etc., from taxpayer-financed public schools.

Moreover, American Marxists are litigious, relentlessly filing barrages of lawsuits in forum-shopped jurisdictions and courtrooms, as well as filing administrative action after administrative action in federal and state bureaucracies, to gather information about government actions and political opponents, as well as bog down bureaucrats with search requests. American patriots should do the same. Information on how to file Freedom of Information Act requests with the federal government can be found at FOIA.gov. Every state has freedom of information rules, which you can easily find on the Internet. In addition, a partial list of conservative and libertarian legal groups can be found at https://conservapedia.com/Conservative_legal_groups, and procedures for making claims against the federal and state governments can be found at https://www.usa.gov/complaint-against-government. In addition, if you gather information on the partisan-political nature of particular Marxist-based organizations, you can also challenge the favorable tax status conferred on them by filing complaints with the Internal Revenue Service (IRS).

As a general matter, where feasible, we must institute *our* BDS movement against the influences of American Marxism, adopt the Cloward and Piven–type approach of overwhelming "the system," crashing the system, then blaming the system, and taking control of the system—but in this case the system being that which has been created and instituted by the Marxist-based movements.

Moreover, Saul Alinsky's *Rules for Radicals* #13 should be used, where appropriate, as well: "Pick the target, freeze it, personalize it, and polarize it."[25] Alinsky wrote, in part: "Obviously there is no point to tactics unless one has a target upon which to center the attacks."[26]

Also, remember that there is power in numbers. The teachers' unions, Antifa, BLM, and others understand this. So must we.

Here are a few specific tactics for action, which should not be viewed as a comprehensive list:

EDUCATION

In every school district in America, local committees of patriotic community activists must organize, as some are already doing. Among other things, they should get involved in virtually every aspect of local public education. We can no longer leave the education of our children and the well-being of our community to "the professionals." As we have learned, especially since the pandemic, the educational bureaucracy does not have the best interests of our children as their top priority, and consequences for such inattention are disastrous. What shall be done?

1. The community committees should ensure that members attend every school board meeting to make certain that the public's interest and that of the students are being served, not the monopoly interests of the teachers' unions, Marxist activists, and other special interests. By this I mean hundreds of patriot activists showing up and being heard at every school board meeting throughout the year. The classrooms and schools must be taken back by the community.

2. The furtive nature and practices of local school systems must come to an end. Community committees should examine classroom curriculum, textbooks, teacher training and seminar materials, the teachers' contract with the school district, and school budgets. Where there is resistance by

the school boards or school administrations to providing transparency, which is likely, activists should use local and state freedom of information procedures and other legal tools to gain the information. Persistence is key. If necessary, seek the services of a local lawyer in the community who is willing to voluntarily assist in accessing the information. While it may be necessary to approach national legal groups for help, the goal here is to create a permanent, local presence and voice of community committees in your school system to counter and monitor the school boards, educational bureaucrats, and unions that have had free run and total control over education up to this point.

3. Community committees should insist that contracts with the teachers' unions prevent teachers from using classrooms and abusing academic freedom to proselytize or indoctrinate students about CRT, Critical Gender Theory, or other movements within the Marxist orbit that have suddenly been imposed upon the students. No more brainwashing of your children with racist hate and contempt for their country. Teachers are paid to teach, and by teach we mean objective, factual, scientific, mathematical learning. Moreover, school administrators should be on notice that you expect them to ensure that the teachers they oversee, and content of course curriculum, are appropriate. For example, students should be taught history, as written by real historians, not the widely condemned and discredited 1619 Project—which is CRT pablum. If they are incapable or unwilling to run a tight ship in this regard, they should be removed.

4. Private attorneys and legal groups are joining together in lawsuits against CRT training and teaching in public schools, arguing discrimination on the basis of race and

color, in addition to sex, gender and religion, in violation of the Civil Rights Act of 1964, and Title VI and Title IX of the Education Amendments of 1972, and the creation of a hostile educational environment based on compelled discriminatory speech and the perpetuation of racial stereotypes.[27] Community committees, parents' groups, and other patriot activists should file their own lawsuits against as many school systems as possible that practice and impose CRT racism and other Marxist-related ideologies. The Legal Insurrection website, founded and operated by Professor William Jacobson, provides some helpful resources concerning CRT in K–12 schools here: https://criticalrace.org/k-12/. Parents Defending Education is one of several grassroots organizations that can also provide assistance. They can be found here: https://defendinged.org/.

5. In states where there are friendly legislatures and governors, community committees should urge them to pass laws preventing the indoctrination of students and training of teachers in the ideologies of the various Marxist-related organizations, including CRT. Some states, but not nearly enough, have passed such laws. Friendly state attorneys general should be urged to use federal and state constitutional and civil rights protections against school districts and teachers' unions that impose racist indoctrination on teachers and students. Moreover, American patriots should demand that state law require schools to teach students civics, the foundational principles in the Declaration of Independence and Constitution, etc. School systems receive significant state funds and this is another way to hold them to account.

6. In most communities, a majority of property taxes go toward funding the local school system, and the majority

of those funds are used to compensate teachers. If school systems refuse to be responsive to the community committees and the public, and if teachers' unions continue to promote their own political and ideological agendas, the community committees of which I speak should organize a taxpayer revolt. The experience of the Tea Party Movement will provide excellent guidance. Although teachers' unions in certain states have the power to strike, the power of the purse is an important and underutilized tool in the struggle for control over public schools.

7. Community committees should demand competition in education. The issue is what is in the best interest of individual students and the public, not entrenched school board members, teachers' unions, and the educational bureaucracy. This triumvirate always oppose school choice, including charter schools, vouchers for private and parochial schools, etc., because they oppose competition. Parents and other taxpayers should insist that tax dollars follow the student, especially now given the radicalization and politicization of our public school systems, and the abuse of power demonstrated by many teachers' unions during the coronavirus pandemic.

8. Community committees should develop and train potential candidates to run for local school boards, or endorse those who share their commitment to true education reform. This has already begun in a few communities.

9. Hopefully, community committees will be established and flourish throughout the country, making possible the sharing of information and tactics among them.

10. There are also steps you can take, in conjunction with other groups or nonprofit legal foundations, respecting the

political and other activities of the National Education Association (NEA) or American Federation of Teachers (AFT) and their state and local affiliates, which are *public* sector unions receiving special tax and other governmental benefits.[28] These include filing requests with the IRS for their tax returns. Moreover, sometimes these unions and other related groups set up tax-exempt organizations. The federal returns of the tax-exempt organizations (Form 990s) are publicly available on the organization's website. The IRS also accepts complaints filed against tax-exempt organizations for alleged noncompliance with their federal tax status, including in many cases teachers' unions. Information can be found here: https://www.irs.gov/charities-non-profits/irs-complaint-process-tax-exempt-organizations.

Higher education presents its own set of difficulties and challenges. It is the breeding ground of American Marxism, where tenured Marxist and radical professors rule the roost. Indeed, the most subversive colleges and universities should be subjected to the kind of BDS movement its students and graduates often unleash against others. There are opportunities for real pushback.

1. In the first place, any parent who is involved in financially supporting a child's tuition to attend a college or university must at least attempt to exercise some control over the child's decision about which school he or she will attend. Here, we have real school choice, and the decision is whether the choice will be a wise one. Thus the parent must become intimately familiar with a school's reputation for academic freedom, free speech, traditional education, and the like, or whether it is a hotbed of Marxist radicalism and intolerance. Moreover, even if you are not assisting financially with tuition, a parent should still use his or

her influence to help direct and guide their child's decision. In addition, if your child may have been accepted into an Ivy League school, you should not be hypnotized by its name and past reputation. For example, among CRT's most ardent founders were Harvard and Stanford law professors. As discussed at length earlier, the Marxist-based Critical Theory (CT) ideology has devoured our colleges and universities and spawned numerous radical movements throughout academia, which have spread throughout our society. Again, the Legal Insurrection website provides a very useful and comprehensive database of CRT activity on college and university campuses, which can be found here: https://legalinsurrection.com/tag/college-insurrection/.

2. Colleges and universities conduct constant fund-raising campaigns, where they reach out to graduates for financial support. Some of these institutions amass huge endowment funds. This is an easy way to cut off a funding source to schools that are breeding grounds for American Marxism. In fact, campaigns should be launched to inform graduates and potential donors that they should withhold their support from certain colleges or universities that engage in silencing academic freedom and free speech, promote Marxism, and are part of the cancel culture. There are also schools, albeit few in number, that should be supported for their traditional approach to a liberal arts education, such as Hillsdale College, Grove City, among others.

3. The tables should be turned on the most radical colleges and universities. Several should be chosen as examples, where they are specifically targeted for BDS-like campaigns—that is, boycotted by parents, students, and donors; divested of private-sector dollars; and sanctioned

by pressure campaigns on local and state governments as well as corporations to slash their support for these schools.

4. State legislatures are the primary governmental sources of funding for colleges and universities, and in some cases the primary source—that is, state taxpayers. Yet they do little to monitor or influence how most of the funds are spent on these campuses. Colleges and universities have become empires unto themselves, insisting on immunity from substantive monitoring and oversight, while using the freedom granted such institutions under the First Amendment and the doctrine of academic freedom to silence nonconforming voices—whether they be professors, students, outside speakers, etc. The time is long overdue when legislatures and governors must be pressured to take immediate actions to rein in the despotic aspects of these institutions—which use their liberties to destroy ours.

For example, academia is overpopulated by radical tenured professors, too many of whom preach sedition, as discussed at length earlier. I also showed that in a survey of hundreds of college and university faculty in 2006, "80 percent were [found to be] solidly left, with well over half of those being extreme left . . . one in five professors in the social sciences self-identified as 'Marxist.' "[29] That was fifteen years ago; imagine how much worse it is today. Moreover, in my book *Plunder and Deceit*, I noted studies showing that "there is . . . an incestuous network of graduates from the top departments in different fields who hire fellow alumni as they move into the highest positions in departments at other colleges and universities"[30] to ensure and promote ideological groupthink among the faculty.

The corrupt manner in which taxpayer-subsidized college and university faculties are recruited, hired, paid, and tenured must be broken up by the state legislatures. In fact, the practice of "tenure" should be eliminated altogether. There is no legitimate or rational basis for the extreme ideological and political lopsidedness of college and university faculties in numerous departments. Furthermore, there is no good reason why taxpayers should pay Marxists to teach generations of students to hate their country, protect them from scrutiny and accountability, and provide them with lifetime job security with tenure. This academic cabal is free to relentlessly advance its ideological causes and effectively control America's college and university campuses. It is they and their administrators who have destroyed academic freedom and free speech. Indeed, if academic freedom and free speech truly existed on these campuses, the few professors who do not conform to the majority ideology and even dare to question it would not be threatened, subjected to cancel culture, and have their careers ruined. Students and student groups that defy the campus Marxists would not be harassed and violently attacked.[31] Guest speakers of all views would be welcome, rather than pro-American speakers being shouted down and chased off campus by angry mobs. Commencement speakers would be more representative of the greater society.[32]

As so many of America's college and university departments have become Marxist-oriented indoctrination mills, it is not surprising that Democratic politicians like Senator Bernie Sanders have proposed free college tuition and eliminating student loans as a way to encourage more young people to attend colleges and universities.[33] The Biden administration has proposed billions more in higher-education spending and grants, and promises much more in the future.[34] And yet, it still is not enough, as college costs, spending, and tuition skyrocket beyond all reason.[35]

Moreover, despite the enormous expenditure of taxpayer dollars to subsidize these schools, their ideological inbreeding appears to immunize most of them from regularized, sustained, and thorough oversight and inspection, certainly by Democrats who control Congress and various state legislatures. But state legislatures that do not condone the transformation of these institutions and their huge price tags should immediately begin to claw back future funding from these schools and demand academic and financial accountability. Again, the power of the purse is a crucial means by which to check these increasingly out-of-control institutions.

5. Since the Biden administration is actually giving cover to colleges and universities that accept untold tens of millions of dollars in foreign subsidies and donations,[36] including from Communist China, which has established "Confucius Institutes" throughout America academia, and despite the Senate's recent action tightening controls on these funds,[37] state legislatures should be pressured to compel these schools to report the receipt of these funds and then ban them. China and other countries are using these funds to buy favorable and supportive propaganda and coursework for their repressive regimes. Should colleges and universities refuse to comply, state legislatures should further slash their funding.

6. Do not overlook that you can use state freedom of information laws to collect all kinds of information from and about public universities, and the federal FOIA applies to the Department of Education, where additional information on these schools undoubtedly exists.

Finally, students obviously have a stake in their own education. If a professor is abusing his role and turning the classroom into a regular indoctrination seminar in support of the many Marxist-related movements, the student should demand that the college or university refund his costs; even join with like-minded students and object to the professor's propagandizing to the school administration; and perhaps even consider litigation along commercial lines for false advertising, bait and switch, etc.

CORPORATIONS

Ayn Rand observed: "The greatest guilt of modern industrialists is not the fumes of their factory smokestacks, but the pollution of this country's intellectual life, which they have condoned, assisted and supported."[38] So true.

For reasons discussed earlier, and as bizarre as it may seem, many major corporations have adopted BLM,[39] other Marxist-oriented movements and agendas related to CT, and the Democratic Party's deceitful voter schemes.[40] In a campaign of repression, many seek to squelch free speech, censor nonconforming opinions and beliefs, and ban or boycott individuals, groups, other usually smaller businesses that do not comply with the new orthodoxy, and even Republican state legislatures. Moreover, they are indoctrinating their workforces with the ideology of various Marxist movements as a condition of employment.[41] Of course, Donald Trump banned the federal government from using CRT in its training and from doing business with companies that use CRT and rejected efforts by the Democratic Party and their surrogate groups to eviscerate pre-2020 state voting laws.[42]

These companies have now openly partnered with the Democratic Party against the Republican Party, withholding financial support from the latter and backing more of the former's candidates.[43] Indeed, Joe Biden was their hands-down candidate for president.[44] And Biden has hired numerous executives from among their ranks.[45] In addition, corporate CEOs are activists and propagandists for these causes, organizing petitions, letters, and other politically motivated, public efforts, and even basing corporate success on achievements in social activism.[46]

Yet, while virtue-signaling here at home, many of these same corporations are doing business with America's most dangerous enemy, Communist China's genocidal regime.[47] They are expanding their ties with China,[48] or trying to enter the Chinese market, and are silent about the horrific human rights violations in China,[49] including the forced harvesting of organs,[50] its massive network of concentration camps,[51] and the torture, rape, and murder of Uyghur Muslims, among other minority groups.[52]

Again, what can be done?

1. Each of us, and our circle of friends, associates, and neighbors, can practice what I call "patriotic commerce"—that is, become an informed patriotic consumer. Together, we have enormous economic clout. Whether purchasing small, everyday products and services, or making larger, life-changing financial decisions, each of us needs to take a little time to determine whether the individual or company with whom we intend to do business shares our worldviews. If they do, or are neutral and stay out of politics, then we should support them. If not, we should not do business with them and even organize boycotts against them as part of our BDS movements. Boycotting is something the American Marxists and their allies and surrogates have been doing for decades, and we must push back. In fact, they have greatly ramped up these activities in recent years.[53]

   Moreover, you should support economically companies that are targeted but refuse to cave to these mob tactics by purchasing their products and services. For example, when

Goya's CEO said supportive words about President Trump, his company was boycotted by the Marxist brigades. But the pushback by patriotic Americans was swift and profound, who rallied to the company's aid by purchasing so many Goya products that store shelves were cleared.[54] The lesson learned is that in addition to personally and collective boycotting companies, we must support pro-American companies as well.

Furthermore, use social media to expose, pressure, and organize protests against politically and ideologically hostile corporations (more on Big Tech later); go to shareholder meetings in large numbers and make your voices heard (this includes corporate media and Big Tech companies). The Free Enterprise Project (FEP) "files shareholder resolutions, engages corporate CEOs and board members at shareholder meetings, petitions the Securities and Exchange Commission (SEC) for interpretative guidance, and sponsors effective media campaigns to create the incentives for corporations to stay focused on their missions," and can assist you in your efforts. FEP can be found here: https://nationalcenter.org/programs/free-enterprise-project. Other groups do as well. You can be a part of patriotic shareholder-driven campaigns.

Lobby state legislators to investigate these corporations, particularly those that do business in and with Communist China, and pressure them to divest all state pension and other funds from these companies.

2. How do you know which corporations have sided with Marxist groups and causes, such as the CRT movement, or are otherwise involved in political and/or policy matters with which you disagree? Of course, the Internet makes available significant information that may provide this information, as do corporate prospectuses (corporations

tend to brag about their "social activism"). There are also organizations that track and rate companies based on their political and ideological activities—including 2ndVote, found here: https://www.2ndvote.com, and the Open-Secrets website tracks donations, found here: https://www.opensecrets.org. Just type in the name of the company. Furthermore, the Media Research Center tracks the corporate sponsors of major network news shows, which can be found here: https://www.mrc.org/conservatives-fight-back.

Where possible, you should also purchase goods and services from smaller, start-up, or neighborhood businesses that are less likely to be involved in the various Marxist-based movements, rather than large international corporations, Amazon, or large warehouse stores that are increasingly aligned with those movements.

3. Support for free market capitalism must no longer be confused with defending corporate oligarchism and crony capitalism. Large corporations have moved into the social activism business and have aligned with Marxist-based movements and the Democratic Party.[55] Therefore, let them live under the iron fist of their newfound partners and experience the consequences. When our allies in government are setting tax and regulatory policies, we must insist that they segregate the treatment of the oligarchical corporations from small and medium-sized businesses. The former's interests do not align with the latter's interests or our interests in preserving our republic. For example, we witnessed how Google, Facebook, Twitter, Apple, etc., teamed up in a brazen effort to destroy the upstart Parler, censor former president Trump, cover up the Hunter Biden scandal pre–general election, enforce coronavirus lockdowns

and ban scientific/expert opinions that differed from that of government bureaucrats, and generally use suppression techniques to stigmatize and silence speech and debate they did not and do not support as political and policy matters. We also witnessed hundreds of corporations collude against the Republican legislature in Georgia and its efforts to judiciously reform the state's election system—as they worked with the Democratic Party and its efforts to establish one-party rule there. These corporations issued letters, petitions, public statements, and some even instituted economic boycotts, including Major League Baseball, which moved its All-Star Game out of Atlanta.[56]

Therefore, when Democratic-controlled state legislatures or congressional Democrats turn on their new corporate allies and, for example, propose significant corporate tax increases, we ought not lift a finger to prevent them. Instead, we should insist that smaller and medium-sized businesses that are not involved in promoting the agenda of American Marxists or the Democratic Party should be protected. Indeed, where appropriate, we should insist on antitrust actions against large corporations that use their clout not only to smother competitors (such as Big Tech) but support political and legislative policies that undermine our country. And if existing antitrust laws are not adequate, they should be updated. Moreover, friendly state legislatures should be lobbied to take on Big Tech, as states are not without statutory recourse, as Florida has demonstrated.[57]

4. Big Media and Big Tech are among the largest corporate oligarchies in the nation. They have demonstrated time and again the use of their corporate clout to repress, censor, and propagandize on behalf of social activism, Marxist-based

movements, and the Democratic Party. Big Media use their corporate clout to try to destroy nonconforming news and opinion organizations (e.g., AT&T-owned CNN repeatedly advocates for de-platforming the Fox News Channel and banning its hosts), and, of course, Big Tech does the same against smaller social media businesses. Let us remember that when cable TV and, later, social media were developed, they were celebrated as providing *more* options and choices for news consumers. Instead, corporate acquisitions and consolidation have led to a relative few corporatists controlling the content and distribution of information throughout the country. This is simply intolerable.

Respecting Big Tech, if you use social media, you should find alternatives to the corporate oligarchs. I am not tech savvy. But I know enough to suggest a few options: Parler, MeWe, and Discord's community forums. Rumble, Vimeo, and Bitchute. And the DuckDuckGo search engine. And there are others you can find on the Internet. Moreover, you can monitor Big Tech's oligopolists' censorship activities by using the Media Research Center's FreeSpeech-America Project and its Censortrack website, found here: https://censortrack.org/.

However, the root cause of Big Tech's power and abuse goes back to the protection granted it by Congress in 1996 under Section 230 of the Community Decency Act. As Rachel Bovard of the Conservative Partnership Institute (CPI), explains: It "protects the Big Tech companies from being sued for the content users post on their sites. The law also creates a liability shield for the platforms to 'restrict access to or availability of material that the provider or user considers to be . . . objectionable, whether or not such material is constitutionally protected.' "[58] She adds: "A handful of Big Tech companies are now controlling the flow of most information in a free society, and they are doing so aided and abetted by government policy. That these are merely private companies exercising their First Amendment rights is a reductive framing which ignores that they do so in a manner that is privileged—they are immune to liabilities to which other First Amendment actors like newspapers are subject—and also that these content moderation decisions occur at an extraordinary and unparalleled scale."[59] Thus, when Republicans next control Congress and the presidency, they must be aggressively pressured to withdraw Section 230 immunity from Big Tech, which President Trump attempted to do but was thwarted by his own party.

Moreover, Facebook billionaire Mark Zuckerberg's interference with and attempted manipulation of elections, including the presidential election in 2020 with hundreds of millions in targeted contributions, as well as Google's manipulation of algorithms, must be investigated and outlawed both at the federal and state level.[60] You can contact friendly state legislators and file complaints against corporations that make what are effectively in-kind contributions with various federal and state agencies and, again, show up at their shareholder meetings and be heard.

Respecting Big Media, and its war on free speech and media competition, large corporations have gobbled up many significant media platforms. I mentioned that AT&T owns CNN. Comcast owns NBC. A partial list of others can be found at Investopedia.com.[61] The lack of self-policing and oversight by these corporations, and their support for the Democratic Party and Marxist-based groups and their agendas, have actually contributed to destroying the purpose of a free, open, and competitive press. Therefore, our BDS efforts should be aimed, as well, at these news organizations and their corporate parents. We should make them as irrelevant as possible by personally refusing to use them, urging our families and circle of friends and associates to boycott them, and attend their shareholder meetings where their politics, ideological social activism, and destruction of freedom of the press are challenged.

In addition, our allegiance, including our viewing and reading habits, should focus on the increased number of independent journalists and news sites that are far more reliable than Big Media outlets. Several such sites are online and do original journalism and report actual news, and others help sort through news stories and aggregate them. A partial list can be found here: https://www.libertynation.com/top-conservative-news-sites. Moreover, there are also cable outlets, including Fox News, Fox Business, One America News Network, Newsmax TV, Sinclair Broadcasting, and other budding news-broadcast platforms; and a relative handful of newspapers, including but not limited to the *New York Post*, the *Washington Examiner*, the *Washington Times*, etc.

5. Professional sports leagues and individual teams are multibillion-dollar corporations as well. Certain leagues, including the National Basketball Association (NBA), as well as teams and players, support, for example, the BLM movement, yet make a great deal of money doing business with the genocidal communist regime in China. Where appropriate, the leagues and teams can be subjected to protests at their corporate headquarters or at the stadiums where they play their games. Professional sports has a huge influence on the culture. Thus far, there has been no pushback. Furthermore, given Major League Baseball's role in

moving the All-Star game from Georgia to Colorado, we must pressure Republicans in Congress to end its special exemption from antitrust laws.

CLIMATE

As discussed earlier, the "climate change" movement (previously, global cooling and global warming) is a degrowth, anticapitalism movement that will impoverish Americans. At bottom, it is a broad-based war on your property rights, liberty, and way of life. More broadly, it is an attack on the most successful economic system known to mankind, and massively expands the power of the federal bureaucracy, politicians, and international/global institutions to manage, dictate, and control infinite aspects of our society and economy through regulations and mandates under the guise of public health and safety, clean air, clean water, and even national security. It will make the abuses of power we saw and experienced from reckless and tyrannical state governments in dealing with the coronavirus pandemic, and the grievous violations of civil and religious liberties, pale by comparison.

I wrote in *Liberty and Tyranny* years ago, "[w]ith the assistance of a pliant or sympathetic media, the Statist uses junk science, misrepresentations, and fear-mongering to promote public health and environmental scares, because he realizes that in a true, widespread health emergency, the public expects the government to act aggressively to address the crisis despite traditional limitations on governmental authority. The more dire the threat, the more liberty people are usually willing to surrender. The government's authority becomes part of the societal frame of reference, only to be built upon during the next 'crisis.' "[62]

As I explained further, the pathology involves "[u]rgent predictions . . . made by cherry-picked 'experts' that the media accept without skepticism or independent investigation and turn into a cacophony of fear. Public officials next clamor to demonstrate that they are taking steps to ameliorate the dangers. New laws are enacted or regulations promulgated that are said to limit the public's exposure to the new 'risk.' "[63]

Indeed, Biden's special presidential envoy for climate, John Kerry, underscored that there will be no limit or end to the encroachment on our liberties in the name of climate change, which is true of all Marxist-spawned movements in America. Kerry declared: "I just remind everybody that that will depend on whether or not we have some breakthrough technologies, some breakthrough innovations, number one, but even if we get to net zero, we still have to get carbon dioxide out of the atmosphere. So, this is a bigger challenge than a lot of people have really grabbed on to yet."[64]

Pushback will require a primarily legal and administrative response. You can access a network of state policy groups, some of which are found here: https://spn.org, and a coalition of property rights groups found here: https://www.property-rts.org, which can provide you with policy advice and legal referrals. You can also use federal and state freedom of information laws and directly contact potentially helpful legal groups (links provided earlier).

Where appropriate, lawsuits can be brought against governmental, private, and nonprofit entities that tortiously interfere with your use of your property or degrade the market value of your property.[65] You can file FOIA requests directly for information with the Environmental Protection Agency (EPA), Interior Department, and other federal agencies to dig into their activities and hold them accountable,[66] as well as slow down regulatory processes and activities. And, again, friendly state attorneys general can be urged to file lawsuits against federal actions, as in Biden's lawless attack against the Keystone XL pipeline.[67]

When Republicans regain majorities in the House and Senate, and win the presidency, they must be pressured to eliminate the special tax-exempt status granted to environmental groups, since they are not nonpartisan charitable foundations; and eliminate their special statutory authority to bring lawsuits on behalf of the public, since their main purpose is to eviscerate our economic system, private property rights, and republican principles. For too long these groups have had a cozy policy and legal relationship with the bureaucrats at the Interior Department, Agriculture Department, Environmental Protection Agency, and other federal departments and agencies.

ANTIFA, BLACK LIVES MATTER, AND RIOTERS

The failure of the federal government to unleash criminal investigations and bring charges against Antifa, BLM, and other domestic terrorist organizations for the mayhem they have unleashed and billions of dollars in damage they have caused in American communities is scandalous.[68] Moreover, the disparate treatment of individuals by federal law enforcement, based on their political beliefs, is shocking.[69]

However, honorable governors can act to protect their citizens, including strengthening their laws against such violence and rioters. In Florida, Governor Ron DeSantis has instituted measures that "[i]ncrease penalties for existing crimes committed during a violent assembly, and protects the communities' law enforcement officers, and victims of these types of acts. The bill also creates specific crimes for mob intimidation and cyber intimidation to ensure that Florida will not be a welcoming place for those wishing to impose their will on innocent civilians and law enforcement by way of mob mentality. Crimes of mob intimidation and cyber intimidation both will become 1st-degree misdemeanors."[70] Governors and state legislators across the country must be pressured to adopt similar laws.

But citizens need not wait for government at all levels to act. There are private civil lawsuits that can be filed against these organizations and individual rioters, depending on each state's statutes, that strike at the finances of these groups and individuals and, hopefully, help compensate victims for their damages. Possible causes of action might include: intentional infliction of emotional distress, tortious interference with contracts, trespass to land and chattels, and conversion of property. State and federal civil RICO lawsuits are possibilities in the most extreme cases, especially with the same organizations showing up at the scene of violent riots.[71]

Moreover, you can ask the IRS to review or investigate financial issues related to organizations such as BLM that you may find in newspaper articles, online sources, etc. For example, questions have been raised about BLM's interlocking operations[72] and transparency.[73]

Furthermore, if you happen to see the license tag of a rioter fleeing a violent scene in a vehicle, report the tag number to your local police department. Your eyes, ears, and video from your cellphones are important crime-fighting tools.

LAW ENFORCEMENT

Law enforcement is under attack by Antifa, BLM, other Marxist-anarchist groups, violent criminals, Democratic politicians, the media, etc. Indeed, since the appearance of BLM and its sympathetic media coverage, a positive view of law enforcement has decreased, particularly among minorities.[74] However, although police are now routinely accused in the media of racist targeting of African Americans and other minorities, the evidence simply does not support these charges.[75] Moreover, 81 percent of black Americans want to retain the local police presence in their communities, with many wanting an increased presence.

Nonetheless, as a consequence of this war on law enforcement, violent crime across America is surging, particularly in our major cities.[76] And law-abiding citizens are paying a steep personal price. Yet, rather than standing up to the mob and their facilitators and appeasers, the war on law enforcement is intensifying.

There are so-called reform efforts under way that are actually intended to further denude police officers and police departments of their ability to protect the citizenry, including legal initiatives that would expose officers to personal harm and financial bankruptcy. Among other things, congressional Democrats and their radical surrogates have been pushing to essentially eliminate qualified immunity and subject officers to endless lawsuits; lower the bar for criminal prosecutions of officers; promote local and state investigations of officers; keep a federal database on all officers; lower the legal standard for determining the justified use of force from "reasonable" to "necessary"; and limit the transfer of "military-style" equipment to police forces.[77]

The result of all of this: across the nation, police recruitment and retention have plummeted.[78] The thin blue line is breaking. And the civil society is descending into chaos. Therefore, in addition to supporting police officers and police departments in any way we can, including speaking out for them, they need our support in specific ways as well. I have one suggestion, in addition to the many you may have as well:

If state law permits, there is no reason why police officers should not bring civil suits against individuals who physically assault them, and even the organizations behind violent riots that result in them being assaulted or injured, such as Antifa and BLM. There are a number of factors that will have to be considered, including the ability to identify the individuals and the group associations, as well as causation. But officers and their unions should consult with a good lawyer to review the law and the facts.[79] You can help by providing financial assistance specifically directed to the legal representation of police officers who bring these lawsuits by contacting your local law enforcement agency, your local police benevolent association, the Law Enforcement Legal Defense Fund found at https://www.policedefense.org; the National Association of Police Organizations found at https://www.napo.org; the Fraternal Order of Police, found here: https://fop.net; and other such groups.

General George S. Patton reportedly said: "Never tell people how to do things. Tell them what to do and they will surprise you with their ingenuity." Thus, at this point, I have provided some concrete ideas and suggestions on how to proceed, but by no means is this an exhaustive list of possible actions or action areas. In the end, it is up to *you* to decide how best to help actively save our republic and what role *you* will choose. That said, Patton also reportedly declared: "No good decision was ever made in a swivel chair."

While this is the end of the book, it is the beginning of a new day.

We choose liberty! Patriots of America, unite!

In loving memory

of Barney Levin

NOTES

CHAPTER ONE: IT'S HERE

1 Mark R. Levin, *Ameritopia: The Unmaking of America* (New York: Threshold Editions, 2012), 3.

2 Andrew Mark Miller, "Black Lives Matter co-founder says group's goal is 'to get Trump out,'" *Washington Examiner*, June 20, 2020, https://www.washingtonexaminer.com/news/black-lives-matter-co-founder-says-groups-goal-is-to-get-trump-out (April 22, 2021).

3 Jason Lange, "Biden staff donate to group that pays bail in riot-torn Minneapolis," Reuters, May 30, 2020, https://www.reuters.com/article/us-minneapolis-police-biden-bail/biden-staff-donate-to-group-that-pays-bail-in-riot-torn-minneapolis-idUSKBN2360SZ (April 22, 2021).

4 Levin, *Ameritopia*, 7.

5 Ted McAllister, "Thus Always to Bad Elites," *American Mind*, March 16, 2021, https://americanmind.org/salvo/thus-always-to-bad-elites/ (April 22, 2021).

6 Ronald Reagan, "Encroaching Control (The Peril of Ever Expanding Government)," in *A Time for Choosing: The Speeches of Ronald Reagan 1961–1982*, eds. Alfred A. Baltizer and Gerald M. Bonetto (Chicago: Regnery, 1983), 38.

CHAPTER TWO: BREEDING MOBS

1 Mark R. Levin, *Ameritopia: The Unmaking of America* (New York: Threshold Editions, 2012), 6–7.
2 Ibid., 7–8.
3 Ibid., 16.
4 Julien Benda, *The Treason of the Intellectuals* (New Brunswick: Transaction, 2014), 2
5 Ibid., 2–3.
6 Capital Research Center, "What Antifa Really Is," December 21, 2020, https://capitalresearch.org/article/is-antifa-an-idea-or-organization/ (April 6, 2021).
7 Scott Walter, "The Founders of Black Lives Matter," *First Things*, March 29, 2021, https://www.firstthings.com/web-exclusives/2021/03/the-founders-of-black-lives-matter (April 6, 2021).
8 Levin, *Ameritopia*, 11.
9 Ibid., 13.
10 Jean-Jacques Rousseau, *Discourse on the Origin and Foundations of Inequality Among Men*, ed. and trans. Donald A. Cress (Indianapolis: Hackett, 2012), 45.
11 Ibid., 87.
12 G. W. F. Hegel, *Elements of the Philosophy of the Right*, trans. S. W. Dyde (Mineola, NY: Dover, 2005), 133.
13 Karl Marx and Friedrich Engels, *The Communist Manifesto* (London: Soho Books, 2010), 36.
14 Ibid., 23.
15 Ibid., 42.
16 Eric Hoffer, *The True Believer: Thoughts on the Nature of Mass Movements* (New York: HarperPerennial, 2010), 12.
17 Ibid., 69.
18 Ibid., 75.
19 Ibid., 76.
20 Ibid.
21 Ibid., 74.
22 Ibid., 80.
23 Ibid., 80–81.
24 Ibid., 85.
25 Ibid., 85–86.
26 Ibid., 87.
27 Tyler O'Neill, "Hacked Soros Documents Reveal Some Big Dark Money

Surprises," PJ Media, August 19, 2016, https://pjmedia.com/news-and-politics/tyler-o-neil/2016/08/19/hacked-soros-documents-reveal-some-big-dark-money-surprises-n47598 (April 6, 2021).

28 Hoffer, *The True Believer*, 98.

29 Ibid., 140.

30 Hannah Arendt, *The Origins of Totalitarianism* (New York: Harcourt, 1976), 307.

31 *Frontiers in Social Movement Theory*, ed. Aldon D. Morris and Carol McClurg Mueller (New Haven: Yale University Press, 1992), x.

32 William A. Gamson, "The Social Psychology of Collective Action," in *Frontiers in Social Movement Theory*, 56. Professor Gamson is a professor of sociology at Boston College and codirects the Media Research and Action Project: https://www.bc.edu/bc-web/schools/mcas/departments/sociology/people/affiliated-emeriti/william-gamson.html (April 6, 2021).

33 Ibid.

34 Ibid., 57.

35 Ibid., 74.

36 Debra Friedman and Doug McAdam, "Collective Identity and Activism: Networks, Choices and the Life of a Social Movement," in *Frontiers in Social Movement Theory*, 157. Professor McAdam is currently the Ray Lyman Wilbur Professor of Sociology (Emeritus) at Stanford University: https://sociology.stanford.edu/people/douglas-mcadam (April 6, 2021).

37 Ibid.

38 Ibid., 169–70.

39 Bert Klandermans, "The Social Construction of Protest and Multiorganizational Fields," in *Frontiers in Social Movement Theory*, 99–100. Professor Klandermans is a professor of sociology at the Free University, Amsterdam, Netherlands: https://research.vu.nl/en/persons/bert-klandermans (April 6, 2021).

40 Aldon D. Morris, "Political Consciousness and Collective Action," in *Frontiers in Social Movement Theory*, 351–52. Professor Morris is the Leon Forrest Professor of Sociology and African American Studies at Northwestern University: https://sociology.northwestern.edu/people/faculty/core/aldon-morris.html (April 6, 2021).

41 Ibid., 357–58.

42 Ibid., 370.

43 Ibid.

44 Ibid.

45 Ibid., 371.

46 Ibid.

47 Ibid.
48 Ibid.
49 Ibid.
50 Ibid.
51 Frances Fox Piven and Richard Cloward, *The Breaking of the American Social Compact* (New York: New Press, 1967), 267.
52 Ibid., 269.
53 Ibid., 287, 288.
54 Ibid., 289.
55 Biden-Sanders Unity Task Force Recommendations, "Combating the Climate Crisis and Pursuing Environmental Justice," https://joebiden.com/wp-content/uploads/2020/08/UNITY-TASK-FORCE-RECOMMENDATIONS.pdf (April 6, 2021).
56 Piven and Cloward, *The Breaking of the American Social Compact*, 289.
57 Ibid.
58 Ibid., 290.
59 Ibid.
60 Ibid., 291.
61 Ibid.
62 Ibid.
63 Ibid., 291–92.
64 Nicholas Fondacaro, "ABC, NBC Spike 'Mostly Peaceful' Protests Leaving $2 Billion in Damages," mrcNewsBusters, September 16, 2020, https://www.newsbusters.org/blogs/nb/nicholas-fondacaro/2020/09/16/abc-nbc-spike-mostly-peaceful-protests-leaving-2-billion (April 6, 2021).
65 Piven and Cloward, *The Breaking of the American Social Compact*, 292.
66 Ibid., 292–93.
67 Frances Fox Piven, "Throw Sand in the Gears of Everything," *Nation*, January 18, 2017, https://www.thenation.com/article/archive/throw-sand-in-the-gears-of-everything/ (April 6, 2021).
68 Ibid.
69 Ibid.
70 Ibid.
71 Allan Bloom, *The Closing of the American Mind* (New York: Simon & Schuster, 1987), 26.
72 Ibid., 55, 56.
73 Ibid., 58.

CHAPTER THREE: HATE AMERICA, INC.

1 Felicity Barringer, "The Mainstreaming of Marxism in U.S. Colleges," *New York Times*, October 29, 1989, https://www.nytimes.com/1989/10/25/us/education-the-mainstreaming-of-marxism-in-us-colleges.html (April 7, 2021).
2 Ibid.
3 Ibid.
4 Ibid.
5 Herbert Croly, "The Promise of American Life," in *Classics of American Political and Constitutional Thought*, vol. 2, eds. Scott J. Hammond, Kevin R. Harwick, and Howard L. Lubert (Indianapolis: Hackett, 2007), 297.
6 Ibid., 313.
7 Herbert D. Croly, *Progressive Democracy* (London: Forgotten Books, 2015), 38–39.
8 Statista, "Percentage of the U.S. Population who have completed four years of college or more from 1940 to 2019," https://www.statista.com/statistics/184272/educational-attainment-of-college-diploma-or-higher-by-gender/ (April 7, 2021).
9 Ibid.
10 John Dewey, *Individualism Old and New* (Amherst, NY: Prometheus Books, 1999), 51.
11 John Dewey, *Democracy and Education* (Simon & Brown, 2012), 234.
12 Ibid., 239, 240, 245.
13 John Dewey, "Ethical Principles Underlying Education," appearing in *The Early Works*, vol. 5, *1882–1898: Early Essays*, ed. Jo Ann Boydston (Carbondale, Ill.: Southern Illinois University Press, 2008), 59–63.
14 John Dewey, "What Are the Russian Schools Doing?" *New Republic*, December 5, 1928, https://newrepublic.com/article/92769/russia-soviet-education-communism (April 7, 2021).
15 Ibid.
16 Ibid.
17 Mark R. Levin, *Unfreedom of the Press* (New York: Threshold Editions, 2019), Chapter 6.
18 Richard M. Weaver, *Ideas Have Consequences* (Chicago: University of Chicago Press, 1948), 2.
19 Ibid.
20 Ibid., 5.
21 Ibid.
22 Ibid., 5–6.

23 Ibid., 6.

24 Ibid., 85.

25 Madeleine Davis, "New Left," *Encyclopaedia Britannica*, https://www.britannica.com/topic/New-Left (April 7, 2021).

26 Ibid.

27 *A-Z Guide to Modern Social and Political Theorists*, eds. Noel Parker and Stuart Sun (London: Routledge, 1997), 238.

28 Herbert Marcuse, *One Dimensional Man* (Boston: Beacon Press: 1964), 3.

29 Ibid.

30 Ibid., 4.

31 Herbert Marcuse, "The Failure of the New Left?" in *New German Critique* 18 (Fall 1979), https://www.marcuse.org/herbert/pubs/70spubs/Marcuse1979FailureNewLeft.pdf (April 7, 2021).

32 Barringer, "The Mainstreaming of Marxism in U.S. Colleges."

33 Ibid.

34 Ibid.

35 Richard Landes, *Heaven on Earth: The Varieties of the Millennial Experience* (Oxford: Oxford University Press, 2011), 12, 13.

36 Ibid., 13.

37 Ibid.

38 Ibid., 14.

39 Ibid., 17.

40 BBC, "Historical Figures, Vladimir Lenin," http://www.bbc.co.uk/history/historic_figures/lenin_vladimir.shtml (April 7, 2021).

41 BBC, "Historical Figures, Mao Zedong," http://www.bbc.co.uk/history/historic_figures/mao_zedong.shtml (April 7, 2021).

42 BBC, "Historical Figures, Pol Pot," http://www.bbc.co.uk/history/historic_figures/pot_pol.shtml (April 7, 2021).

43 Lois Weis, "For Jean Anyon, my colleague and friend," *Perspectives on Urban Education*, University of Pennsylvania, https://urbanedjournal.gse.upenn.edu/archive/volume-11-issue-1-winter-2014/jean-anyon-my-colleague-and-friend (April 7, 2021).

44 Jean Anyon, *Marx and Education* (New York: Routledge, 2011), 7

45 Ibid., 7, 8.

46 Raymond Aron, *The Opium of the Intellectuals* (New Brunswick, NJ: Transaction, 1957), 94.

47 Anyon, *Marx and Education*, 8–9 (quoting Marx and Engels).

48 Jeffry Bartash, "Share of union workers in the U.S. falls to a record low in 2019," *Marketwatch*, January 31, 2020, https://www.marketwatch.com

/story/share-of-union-workers-in-the-us-falls-to-a-record-low-in-2019-2020-01-22 (April 8, 2021).

49 Richard Epstein, "The Decline of Unions Is Good News," Ricochet, January 28, 2020, https://ricochet.com/717005/archives/the-decline-of-unions-is-good-news/ (April 8, 2021).

50 Anyon, *Marx and Education*, 9–10 (quoting Marx).

51 Aron, *The Opium of the Intellectuals*, 94–95.

52 Anyon, *Marx and Education*, 11.

53 Ibid., 12–13 (quoting Marx).

54 Lance Izumi, "Why Are Teachers Mostly Liberal?" Pacific Research Institute, April 3, 2019, https://www.pacificresearch.org/why-are-teachers-mostly-liberal/ (April 8, 2021).

55 Alyson Klein, "Survey: Educator's Political Leanings, Who They Voted For, Where They Stand on Key Issues," *Education Week*, December 12, 2017, https://www.edweek.org/leadership/survey-educators-political-leanings-who-they-voted-for-where-they-stand-on-key-issues/2017/12 (April 8, 2021).

56 Anyon, *Marx and Education*, 19.

57 Ibid., 35.

58 Ibid., 36–37.

59 Ibid., 96–97.

60 Ibid., 97.

61 Ibid., 98.

62 Ibid., 99.

63 Ibid.

64 Ibid., 99–100.

65 Ibid., 100–101.

66 Ibid., 103–4.

67 Jean Anyon, *Radical Possibilities: Public Policy, Urban Education, and a New Social Movement* (New York: Routledge, 2014), 140–41.

68 John M. Ellis, *The Breakdown of Higher Education* (New York: Encounter Books), 30, 31.

69 Ibid., 31.

CHAPTER FOUR: RACISM, GENDERISM, AND MARXISM

1 Uri Harris, "Jordan B. Peterson, Critical Theory, and the New Bourgeoisie," *Quillette*, January 17, 2018, https://quillette.com/2018/01/17/jordan-b-peterson-critical-theory-new-bourgeoisie/ (April 8, 2021).

2 Ibid.
3 Ibid.
4 Ibid.
5 Ibid.
6 Ibid.
7 Ibid.
8 Ibid.
9 Jonathan Butcher and Mike Gonzalez, "Critical Race Theory, the New Intolerance, and Its Grip on America," Heritage Foundation, December 7, 2020, https://www.heritage.org/civil-rights/report/critical-race-theory-the-new-intolerance-and-its-grip-america (April 8, 2021).
10 George R. La Noue, "Critical Race Training or Civil Rights Law: We Can't Have Both," Liberty & Law, November 4, 2020, https://lawliberty.org/critical-race-theory-or-civil-rights-law-we-cant-have-both/ (April 8, 2021).
11 Ibid.
12 Thomas Sowell, *Intellectuals and Society* (New York: Basic Books, 2011), 468.
13 Ibid., 469.
14 Ibid.
15 Ibid.
16 Herbert Marcuse, *One-Dimensional Man: Studies in the Ideology of Advanced Industrial Society* (Boston: Beacon Press, 1991), 256–57.
17 Faith Karimi, "What critical race theory is—and isn't," CNN, October 1, 2020, https://www.cnn.com/2020/10/01/us/critical-race-theory-explainer-trnd/index.html (April 8, 2021).
18 Ibid.
19 Richard Delgado and Jean Stefancic, *Critical Race Theory* (New York: New York University Press, 2017), 3.
20 Ibid., 8.
21 Ibid.
22 Ibid., 9.
23 Ibid.
24 Ibid., 10, 11.
25 Ibid., 8.
26 "Thomas Sowell Hammers 'Despicable' Derrick Bell; Compares to Hitler," Breitbart, March 7, 2012, https://www.breitbart.com/clips/2012/03/07/sowell%20on%20bell/ (video interview dated May 24, 1990) (April 8, 2021).

27 Thomas Sowell, *Inside American Education: The Decline, the Deception, the Dogmas* (New York: Free Press, 1993), 154.

28 Derrick A. Bell, "*Brown v. Board of Education* and the Interest-Convergence Dilemma," *Harvard Law Review*, January 11, 1980, https://harvardlawreview.org/1980/01/brown-v-board-of-education-and-the-interest-convergence-dilemma/ (April 8, 2021).

29 Derrick A. Bell, "Who's Afraid of Critical Race Theory?" *University of Illinois Law Review*, February 23, 1995, https://sph.umd.edu/sites/default/files/files/Bell_Whos%20Afraid%20of%20CRT_1995UIllLRev893.pdf (April 8, 2021), 901.

30 Ibid.

31 Steve Klinsky, "The Civil Rights Legend Who Opposed Critical Race Theory," RealClearPolitics, October 12, 2020, https://www.realclearpolitics.com/articles/2020/10/12/the_civil_rights_legend_who_opposed_critical_race_theory_144423.html (April 8, 2021).

32 Ibid.

33 Ibid.

34 Ibid.

35 Delgado and Stefancic, *Critical Race Theory*, 45, 46.

36 Butcher and Gonzalez, "Critical Race Theory, the New Intolerance, and Its Grip on America."

37 Robin DiAngelo, *White Fragility* (Boston: Beacon Press, 2018), 28.

38 Delgado and Stefancic, *Critical Race Theory*, 29.

39 Chris Demaske, "Critical Race Theory," First Amendment Encyclopedia, https://www.mtsu.edu/first-amendment/article/1254/critical-race-theory, (April 9, 2021).

40 Delgado and Stefancic, *Critical Race Theory*, 125.

41 Ibid., 127, 128.

42 Ibid., 132, 133.

43 Butcher and Gonzalez, "Critical Race Theory, the New Intolerance, and Its Grip on America."

44 Ozlem Sensoy and Robin DiAngelo, *Is Everyone Really Equal?* (New York: Teachers College Press, 2017), xii.

45 Ibid., vii.

46 Ibid., xxi, xxii, xxiii, xxiv.

47 Ibid., xxiv.

48 "Critical Race Training In Education," Legal Insurrection Foundation, https://criticalrace.org/ (April 9, 2021).

49 Krystina Skurk, "Critical Race Theory in K–12 Education," RealClear-

PublicAffairs, July 12, 2020, https://www.realclearpublicaffairs.com/articles/2020/07/16/critical_race_theory_in_k-12_education_498969.html (April 9, 2021).

50 Ibid.

51 Ibid.

52 Peter W. Wood, *1620: A Critical Response to the 1619 Project* (New York: Encounter Books, 2020), 1 (quoting Jake Silverstein, *New York Times Magazine*).

53 Ibid., 4.

54 Ibid., 5.

55 Ibid., 6.

56 "We Respond to the Historians Who Critiqued the 1619 Project," *New York Times Magazine*, December 20, 2019, https://www.nytimes.com/2019/12/20/magazine/we-respond-to-the-historians-who-critiqued-the-1619-project.html (April 9, 2021).

57 Ibid.

58 Ibid.

59 Ibid.

60 Adam Serwer, "The Fight Over the 1619 Project Is Not About Facts," *Atlantic*, December 23, 2019, https://www.theatlantic.com/ideas/archive/2019/12/historians-clash-1619-project/604093/ (April 9, 2021).

61 Mark R. Levin, *Unfreedom of the Press* (New York: Threshold Editions, 2019), chapter 6.

62 Glenn Garvin, "Fidel's Favorite Propagandist," *Reason*, March 2007, https://reason.com/2007/02/28/fidels-favorite-propagandist/ (April 9, 2021).

63 Zach Goldberg, "How the Media Led the Great Racial Awakening," *Tablet*, August 4, 2020, https://www.tabletmag.com/sections/news/articles/media-great-racial-awakening (April 9, 2021).

64 Ibid.

65 Ibid.

66 Ibid.

67 Ibid.

68 Executive Order 13950, "Combating Race and Sex Stereotyping," September 22, 2020, https://www.federalregister.gov/documents/2020/09/28/2020-21534/combating-race-and-sex-stereotyping (April 9, 2021).

69 Ibid.

70 Ibid.

71 "Executive Order on Advancing Racial Equity and Support for Underserved Communities Through the Federal Government," January 20, 2021, https://www.whitehouse.gov/briefing-room/presidential-actions/2021/01/20/executive-order-advancing-racial-equity-and-support-for-underserved-communities-through-the-federal-government/ (April 9, 2021).

72 Bradford Betz, "What is China's social credit system?" Fox News, May 4, 2020, https://www.foxnews.com/world/what-is-china-social-credit-system (April 9, 2021).

73 Ibid.

74 President's Advisory 1776 Commission, "The 1776 Report," January 2021, https://ipfs.io/ipfs/QmVzW5NfySnfTk7ucdEoWXshkNUXn3dseBA7ZVrQMBfZey (April 9, 2021).

75 Ibid.

76 MSNBC, January 19, 2021.

77 Delgado and Stefancic, *Critical Race Theory*, 154, 155.

78 Patrisse Cullors, "Trained Marxist Patrisse Cullors, Black Lives Matter BLM," YouTube, June 2020, https://www.youtube.com/watch?v=1noLh25FbKI (April 9, 2021).

79 https://www.dailywire.com/news/fraud-blm-co-founder-patrisse-cullors-blasted-over-real-estate-buying-binge.

80 Mike Gonzalez, "To Destroy America," *City Journal*, September 1, 2020, https://www.city-journal.org/marxist-revolutionaries-black-lives-matter (April 9, 2021).

81 Ibid.

82 Scott Walter, "A Terrorist's Ties to a Leading Black Lives Matter Group," Capital Research Center, June 24, 2020, https://capitalresearch.org/article/a-terrorists-ties-to-a-leading-black-lives-matter-group/ (April 9, 2021).

83 Gonzalez, "To Destroy America."

84 Laura Lambert, "Weather Underground," *Encyclopaedia Britannica*, https://www.britannica.com/topic/Weathermen (April 9, 2021).

85 "Celebrating four years of organizing to protect black lives," *Black Lives Matter*, 2013, https://drive.google.com/file/d/0B0pJEXffvS0uOHdJREJnZ2JJYTA/view (April 9, 2021).

86 Karl Marx, *Manifesto of the Communist Party* (Marxists.org), https://www.marxists.org/archive/marx/works/1848/communist-manifesto/ch02.htm (April 9, 2021), chapter 2.

87 Lindsay Perez Huber, "Using Latina/o Critical Race Theory (LATCRIT) and Racist Nativism to Explore Intersectionality in the Education Experiences of Undocumented Chicana College Students," *Educational Foun-*

dations, Winter–Spring 2010, https://files.eric.ed.gov/fulltext/EJ885982.pdf (April 9, 2021), 77, 78, 79.

88 Ibid., 79, 80.

89 Ibid., 80, 81.

90 Jean Stefancic, "Latino and Latina Critical Theory: An Annotated Bibliography," *California Law Review*, 1997, 423.

91 Rodolfo F. Acuna, *Occupied America: A History of Chicanos* (New York: Pearson, 1972), 1.

92 Abby Budiman, "Key findings about U.S. immigrants," Pew Research Center, August 20, 2020, https://www.pewresearch.org/fact-tank/2020/08/20/key-findings-about-u-s-immigrants/ (April 9, 2021).

93 Ricardo Castro-Salazar and Carl Bagley, *Navigating Borders: Critical Race Theory Research and Counter History of Undocumented Americans* (New York: Peter Lang, 2012), 4.

94 Ibid., 5.

95 Ibid., 27.

96 Ibid., 26, 27.

97 Ibid., 27.

98 Ibid., 37.

99 Robert Law, "Biden's Executive Actions: President Unilaterally Changes Immigration Policy," Center for Immigration Studies, March 15, 2021, https://cis.org/Report/Bidens-Executive-Actions-President-Unilaterally-Changes-Immigration-Policy (April 9, 2021).

100 Ashley Parker, Nick Miroff, Sean Sullivan, and Tyler Pager, " 'No end in sight': Inside the Biden administration's failure to contain the border surge," *Washington Post*, March 20, 2021, https://www.washingtonpost.com/politics/biden-border-surge/2021/03/20/21824e94-8818-11eb-8a8b-5cf82c3dffe4_story.html (April 9, 2021).

101 Ibid.

102 Ruth Igielnik and Abby Budiman, "The Changing Racial and Ethnic Composition of the U.S. Electorate," Pew Research Center, September 23, 2020, https://www.pewresearch.org/2020/09/23/the-changing-racial-and-ethnic-composition-of-the-u-s-electorate/ (April 9, 2021).

103 Jim Clifton, "42 Million Want to Migrate to U.S.," Gallup, March 24, 2021, https://news.gallup.com/opinion/chairman/341678/million-migrate.aspx (April 9, 2021).

104 Scott Yenor, "Sex, Gender, and the Origin of the Culture Wars," Heritage Foundation, June 30, 2017, https://www.heritage.org/gender/report/sex-gender-and-the-origin-the-culture-wars-intellectual-history (April 9, 2021).

105 Veronica Meade-Kelly, "Male or Female? It's not always so simple," UCLA, August 20, 2015, https://newsroom.ucla.edu/stories/male-or-female (April 9, 2021).

106 Kadia Goba, "He/she could be they in the new Congress," *Axios*, January 2, 2021, https://www.axios.com/congress-gender-identity-pronouns-rules-40a4ab56-9d5c-4dfc-ada3-4a683882967a.html (April 9, 2021).

107 Russell Goldman, "Here's a list of 58 gender options for Facebook users," ABC News, February 13, 2014, https://abcnews.go.com/blogs/headlines/2014/02/heres-a-list-of-58-gender-options-for-facebook-users/ (April 9, 2021).

108 "Executive Order on Preventing and Combating Discrimination on the Basis of Gender Identity or Sexual Orientation," White House, January 20, 2021, https://www.whitehouse.gov/briefing-room/presidential-actions/2021/01/20/executive-order-preventing-and-combating-discrimination-on-basis-of-gender-identity-or-sexual-orientation/ (April 9, 2021).

109 "Joe Biden's War on Women," *National Review*, January 25, 2021, https://www.nationalreview.com/2021/01/joe-bidens-war-on-women/ (April 9, 2021).

110 Ibid.

111 "Transgender Children & Youth: Understanding the Basics," Human Rights Campaign, https://www.hrc.org/resources/transgender-children-and-youth-understanding-the-basics (April 9, 2021).

112 Michelle Cretella, "I'm a Pediatrician. How Transgender Ideology Has Infiltrated My Field and Produced Large-Scale Child Abuse," *Daily Signal*, July 3, 2017, https://www.dailysignal.com/2017/07/03/im-pediatrician-transgender-ideology-infiltrated-field-produced-large-scale-child-abuse/ (April 9, 2021).

113 Ibid.

114 Christine Di Stefano, "Marxist Feminism," Wiley Online Library, September 15, 2014, https://onlinelibrary.wiley.com/doi/abs/10.1002/9781118474396.wbept0653 (April 9, 2021).

115 Sue Caldwell, "Marxism, feminism, and transgender politics," *International Socialism*, December 19, 2017, http://isj.org.uk/marxism-feminism-and-transgender-politics/ (April 9, 2021).

116 Ibid.

117 Natalie Jesionka, "Social Justice for toddlers: These new books and programs start the conversation early," *Washington Post*, March 18, 2021, https://www.washingtonpost.com/lifestyle/2021/03/18/social-justice-antiracist-books-toddlers-kids/ (April 9, 2021).

118 Ibid.

119 "Sexual Ideology Indoctrination: The Equality Act's Impact on School Curriculum and Parental Rights," Heritage Foundation, May 15, 2019, https://www.heritage.org/civil-society/report/sexual-ideology-indoctrination-the-equality-acts-impact-school-curriculum-and (April 9, 2021).

120 Ibid.

121 Ibid.

CHAPTER FIVE: "CLIMATE CHANGE" FANATICISM

1 George Reisman, *Capitalism* (Ottawa, IL: Jameson Books, 1990), 19.

2 F. A. Hayek, *The Fatal Conceit: The Errors of Socialism* (Chicago: University of Chicago Press, 1988), 6, 7.

3 Milton Friedman, *Capitalism and Freedom* (Chicago: University of Chicago Press, 2002), 7, 8.

4 Ibid., 9.

5 Ibid., 10.

6 Reisman, 77.

7 Ibid.

8 Federico Demaria, Francois Schneider, Filka Sekulova, and Joan Martinez-Alier, "What Is Degrowth? From Activist Slogan to a Social Movement," *Environmental Values* 22, no. 1 (2013), 192.

9 Ibid., 194.

10 Ibid.

11 Mark R. Levin, *Plunder and Deceit* (New York: Threshold Editions, 2015), 112; Demaria, Schneider, Sekulova, and Martinez-Alier, "What is Degrowth?"

12 Mackenzie Mount, "Green Biz, Work Less to Live More," Sierra Club, March 6, 2014, https://contentdev.sierraclub.org/www/www/sierra/2014-2-march-april/green-biz/work-less-live-more (April 10, 2021).

13 "Serge Latouche," famouseconomists.net, https://www.famouseconomists.net/serge-latouche (April 10, 2021).

14 Serge Latouche, *Farewell to Growth* (Cambridge: Polity Press, 2009), 89.

15 Ibid., 90–91.

16 Ibid., 31, 32.

17 George A. Gonzalez, "Urban Sprawl, Climate Change, Oil Depletion, and Eco-Marxism," in *Political Theory and Global Climate Change*, ed. Steve Vanderheiden (Cambridge, MA: MIT Press, 2008), 153.

18 Ibid.

19 Giorgos Kallis, *In Defense of Degrowth: Opinions and Minifestos* (Brussels: Uneven Earth Press, 2017), 10.

20 Ibid., 12.

21 Ibid., 13, 14.

22 Ibid., 71.

23 Ibid., 72.

24 Ayn Rand, *Return of the Primitive: The Anti-Industrial Revolution* (New York: Meridian, 1998), 280, 281.

25 Ibid., 282.

26 Ibid., 285.

27 Ibid.

28 Timothy W. Luke, "Climatologies as Social Critique: The Social Construction/Creation of Global Warming, Global Dimming, and Global Cooling," in *Political Theory and Global Climate Change*, ed. Steve Vanderheiden (Cambridge, MA: MIT Press, 2008), 128.

29 Ibid., 145.

30 Rand, *Return of the Primitive*, 277.

31 Ibid., 278.

32 Luke, "Climatologies as Social Critique," 145.

33 Karl Marx and Friedrich Engels, *The Communist Manifesto* (London: Soho Books, 2010) 21.

34 Rand, *Return of the Primitive*, 285, 286.

35 David Naguib Pellow, *What Is Critical Environmental Justice?* (Cambridge, U.K.: Polity Press, 2018), 4.

36 Ibid., 4, 5.

37 Ibid., 18.

38 Ibid., 18–19.

39 Ibid., 22.

40 Ibid., 23.

41 "Declaration of Independence: A Transcription," https://www.archives.gov/founding-docs/declaration-transcript (April 10, 2021).

42 Pellow, *What Is Critical Environmental Justice?*, 26, 30.

43 Ibid., 30, 31.

44 "The Margarita Declaration on Climate Change," July 15–18, 2014, https://redd-monitor.org/2014/08/08/the-margarita-declaration-on-climate-change-we-reject-the-implementation-of-false-solutions-to-climate-change-such-as-carbon-markets-and-other-forms-of-privatization-and-commodification-of-life/ (April 10, 2021).

45 Hayek, *The Fatal Conceit*, 8.

46 "The Margarita Declaration on Climate Change."
47 Thomas Sowell, *The Quest for Cosmic Justice* (New York: Touchstone, 1999), 99.
48 Ibid., 131, 132.
49 "The Margarita Declaration on Climate Change."
50 Ibid.
51 Reisman, *Capitalism*, 63.
52 Ibid., 65.
53 Ibid.
54 Ibid., 71.
55 Ibid.
56 "There is no climate emergency," Letter to United Nations Secretary General, September 23, 2019, https://clintel.nl/wp-content/uploads/2019/09/ecd-letter-to-un.pdf (April 10, 2021).
57 Ibid.
58 Ibid.
59 Ian Pilmer, "The Science and Politics of Climate Change," in *Climate Change: The Facts*, ed. Alan Moran (Woodsville, NH: Stockade Books, 2015), 10, 11.
60 Ibid., 21.
61 Ibid., 24, 25.
62 Patrick J. Michaels, "Why climate models are failing," in *Climate Change: The Facts*, 27.
63 Richard S. Lindzen, "Global warming, models and language," in *Climate Change: The Facts*, 38.
64 Robert M. Carter, "The scientific context," in *Climate Change: The Facts*, 81.
65 Ibid., 82.
66 H. Res. 109, 116th Cong. (2019–2020), https://www.congress.gov/bill/116th-congress/house-resolution/109 (April 10, 2021).
67 Milton Ezrati, "The Green New Deal and the Cost of Virtue," *Forbes*, February 2, 2019, https://www.forbes.com/sites/miltonezrati/2019/02/19/the-green-new-deal-and-the-cost-of-virtue/?sh=6fe12ccd3dec (April 10, 2021).
68 Ibid.
69 Ibid.
70 Ibid.
71 Kevin Dayaratna and Nicolas Loris, "A Glimpse of What the Green New Deal Would Cost Taxpayers," *Daily Signal*, March 25, 2019, https://

www.dailysignal.com/2019/03/25/a-glimpse-of-what-the-green-new-deal-would-cost-taxpayers/ (April 10, 2021).

72 Douglas Holtz-Eakin, Dan Bosch, Ben Gitis, Dan Goldbeck, and Philip Rossetti, "The Green New Deal: Scope, Scale, and Implications," American Action Forum, February 25, 2019, https://www.americanactionforum.org/research/the-green-new-deal-scope-scale-and-implications/ (April 10, 2021).

73 "Paris Agreement," November 2015, https://unfccc.int/files/meetings/paris_nov_2015/application/pdf/paris_agreement_english_.pdf (April 10, 2021).

74 "U.S. Declares China committing 'genocide' against Uighurs," Associated Foreign Press, January 19, 2021, https://www.msn.com/en-au/news/world/us-declares-china-committing-genocide-against-uighurs/ar-BB1cTEIz (April 10, 2021).

75 Ibid.

76 Barbara Boland, "Biden: China's Genocide of Uighurs Just Different Norms," *American Conservative*, February 28, 2021, https://www.theamericanconservative.com/state-of-the-union/biden-chinas-genocide-of-uighurs-just-different-norms/ (April 10, 2021).

77 Brian Zinchuk, "This is the executive order killing Keystone XL, citing the reasons why Biden did it," *Toronto Star*, January 20, 2021, https://www.thestar.com/news/canada/2021/01/20/this-is-the-executive-order-killing-keystone-xl-citing-the-reasons-why-biden-did-it.html (April 10, 2021).

78 "Fact Sheet: President Biden Takes Executive Actions to Tackle the Climate Crisis at Home and Abroad, Create Jobs, and Restore Scientific Integrity Across Federal Government," White House, January 27, 2021, https://www.whitehouse.gov/briefing-room/statements-releases/2021/01/27/fact-sheet-president-biden-takes-executive-actions-to-tackle-the-climate-crisis-at-home-and-abroad-create-jobs-and-restore-scientific-integrity-across-federal-government/ (April 10, 2021).

79 Megan Henney, "Progressives pressure Biden to pass $10T green infrastructure, climate justice bill," FoxBusiness, March 30, 2021, https://www.foxbusiness.com/economy/progressives-pressure-biden-green-infrastructure-climate-justice-bill (April 10, 2021).

80 "Pork wrapped in a stimulus," *Washington Times*, March 9, 2021, https://www.washingtontimes.com/news/2021/mar/9/editorial-democrats-coronavirus-stimulus-91-percen/ (April 10, 2021).

81 Brad Polumbo, "9 Crazy Examples of Unrelated Waste and Partisan Spending in Biden's $2 Trillion 'Infrastructure' Proposal," Foundation for Economic Education, March 31, 2021, https://fee.org/articles/9-crazy-examples-of-unrelated-waste-and-partisan-spending-in-biden-s-2t-infrastructure-proposal/ (April 10, 2021).

82 Katelyn Caralle, "AOC leads left's claim $2 trillion infrastructure bill is NOT enough," *Daily Mail*, March 31, 2021, https://www.msn.com/en-us/news/politics/aoc-leads-lefts-claim-dollar2-trillion-infrastructure-bill-is-not-enough/ar-BB1far2x (April 10, 2021).

83 "Recognizing the duty of the Federal Government to implement an agenda to Transform, Heal, and Renew by Investing in a Vibrant Economy ('THRIVE')," S. Res.____, MUR21083, https://www.markey.senate.gov/imo/media/doc/(2.8.2021)%20THRIVE.pdf (April 10, 2021).

84 Collin Anderson, "Progressives Push Biden to Include $10 Trillion Climate Plan in Infrastructure Package," *Washington Free Beacon*, March 31, 2021, https://freebeacon.com/policy/progressives-push-biden-to-include-10-trillion-climate-plan-in-infrastructure-package/ (April 10, 2021).

85 Michael Shellenberger, "Why California's Climate Policies Are Causing Electricity Blackouts," *Forbes*, August 15, 2020, https://www.forbes.com/sites/michaelshellenberger/2020/08/15/why-californias-climate-policies-are-causing-electricity-black-outs/?sh=43991d831591 (April 10, 2021).

86 Ibid.

87 "Understanding the Texas Energy Predicament," Institute for Energy Research, February 18, 2021, https://www.instituteforenergyresearch.org/the-grid/understanding-the-texas-energy-predicament/ (April 10, 2021).

88 Ibid.

89 Ibid.

90 Benji Jones, "The Biden administration has a game-changing approach to nature conservation," *Vox*, May 7, 2021, https://www.vox.com/2021/5/7/22423139/biden-30-by-30-conservation-initiative-historic.

91 Mark R. Levin, *Plunder and Deceit* (New York: Threshold Editions, 2015), 111.

CHAPTER SIX: PROPAGANDA, CENSORSHIP, AND SUBVERSION

1 "Marx the Journalist, an Interview with James Ledbetter," *Jacobin*, May 5, 2018, https://www.jacobinmag.com/2018/05/karl-marx-journalism-writings-newspaper (April 11, 2021).

2 Ibid.

3 Ibid.
4 Ibid.
5 Ibid.
6 Richard M. Weaver, *Ideas Have Consequences* (Chicago: University of Chicago, 1948), 87–88.
7 Ibid., 88.
8 Ibid., 88, 89.
9 Ibid., 89–90.
10 Ibid., 101.
11 Edward Bernays, *Propaganda* (Brooklyn: IG, 1928), 52, 53.
12 Ibid., 47–48.
13 Richard Gunderman, "The manipulation of the American mind—Edward Bernays and the birth of public relations," Phys.org, July 9, 2015, https://phys.org/news/2015-07-american-mindedward-bernays-birth.html (April 11, 2021).
14 Harold Dwight Lasswell, *Propaganda Technique in the World War* (Boston: MIT Press, 1927), 221.
15 Hannah Arendt, *The Origins of Totalitarianism* (Orlando: Harcourt, 1968), 352.
16 Ibid., 353.
17 Mark R. Levin, *Ameritopia* (New York: Threshold Editions, 2012), 7, 8.
18 Daniel J. Boorstin, *The Image: A Guide to Pseudo-Events in America* (New York: Vintage Books, 1961), 35.
19 Ibid.
20 Ibid.
21 Ibid., 37.
22 Ibid.
23 Ibid., 182, 183.
24 John Dewey, *Liberalism and Social Action* (Amherst, NY: Prometheus Books, 1935), 65–66.
25 Ibid., 66.
26 Michael Schudson, "What Public Journalism Knows about Journalism but Doesn't Know about 'Public,' " in *The Idea of Public Journalism*, ed. Theodore L. Glasser (New York: Guilford Press, 1999), 123.
27 Theodore Glasser, "The Ethics of Election Coverage," *Stanford Magazine*, October 2016, https://stanfordmag.org/contents/the-ethics-of-election-coverage (April 11, 2021).
28 Ibid.
29 Davis "Buzz" Merritt, *Public Journalism and Public Life: Why Telling the News Is Not Enough* (New York: Routledge, 1998), 96, 97.

30 Davis Merritt, "Stop Trump? But who will bell the cat?" *Wichita Eagle*, December 8, 2018, https://www.kansas.com/opinion/opn-columns-blogs/article48524730.html (April 11, 2021).
31 Ibid.
32 Merritt, *Public Journalism and Public Life*, 7.
33 Jay Rosen, *What Are Journalists For?* (New Haven, CT: Yale University Press, 1999), 20.
34 Ibid., 19–20.
35 Jay Rosen, "Donald Trump Is Crashing the System. Journalism Needs to Build a New One," *Washington Post*, July 13, 2016, https://www.washingtonpost.com/news/in-theory/wp/2016/07/13/donald-trump-is-crashing-the-system-journalists-need-to-build-a-new-one/ (April 11, 2021).
36 Ibid.
37 Martin Linsky, "What Are Journalists For?" *American Prospect*, November 14, 2001, https://prospect.org/features/journalists-for/ (April 11, 2021).
38 "Marx the Journalist, an Interview with James Ledbetter," *Jacobin*, May 5, 2018, https://www.jacobinmag.com/2018/05/karl-marx-journalism-writings-newspaper (April 11, 2021).
39 Saul D. Alinsky, *Rules for Radicals: A Pragmatic Primer for Realistic Radicals* (New York: Vintage Books, 1971), xxii, xxiii.
40 Ibid., 130, 131, 133.
41 Chuck Todd, *Meet the Press*, December 30, 2018, https://www.nbcnews.com/meet-the-press/meet-press-december-30-2018-n951406 (April 11, 2021).
42 "Global Warming," mrcNewsBusters, https://www.newsbusters.org/issues-events-groups/global-warming (April 11, 2021).
43 Zach Goldberg, "How the Media Led the Great Racial Awakening," *Tablet*, August 4, 2020, https://www.tabletmag.com/sections/news/articles/media-great-racial-awakening (April 11, 2021).
44 Ibid.
45 Ibid.
46 Ibid.
47 Ted Johnson, "CNN Announces Expansion of Team Covering Race Beat," *Deadline*, July 13, 2020, https://deadline.com/2020/07/cnn-jeff-zucker-race-beat-1202984234/ (April 11, 2021).
48 Martin Luther King Jr., "I Have a Dream," 1963, *Encyclopaedia Britannica*, https://www.britannica.com/topic/I-Have-A-Dream (April 11, 2021).
49 Robert Henderson, "Tell Only Lies," *City Journal*, December 27, 2020, https://www.city-journal.org/self-censorship (April 11, 2021).

50 Ibid.

51 Ibid.

52 Ibid.

53 Eric Kaufmann, "Academic Freedom in Crisis: Punishment, Political Discrimination, and Self-Censorship," Center for the Study of Partisanship and Ideology, March 1, 2021, https://cspicenter.org/wp-content/uploads/2021/03/AcademicFreedom.pdf (April 11, 2021).

54 Kelsey Ann Naughton, "Speaking Freely: What Students Think about Expression at American Colleges," Foundation for Individual Rights in Education, October 2017, https://d28htnjz2elwuj.cloudfront.net/wp-content/uploads/2017/10/11091747/survey-2017-speaking-freely.pdf (April 11, 2021).

55 Diane Ravitch, *The Language Police: How Pressure Groups Restrict What Students Learn* (New York: Vintage, 2003), 3–4.

56 Ibid., 160.

57 Krystina Skurk, "Critical Race Theory in K–12 Education," RealClearPublicAffairs, https://www.realclearpublicaffairs.com/articles/2020/07/16/critical_race_theory_in_k-12_education_498969.html (April 11, 2021); Max Eden, "Critical Race Theory in American Classrooms," *City Journal*, September 18, 2020, https://www.city-journal.org/critical-race-theory-in-american-classrooms (April 11, 2021).

58 Todd Starnes, "Parents furious over school's plan to teach gender spectrum, fluidity," Fox News, May 15, 2015, https://www.foxnews.com/opinion/parents-furious-over-schools-plan-to-teach-gender-spectrum-fluidity (April 11, 2021).

59 Charles Fain Lehman, "American High Schools Go Woke," *Washington Free Beacon*, November 30, 2020, https://freebeacon.com/campus/american-high-schools-go-woke/ (April 11, 2021).

60 UN Climate Change Learning Platform, https://www.uncclearn.org/ (April 11, 2021).

61 Allison Graham, "Why Should Schools Teach Climate Education?" Medium.com, July 12, 2018, https://medium.com/uncclearn/why-should-schools-teach-climate-education-f1e101ebc56e (April 11, 2021).

62 Ibid.

63 Charles Gasparino, "How corporations surrendered to hard-left wokeness," *New York Post*, February 13, 2021, https://nypost.com/2021/02/13/how-corporations-surrendered-to-hard-left-wokeness/ (April 11, 2021).

64 Ibid.

65 Brooke Kato, "What is cancel culture? Everything to know about the toxic online trend," *New York Post*, March 10, 2021, https://nypost.com

/article/what-is-cancel-culture-breaking-down-the-toxic-online-trend/ (April 11, 2021).

66 "A Letter on Justice and Open Debate," *Harper's Magazine*, July 7, 2020, https://harpers.org/a-letter-on-justice-and-open-debate/ (April 11, 2021).

67 Heather Moon, "Top 10 Worst Cases of Big Tech Censorship in 2020," mrcNewsBusters, January 4, 2021, https://www.newsbusters.org/blogs/free-speech/heather-moon/2021/01/04/top-10-worst-cases-big-tech-censorship-2020 (April 11, 2021).

68 "FACEBOOK INSIDER LEAKS: Hours of Video of Zuckerberg & Execs Admitting They Have 'Too Much Power' . . . FB Wants to 'Work . . . with [Biden] on Some of Their Top Priorities' . . . 'Biden Issued a Number of Exec Orders . . . We as a Company Really Care Quite Deeply About,' " Project Veritas, January 31, 2021, https://www.projectveritas.com/news/facebook-insider-leaks-hours-of-video-of-zuckerberg-and-execs-admitting-they/ (April 11, 2021).

69 Ibid.

70 Allum Bokhari, "Exclusive: Unreleased Federal Report Concludes 'No Evidence' that Free Speech Online 'Causes Hate Crimes,' " Breitbart, March 3, 2021, citing "The Role of Information and Communication Technologies in Hate Crimes: An Update to the 1993 Report," U.S. Department of Commerce, https://www.slideshare.net/AllumBokhari/ntia-hate-crimes-report-january-2021/1 (April 11, 2021).

71 Ibid.

72 Emily Jacobs, "Democrats demand more censorship from Big Tech bosses," *New York Post*, November 18, 2020, https://nypost.com/2020/11/18/democrats-use-big-tech-hearings-to-demand-more-censorship/ (April 11, 2021).

73 "The War on Free Speech," *Pittsburgh Post-Gazette*, January 26, 2021, https://www.post-gazette.com/opinion/editorials/2021/01/26/The-war-on-free-speech-Parler-Social-Media-technology/stories/202101140041 (April 11, 2021).

74 Krystal Hur, "Big tech employees rally behind Biden campaign," Opensecrets.org, January 12, 2021, https://www.opensecrets.org/news/2021/01/big-tech-employees-rally-biden/ (April 11, 2021).

75 Ari Levy, "Here's the final tally of where tech billionaires donated for the 2020 election," CNBC, November 2, 2020, https://www.cnbc.com/2020/11/02/tech-billionaire-2020-election-donations-final-tally.html (April 11, 2021).

76 Chuck Ross, "Biden Has Ties to 5 Major Tech Companies," *Daily Caller*,

January 10, 2021, https://dailycaller.com/2021/01/10/biden-big-tech-apple-facebook-trump-parler/ (April 11, 2021).

77 Ryan Lizza, Daniel Lippman, and Meridith McGraw, "AOC wants to cancel those who worked for Trump. Good luck with that, they say," *Politico*, November 9, 2020, https://www.politico.com/news/2020/11/09/aoc-cancel-worked-for-trump-435293 (April 11, 2021).

78 Representatives Anna G. Eshoo and Jerry McNerney, "February 22, 2021 Letter to Mr. John T. Stankey," https://mcnerney.house.gov/sites/mcnerney.house.gov/files/McNerney-Eshoo%20TV%20Misinfo%20Letters%20-%202.22.21.pdf (April 11, 2021).

79 Andrew Kerr, "Media Matters Study on Fox News 'Misinformation' Is Riddled with Misrepresentations, Flagged Objectively True Statements," *Daily Caller*, February 22, 2021, https://dailycaller.com/2021/02/22/media-matters-fox-news-disinformation/ (April 11, 2021).

80 Eshoo and McNerney, "February 22, 2021 Letter to Mr. John T. Stankey."

81 Tom Elliot, "Now CNN's @oliverdarcy is going after cable companies for carrying Fox News," Twitter, January 8, 2021 (screenshot of @oliverdarcy), https://twitter.com/tomselliott/status/1347465189252341764?lang=en (April 11, 2021).

82 Ibid.

83 Alinsky, *Rules for Radicals*, 130.

84 Nicholas Kristoff, "Can We Put Fox News on Trial with Trump?" *New York Times*, February 10, 2021, https://www.nytimes.com/2021/02/10/opinion/fox-news-accountability.html (April 11, 2021).

85 Ibid.

86 Ibid.

87 Ibid.

88 Harry Hodgkinson, *Double Talk: The Language of Communism* (London: George Allen & Unwin, 1955), v, vi.

89 Ibid., 44

90 Ibid., 122.

CHAPTER SEVEN: *WE CHOOSE LIBERTY!*

1 J. Christian Adams, "Read the Shocking Pentagon Training Materials Targeting Conservatives in the Military," PJ Media, March 22, 2021, https://pjmedia.com/jchristianadams/2021/03/22/read-the-pentagon-training-materials-targeting-conservatives-in-the-military-n1434071 (April 22, 2021); "Reversing Trump, Pentagon to release new transgen-

der policy," Associated Press, March 31, 2021, https://www.foxnews.com/us/reversing-trump-pentagon-new-transgender-policy (April 22, 2021).

2 Charles Creitz, "Rep. Waltz slams West Point 'White rage' instruction: Enemy's ammo 'doesn't care about race, politics,' " Fox News, April 8, 2021, https://www.foxnews.com/politics/rep-michael-waltz-slams-west-point-white-rage-instruction-enemys-ammo-doesnt-care-about-race-politics (April 22, 2021).

3 Aaron Mehta, "Climate change is now a national security priority for the Pentagon," *DefenseNews*, January 27, 2021, https://www.defensenews.com/pentagon/2021/01/27/climate-change-is-now-a-national-security-priority-for-the-pentagon/ (April 22, 2021).

4 "Facts and Figures," National Law Enforcement Officers Memorial Fund, https://nleomf.org/facts-figures (April 22, 2021).

5 Jeffrey James Higgins, "Enough of the lying—just look at the data. There's no epidemic of racist police officers killing black Americans," *Law Enforcement Today*, June 26, 2020, https://www.lawenforcementtoday.com/systematic-racism-in-policing-its-time-to-stop-the-lying/ (April 22, 2021).

6 Victor Davis Hanson, "Obama: Transforming America," RealClearPolitics, October 1, 2013, https://www.realclearpolitics.com/articles/2013/10/01/obama_transforming_america_120170.html (April 22, 2021).

7 "Less Policing = More Murders," Law Enforcement Legal Defense Fund, http://www.policedefense.org/wp-content/uploads/2021/04/Depolicing_April14.pdf (April 22, 2021).

8 George Thomas, "Demoralized and Demonized: Police Departments Face 'Workforce Crisis' as Officers Leave in Droves," CBN News, September 9, 2020, https://www1.cbn.com/cbnnews/us/2020/september/demoralized-and-demonized-police-departments-face-workforce-crisis-as-officers-leave-in-droves (April 22, 2021).

9 Jack Kelly, "Cities Will See Citizens Flee, Fearing Continued Riots and the Reemergence of Covid-19," *Forbes*, June 2, 2020, https://www.forbes.com/sites/jackkelly/2020/06/02/cities-will-see-citizens-flee-fearing-continued-riots-and-the-reemergence-of-covid-19/?sh=627a0593d30d (April 22, 2021).

10 Dave Huber, "National Education Association reps show support for abortion, 'white fragility,' " College Fix, July 13, 2019, https://www.thecollegefix.com/national-education-association-reps-show-support-for-abortion-white-fragility/ (April 22, 2021).

11 Ashley S. Boyd and Janine J. Darragh, "Teaching for Social Justice: Using

All American Boys to Confront Racism and Police Brutality," American Federation of Teachers, Spring 2021, https://www.aft.org/ae/spring2021/boyd_darragh (April 22, 2021).

12 Jonathan Butcher and Mike Gonzalez, "Critical Race Theory, the New Intolerance, and Its Grip on America," Heritage Foundation, December 7, 2020, https://www.heritage.org/sites/default/files/2020-12/BG3567.pdf (April 22, 2021), 15.

13 Ibid., 16.

14 Ibid., 18.

15 Jackson Elliott, "Parents too afraid to oppose critical race theory in schools, says activist," *Christian Post*, January 25, 2021, https://www.christianpost.com/news/parents-too-afraid-to-oppose-crt-in-schools-says-activist.html (April 22, 2021).

16 Jay Schalin, "The Politicization of University Schools of Education: The Long March through the Education Schools," James G. Marin Center for Academic Renewal, February 2019, https://files.eric.ed.gov/fulltext/ED594180.pdf (April 22, 2021), 1.

17 Ibid., 94.

18 Lily Zheng, "We're Entering the Age of Corporate Social Justice," *Harvard Business Review*, June 15, 2020, https://hbr.org/2020/06/were-entering-the-age-of-corporate-social-justice (April 22, 2021).

19 Dan McLaughlin, "The Party in Power Is Directing a Corporate Conspiracy against Its Political Opposition," *National Review*, April 13, 2021, https://www.nationalreview.com/2021/04/the-party-in-power-is-directing-a-corporate-conspiracy-against-its-political-opposition/ (April 22, 2021).

20 Zachary Evans, "Amazon, Google Join Hundreds of American Corporations in Signing Letter Opposing Voting Limits," *National Review*, April 14, 2021, https://www.nationalreview.com/news/amazon-google-join-hundreds-of-american-corporations-in-signing-letter-opposing-voting-limits/ (April 22, 2021).

21 Phill Kline, "How Mark Zuckerberg's $350 million threatens democracy," *Washington Examiner*, October 21, 2020, https://www.msn.com/en-us/news/politics/how-mark-zuckerbergs-dollar350-million-threatens-democracy/ar-BB1afARG (April 22, 2021); J. Christian Adams, "The Real Kraken: What Really Happened to Donald Trump in the 2020 Election," PJ Media, December 2, 2020, https://pjmedia.com/jchristianadams/2020/12/02/the-real-kraken-what-really-happened-to-donald-trump-in-the-2020-election-n1185494 (April 22, 2021).

22 Mark R. Levin, *Liberty and Tyranny* (New York: Threshold Editions, 2009), 195.

23 Thomas Paine, *The American Crisis*, ed. Steve Straub, The Federalist Papers Project, https://thefederalistpapers.org/wp-content/uploads/2013/08/The-American-Crisis-by-Thomas-Paine-.pdf (April 22, 2021) 5.

24 Ibid., 8.

25 Saul D. Alinsky, *Rules for Radicals: A Pragmatic Primer for Realistic Radicals* (New York: Vintage Books, 1971), 130.

26 Ibid., 131.

27 Sam Dorman, "Nevada charter school's students were instructed to link aspects of their identity with oppression: Lawsuit," Fox News, December 23, 2020, https://www.foxnews.com/us/lawsuit-nevada-race-christianity-william-clark (April 22, 2021); Chris F. Rufo, tweet, January 20, 2021, https://twitter.com/realchrisrufo/status/1352033792458776578?lang=en (April 22, 2021).

28 Jeff Archer, "Complaints Point Up 'Murky' Areas in Union Activism," *Education Week*, November 1, 2000, https://www.edweek.org/teaching-learning/complaints-point-up-murky-areas-in-union-activism/2000/11 (April 25, 2021); Dave Kendrick, "Landmark Sues Fla., N.J. Unions for Tax Violations," National Legal and Policy Center, January 17, 2005, https://nlpc.org/2005/01/17/landmark-sues-fla-nj-unions-tax-violations/ (April 25, 2021).

29 John M. Ellis, *The Breakdown of Higher Education* (New York: Encounter Books, 2020), 30, 31.

30 Mark R. Levin, *Plunder and Deceit* (New York: Threshold Editions, 2015), 87, 88.

31 Alana Mastrangelo, "Top 10 Craziest Attacks on Campus Conservatives of 2019," Breitbart, January 1, 2020, https://www.breitbart.com/tech/2020/01/01/top-10-craziest-attacks-on-campus-conservatives-of-2019/ (April 22, 2021).

32 Spencer Brown, "Conservative Voices Once Again Excluded from Commencement Season," Young America's Foundation, June 16, 2020, https://www.yaf.org/news/conservative-voices-once-again-excluded-from-commencement-season/ (April 22, 2021).

33 Anya Kamenetz and Eric Westervelt, "Fact-Check: Bernie Sanders Promises Free College. Will It Work?" NPR, February 17, 2016, https://www.npr.org/sections/ed/2016/02/17/466730455/fact-check-bernie-sanders-promises-free-college-will-it-work (April 22, 2021).

34 Lilah Burke, "A Big Budget from Biden," *Inside Higher Education*, April 12, 2021, https://www.insidehighered.com/news/2021/04/12/bidens-proposed-budget-increases-funding-pell-hbcus-research (April 22, 2021).

35 Stuart Shepard and James Agresti, "Government Spending on Education

Is Higher than Ever. And for What?" Foundation for Economic Education, March 1, 2018, https://fee.org/articles/government-spending-on-education-is-higher-than-ever-and-for-what/ (April 22, 2021).

36 Winfield Myers, "Time to End Hostile Powers' Influence Operations at American Universities," *American Spectator*, February 16, 2021, https://spectator.org/confucius-institute-foreign-influence-american-universities/ (April 22, 2021).

37 Christian Nunley, "Senate approves bill to tighten controls on China-funded Confucius Institutes on U.S. university campuses," CNBC, March 5, 2021, https://www.cnbc.com/2021/03/05/us-senate-approves-bill-against-china-funded-confucius-institutes.html (April 22, 2021).

38 Ayn Rand, *Return of the Primitive: The Anti-Industrial Revolution* (London: Meridian, 1970), 283.

39 Aaron Morrison, "AP Exclusive: Black Lives Matter opens up about its finances," Associated Press, February 23, 2021, https://apnews.com/article/black-lives-matter-90-million-finances-8a80cad199f54c0c4b9e74283d27366f (April 22, 2021).

40 Wendell Husebo, "200 Companies Oppose Voter ID Laws—Many Require IDs for Use of Service," Breitbart, April 5, 2021, https://www.breitbart.com/politics/2021/04/05/200-companies-oppose-voter-id-laws-many-require-ids-for-use-of-service/ (April 22, 2021).

41 Joanna Williams, "The racism racket: Diversity training in the workplace and beyond is worse than useless," Spiked, April 9, 2021, https://www.spiked-online.com/2021/04/09/the-racism-racket/ (April 22, 2021).

42 Megan Fox, "Trump Bans Companies That Use 'Critical Race Theory' from Getting Govt. Contracts," PJ Media, September 23, 2020, https://pjmedia.com/news-and-politics/megan-fox/2020/09/23/trump-bans-companies-that-use-critical-race-theory-from-getting-govt-contracts-n958223 (April 22, 2021).

43 Lachlan Markay, "Republican leaders raked in sizable donations from grassroots supporters," *Axios*, April 18, 2021, https://news.yahoo.com/republican-leaders-raked-sizable-donations-210114067.html (April 22, 2021); Alex Gangitano, "Tom Cotton: Chamber of Commerce is 'a front service for woke corporations,' " *Hill*, March 16, 2021, https://www.msn.com/en-us/news/politics/tom-cotton-chamber-of-commerce-is-a-front-service-for-woke-corporations/ar-BB1eEhPz (April 22, 2021).

44 Neil Munro, "New York Times: Wall Street Backs Joe Biden," Breitbart, August 9, 2020, https://www.breitbart.com/2020-election/2020/08/09/new-york-times-wall-street-backs-joe-biden/ (April 22, 2021).

45 Chuck Ross, "Biden Has Ties to 5 Major Tech Companies," *Daily Caller*, January 10, 2021, https://dailycaller.com/2021/01/10/biden-big-tech-apple-facebook-trump-parler/ (April 22, 2021).

46 Michael Bloomberg, "US CEOs sign statement against 'discriminatory' voting laws," AFP, April 14, 2021, https://www.yahoo.com/lifestyle/us-ceos-sign-statement-against-145620338.html (April 25, 2021); Sophie Mann, "CEOs answer the call of the woke by pivoting to 'stakeholder' capitalism," *Just the News*, April 24, 2021, https://justthenews.com/politics-policy/finance/hold-ceos-answer-call-woke-changing-their-goals-and-pivoting-stakeholder (April 25, 2021).

47 "Here Are the Fortune 500 Companies Doing Business in Xinjiang," ChinaFile, October 2, 2018, https://www.chinafile.com/reporting-opinion/features/here-are-fortune-500-companies-doing-business-xinjiang (April 25, 2021).

48 Tom Mitchell, Thomas Hale, and Hudson Lockett, "Beijing and Wall Street deepen ties despite geopolitical rivalry," *Financial Times*, October 26, 2020, https://www.ft.com/content/8cf19144-b493-4a3e-9308-183bbcc6e76e (April 25, 2021).

49 Houston Keene, "Companies ripping Georgia do business in China, silent on human rights violations," Fox Business, April 1, 2021, https://www.foxbusiness.com/politics/georgia-bill-criticized-delta-apple-coca-cola-silent-china-uyghur-genocide (April 25, 2021).

50 Saphora Smith, "China forcefully harvests organs from detainees, tribunal concludes," NBC News, June 18, 2019, https://www.nbcnews.com/news/world/china-forcefully-harvests-organs-detainees-tribunal-concludes-n1018646 (April 25, 2021).

51 Emma Graham-Harrison, "China has built 380 internment camps in Xinjiang, study finds," *Guardian*, September 23, 2020, https://www.theguardian.com/world/2020/sep/24/china-has-built-380-internment-camps-in-xinjiang-study-finds (April 25, 2021).

52 Alex Winter, "LIVING HELL: China has locked up 8 MILLION people in terrifying 're-education' camps in last six years, leaked docs reveal," *U.S. Sun*, September 18, 2020, https://www.the-sun.com/news/us-news/1495061/china-document-8-million-training-detention-camps/ (April 25, 2021).

53 "Church leaders seek Home Depot boycott on Georgia voting law," *Canadian Press*, April 21, 2021, https://www.msn.com/en-ca/money/topstories/church-leaders-seek-home-depot-boycott-on-georgia-voting-law/ar-BB1fRzT0 (April 25, 2021).

54 Evie Fordham, "Goya 'buy-cott' begins as customers load up on product

after Trump backlash," Fox Business, July 12, 2020, https://www.foxbusiness.com/markets/goya-food-sales-trump-controversy (April 25, 2021).

55 Mann, "CEOs answer the call of the woke by pivoting to 'stakeholder' capitalism."

56 John Binder, "Wall Street, Corporations Team Up with Soros-Funded Group to Pressure States Against Election Reforms," Breitbart, April 13, 2021, https://www.breitbart.com/politics/2021/04/13/wall-street-corporations-team-up-with-soros-funded-group-to-pressure-states-against-election-reforms/ (April 25, 2021).

57 David Aaro, "Ron DeSantis pushes bill aimed to take power away from Big Tech," Fox News, February 16, 2021, https://www.foxnews.com/tech/desantis-pushes-bill-to-aimed-to-take-power-away-from-big-tech (April 25, 2021).

58 Rachel Bovard, "Section 230 protects Big Tech from lawsuits. But it was never supposed to be bulletproof," *USA Today*, December 13, 2020, https://www.usatoday.com/story/opinion/2020/12/13/section-230-big-tech-free-speech-donald-trump-column/3883191001/ (April 25, 2021).

59 Ibid.

60 John Solomon, "Zuckerberg money used to pay election judges, grow vote in Democrat stronghold, memos reveal," *Just the News*, October 20, 2020, https://justthenews.com/politics-policy/elections/memos-show-zuckerberg-money-used-massively-grow-vote-democrat-stronghold (April 25, 2021); Libby Emmons, "BREAKING: Project Veritas exposes Google manager admitting to election interference," *Post Millennial*, October 19, 2020, https://thepostmillennial.com/breaking-project-veritas-exposes-google-manager-admitting-to-election-influence (April 25, 2021).

61 Unlike most of the corporations listed, the Fox news platforms, such as the Fox News Channel, for which I host a Sunday program, and the Fox Business Channel, were actually created, not acquired, by Fox.

62 Levin, *Liberty and Tyranny*, 114.

63 Ibid., 115.

64 Maydeen Merino, " 'Net Zero Is Not Enough': John Kerry Says We Need to Remove Carbon Dioxide from the Atmosphere," *Daily Caller*, April 22, 2021, https://dailycaller.com/2021/04/22/john-kerry-remove-carbon-atmosphere-leaders-summit-climate-change/ (April 25, 2021).

65 "The Government Is on My Property. What Are My Rights?" Owners' Counsel of America, April 11, 2016, https://www.ownerscounsel.com/the-government-is-on-my-property-what-are-my-rights/ (April 25, 2021).

66 Wilson P. Dizard, "Lamberth finds EPA in contempt for e-document

purge," GCN, July 25, 2003, https://gcn.com/articles/2003/07/25/lamberth-finds-epa-in-contempt-for-edocument-purge.aspx (April 25, 2021).

67 Melissa Quinn, "21 states sue Biden for revoking Keystone XL pipeline permit," CBS News, March 18, 2021, https://www.cbsnews.com/news/keystone-pipeline-21-states-sue-biden/ (April 25, 2021).

68 Teny Sahakian, "NY Times ignores 18 deaths, nearly $2 billion in damage when bashing GOP bills targeting rioters," Fox News, April 23, 2021, https://www.foxnews.com/us/ny-times-ignores-18-deaths-nearly-2-billion-dollars-in-damage-when-bashing-gop-bills-targeting-rioters (April 25, 2021).

69 Josh Gerstein, "Leniency for defendants in Portland clashes could affect Capitol riot cases," *Politico*, April 14, 2021, https://www.politico.com/news/2021/04/14/portland-capitol-riot-cases-481346 (April 25, 2021).

70 "Governor Ron DeSantis Signs Hallmark Anti-Rioting Legislation Taking Unapologetic Stand for Public Safety," Office of the Governor press release, April 19, 2021, https://www.flgov.com/2021/04/19/what-they-are-saying-governor-ron-desantis-signs-hallmark-anti-rioting-legislation-taking-unapologetic-stand-for-public-safety/ (April 25, 2021).

71 "Racketeer Influenced and Corrupt Organizations (RICO) Law," Justia.com, https://www.justia.com/criminal/docs/rico/ (April 25, 2021).

72 Meira Gebel, "The story behind Thousand Currents, the charity that doles out the millions of dollars Black Lives Matter generates in donations," *Insider*, June 25, 2020, https://www.insider.com/what-is-thousand-currents-black-lives-matter-charity-2020-6 (April 25, 2021).

73 Morrison, "AP Exclusive: Black Lives Matter opens up about its finances"; "Black Lives Matter Global Network Foundation," Influence Watch, https://www.influencewatch.org/non-profit/black-lives-matter-foundation/ (April 25, 2021).

74 N'dea Yancy-Bragg, "Americans' confidence in police falls to historic low, Gallup poll shows," *USA Today*, August 12, 2020, https://www.usatoday.com/story/news/nation/2020/08/12/americans-confidence-police-falls-new-low-gallup-poll-shows/3352910001/ (April 25, 2021).

75 John R. Lott, "Data Undercuts Myth of 'Racism' in Police Killings," RealClearPolitics, April 22, 2021, https://www.realclearpolitics.com/articles/2021/04/22/data_undercuts_myth_of_racism_in_police_killings_145640.html (April 25, 2021); John R. Lott and Carlisle E. Moody, "Do White Police Officers Unfairly Target Black Suspects?" SSRN, June 3, 2020, https://papers.ssrn.com/sol3/papers.cfm?abstract_id=2870189 (April 25, 2021); Ryan Saavedra, "Mac Donald: Statistics Do Not Sup-

port the Claim of 'Systemic Police Racism,' " *Daily Wire*, June 3, 2020, https://www.dailywire.com/news/mac-donald-statistics-do-not-support-the-claim-of-systemic-police-racism (April 25, 2021).

76 Jason Johnson, "Why violent crime surged after police across America retreated," *USA Today*, April 9, 2021, https://www.usatoday.com/story/opinion/policing/2021/04/09/violent-crime-surged-across-america-after-police-retreated-column/7137565002/ (April 25, 2021).

77 Morgan Phillips, " 'Justice in Policing Act': What's in the Democratic police reform bill," Fox News, June 8, 2020, https://www.foxnews.com/politics/justice-in-policing-act-whats-in-the-democratic-police-reform-bill (April 25, 2021).

78 Luke Barr, "US police agencies having trouble hiring, keeping officers, according to a new survey," ABC News, September 17, 2019, https://abcnews.go.com/Politics/us-police-agencies-trouble-hiring-keeping-officers-survey/story?id=65643752 (April 25, 2021).

79 Lieutenant Dan Marcou, "You can sue: Cops' legal recourse against assailants and others," Police1.com, June 8, 2016, https://www.police1.com/legal/articles/you-can-sue-cops-legal-recourse-against-assailants-and-others-YWtiK8fzBSZBNwfc/ (April 25, 2021).